THE SEA

JULES MICHELET

The Sea

TRANSLATED FROM THE FRENCH
by
Katia Sainson

GREEN INTEGER
KØBENHAVN & LOS ANGELES
2012

GREEN INTEGER
Edited by Per Bregne
København / Los Angeles
Distributed in the United States by Consortium Book
Sales and Distribution/Perseus
Distributed in England and throughout Europe by
Turnaround Publisher Services
Unit 3, Olympia Trading Estate
Coburg Road, Wood Green, London N22 6TZ
44 (0)20 88293009
ON NET available through Green Integer
(323) 857-1115 / http://www.greeninteger.com

Green Integer
6022 Wilshire Boulevard, Suite 202C
Los Angeles, California 90036 USA

Series Design: Per Bregne
Book Design and Typography: Rebecca Chamlee
Cover photograph: Jules Michelet

LIBRARY OF CONGRESS IN PUBLICATION DATA
Jules Michelet (1798-1874)
The Sea
ISBN: 9781933382111
p. cm – Green Integer 188
I. Title II. Series III. Translator: Katia Sainson
Green Integer books are published for Douglas Messerli
Printed in the United States of America on acid-free paper.

Table of Contents

Translator's Introduction   7

BOOK I: *Gazing Over the Seas*

The Sea as Viewed from Shore   16
Beaches, Shores and Cliffs   25
Beaches, Shores and Cliffs (continued)   32
The Sea's Rivers: The Circle of Water and
     the Circle of Fire   40
The Sea's Pulse   52
Storms   63
The Storm of October 1859   71
Lighthouses   87

BOOK II: *The Genesis of the Sea*

Fertility   98
The Sea of Milk   107
The Atom   119
The Blood Flower   130
The Makers of Worlds   140
Daughter of the Sea   151
The Stone Workers   164
Shells, Mother-of-pearl, Pearls   173
Pirates of the High Seas: Octopi, etc.   186
Crustaceans: War and Intrigue   194

The Fish   204
The Whale   219
The Sirens   231

BOOK III: *The Conquest of the Sea*

The Harpoon   246
The Discovery of the Three Oceans   255
The Law of Storms   269
Polar Seas   282
The War Against the Races of the Sea   297
The Rights of the Sea   309

BOOK IV: *Rebirth through the Sea*

The Origins of Bathing in the Sea   320
Choosing a Beach   332
The Residence   342
The Initial Yearning for the Sea   354
Bathing—The Renaissance of Beauty   363
The Rebirth of the Heart and of Fraternity   371
Vita Nuova of Nations   381

Translator's Introduction

With the coup d'état that established the Second Empire in 1852, Jules Michelet (1798-1874), who until that time had held a position in the National Archives as well as at the Collège de France as a popular, yet controversial, liberal history professor whose courses had twice been suspended, began a new chapter in his life. Forced to leave both of these positions because he refused to sign an oath of allegiance to France's new Emperor, Napoleon III, he began the most productive period of his intellectual life. This period of professional turmoil was also one of personal discovery for France's most important nineteenth-century historian. He met and married his second wife, Athénaïs Mialaret, a woman thirty years his junior, at this time. His new wife not only sparked his interest in natural history but she was the model for his sexualized natural universe.

After 1852, Michelet continued writing the monumental works of historiography for which he is best known: the *History of the Revolution* (in 7 volumes, published between 1847 and 1853) and the *History of France* (whose 7 volumes dealing with the periods from the Renaissance to the 18th century were published between 1857 and 1867). Along with those works, he produced a parallel series of books on natural history, which included *The Bird* (1856), *The Insect* (1857), *The Sea* (1861) and *The Mountain* (1868). With these works, he hoped to appeal to and enlighten a readership beyond the intellectual elite he spoke to in his lectures and his more scholarly historical works. These books were part of his pedagogical mission to create texts that would inform a mass reading public about the ground-breaking theories of contemporary natural history in the years before Darwin's theory of evolution had yet to make an impact in France, but when the proto-evolutionary theories of Lamarck and Geoffroy Saint-Hilaire had already captured the imaginations of many intellectuals outside scientific circles. In these texts, which are a testament to the colliding paradigms of history and natural history that was perhaps the nineteenth century's greatest intellectual encounter, Michelet presents revolutionary concepts of time and the history of life on earth in simple and yet lyrical language. Moreover, Michelet's natural world reveals the same civic ideals based on love and family that were at the core of the Revolutionary ideals that he championed in his historiography.

The Sea, which is translated here for the first time since 1861, is a work that is part scientific popularization, part history, part travelogue, part prose poem and part autobiography. Written by the author that Gustave Flaubert dubbed the *only* French Romantic, this gripping and fantastical description of the primordial sea later impacted such divergent contemporary imaginings of the sea as Jules Verne's *Twenty Thousand Leagues under the Sea* (in which the author dutifully echoes Michelet's theories on sea life) and Lautréamont's *Chant de Maldoror*, with its twisted dark parody of Michelet's portrayal of shark passion.

Michelet does battle against the perspective of the land-dweller, for whom the sea has often been a fatal boundary that separates two very different worlds. It is a site of darkness, a desert, a monster, an enemy and an agent of death that is constantly threatening those on earth with a return to chaos. He dismisses this conventional perspective of the sea as a sterile, foreboding desert and reveals the sea's true nature as the world's life-blood.

Emphasizing the link between the sea [*la mer*] and the mother [*la mère*], Michelet explores the multi-dimensional relationship between man and this mother of all life. Michelet's sea, which is teeming with fertility, is where life began through the process of spontaneous generation. It is at once a figure of maternal nurturing and of unrelenting desire. The sea, which is unendingly conceiving and giving birth, is Michelet's "great female of the earth."

In this work, Michelet gives his own version of the *genesis* of life that is heavily influenced by the natural philosophy of thinkers such as Etienne Geoffroy Saint-Hilaire, from whom Michelet took his vision of nature's unity and whose natural philosophy was championed by such authors as Goethe, Balzac and Sand, Jean Baptiste Lamarck, Michelet's "blind Homer of the Museum" and Felix Pouchet, the last great theorist of spontaneous generation and nemesis of Pasteur. In his "Genesis of the Sea" the historian explains that what he calls sea mucus is the building block for all life on earth, the universal element of life, or as Michelet writes, it is "life itself."

The author's natural history of the sea consists of a chain of being that goes from the simplest and most primitive creatures to the more complex forms that evolved into land animals and those that developed deeper social relationships. This evolutionary chain is presented in the form of individual histories or portraits featuring microscopic organisms, jellyfish, sea urchins, fish and ending with whales and seals. In these tableaux, which are prose poems of sorts, Michelet gives voice to the silent workers such as atomies, polyps and sea urchins, just as he gave voice to the people—those voiceless laborers—in his earlier books. In the same way that Michelet's histories attempted to resurrect the voices of the past that had been silenced, in this book on the sea, he proposes to expose the creatures that cannot speak to the world and yet are its creators.

In juxtaposition to these silent creative forces of nature Michelet presents a harsh analysis of man's conquest of the sea and his role as the "tyrannical God" of Nature. In a complete reversal from the author's initial perspective on the sea as a threat to man it is European man that becomes the cruel enemy of the sea. Michelet offers a scathing indictment of the West's barbarity towards nature that goes hand in hand with a denunciation of colonization. Demonstrating the interrelationship between the advance of science and the lust for economic power, Michelet describes the blind and violent pillaging of the sea. In light of the devastation brought about by Europeans, he calls for the promulgation of a "Rights of the Sea" (comparable to the French Revolution's Rights of Man) that would put an end to such annihilating practices as whaling.

In the final analysis however, Michelet always returns to the restorative properties of the sea. Having embraced innovative contemporary ideas on the benefits of bathing in seawater, Michelet lays out to a public, who is just beginning to discover leisure by the sea, the manner by which the mother of all life can repair the soul and the body. He presents the methods by which bathing can enhance the health of all his contemporaries, most notably women and children. He argues that for late nineteenth-century Europeans whose lives have been made too fast-paced by new technologies and whose bodies are weakening under the degradation of urban living, the sea with its embryonic mucus from which man was born is the place in which he can be reborn.

*　　*　　*

As Jean Borie has written, Michelet provides "science and scholarship [...] but a science and scholarship that has been kindly relegated to parentheses so as not fatigue the reader". The impressive amount of source material in *The Sea* was often culled from articles read in such journals as *La Revue des deux mondes*, *La Revue germanique* and *La Revue britannique* with their offerings of scientific popularizations and travelogues. Michelet also heavily relied upon encyclopedias and dictionaries such as D'Orbigny's *Dictionnaire universel d'histoire naturelle*. The historian had long been an avid reader of such naturalists as Geoffroy, Lamarck and his good friend Pouchet. Although Michelet was not familiar with Darwin's *Origin of Species* (1859) at the time of the writing of *The Sea*, he does refer to Darwin's work on corals. Another important scientific source for *The Sea* was the work of the American Matthew Maury (1806-1873) who was the head of the US Naval Observatory and the author of a classic work of oceanography, *The Physical Geography of the Sea* (1855) as well as a work entitled *Sailing Directions* (1850) in which the author collected data from the logbooks from naval vessels and merchant marine ships in order to establish standardized data on winds and sea currents in the world's oceans.

The Sea also contains many references to nineteenth-century travel accounts. Among others Michelet cites: Alexander von Humboldt (1796-1859) who with the botanist Aimé Bonpland made a research tour of the Spanish colonies through what is now Venezuela, Columbia, Peru, Ecuador and Mexico; James Ross (1800-1862), an English Naval officer and expert in magnetic observations, who explored the Antarctic region where he discovered Victoria Land and Mount Erebus, a 12,000 foot volcano; François Péron (1775-1810), who accompanied Nicolas Baudin on his expedition to explore what is today known as Australia and who upon his return began writing his *Voyage de découverte aux terres Australes* (1807-1816); Louis Claude Desaulses de Freycinet (1779-1842), who was also on the Baudin expedition and completed Péron's *Voyage* upon his death and who later circumnavigated the globe in an expedition which was described in his *Voyage autour du monde* (1824-1844); Jules Sebastien César Dumont d'Urville (1790-1842) who not only circumnavigated the world twice but as recounted in his *Voyage au pole sud et dans l'Océanie sur les corvettes l'Astrolabe et la Zelée*, (1842) explored the Antarctic; and Elisha Kent Kane (1820-1857) an American Arctic explorer who led an unsuccessful expedition to find the explorer Sir John Franklin in 1850 and who was the author of the book *Arctic Explorations*.

—*Katia Sainson*

BOOK I

Gazing Over the Seas

CHAPTER I

The Sea as Viewed from Shore

A brave Dutch sailor, a steady and cool observer, who has spent his life on the sea, says that frankly, one's first impression of it is one of fear. For any terrestrial being, water is the unbreathable, asphyxiating element. It is the fatal and eternal barrier, which irreversibly separates two worlds. It should come as no surprise that the enormous mass of water that we call the sea, whose profound depth remains unknown and obscure, has always appeared formidable to the human imagination.

Orientals see it as none other than a bitter chasm—the *Night of the Abyss*. In all the ancient languages, in those of India and of Ireland, the term for *sea* is synonymous or analogous to the *desert* and the *night*.

It is with great sorrow that every night we see the sun—the world's joy and the father of all life—sink into and be engulfed by the waves. The world and especially the West mourn it daily. And although we see this spectacle everyday, it holds the same power over us; it has the same melancholic effect.

When diving into the sea to a certain depth, one is quickly deprived of light and enters a twilight where only a single color persists—a sinister red. Then, even that disappears and total darkness descends. It is absolute darkness, except perhaps for certain extraordinary phosphorescent phenomena. Immense in its expanse, enormous in its depth, this mass, which extends over the majority of the globe, seems a world of obscurity. This, above all, is what unnerved and intimidated the earliest men. It was believed that life ceased where there was an absence of light and that with the exception of its surface layers, the rest of the sea's unfathomable depths, its bottom (if an abyss has a bottom), was a black lonely expanse. There, lay only arid sand and stones, along with bones and debris, so many lost goods that this miserly element is constantly taking and never returns, and which are jealously hidden in the deep treasury of shipwrecks.

Seawater does not offer a reassuring transparency. Unlike engaging nymphs of springs or crystal-clear fountains, this water is dark and heavy. It strikes hard. To venture into the sea is to feel strongly transported. It is true that seawater helps the swimmer but it also controls him, he feels like a weak child, cradled by a powerful hand that could just as well crush him.

Once a boat is adrift, who knows where a sudden wind and an irresistible current can carry it? Thus, northern fishermen, in spite of themselves, found polar America and returned with terror-filled accounts about a mournful Greenland. Every nation has its stories, its tales about the sea. Homer and *The Arabian Nights* preserve for us much of this frightening lore: the reefs and storms; doldrums that are no less deadly where one dies of thirst while surrounded by water; man-eaters; sea-monsters; leviathans; krakens and great sea serpents. "The land of fear," as the desert is known, could have also been used to designate the great maritime desert. The boldest sailors, the Phoenicians and Carthaginians, the conquering Arabs who wanted to annex the world, enticed by stories about the land of the Hesperides with all its gold, went beyond the Mediterranean, set off on the great sea, but soon they stopped. The dark line eternally shrouded in clouds, encountered before reaching the equator, filled them with awe. They stopped. They said: "This is the Sea of Darkness." And they returned home. "It would be impious to violate this sanctuary. Woe to anyone who follows his sacrilegious curiosity! On the last islands, we saw a giant, a menacing figure who said: 'Don't go any further.'"

These rather childlike fears of the old world are no different than the obvious emotions of a neophyte or a simple person who, having come from the interior, suddenly catches sight of the sea. Anyone, who has had this sudden unexpected surprise, feels the same way. Animals are visibly disturbed by it. Horses are uneasy even at ebb tide, when the water, which is weary and weak, drags sluggishly along the shore. They shudder and often refuse to walk through the languid waves. Dogs back away and bark, in their own way reviling the waves that they fear. They never make peace with this dubious and seemingly hostile element. According to one traveler, the dogs of Kamchatka peninsula that are used to this spectacle are nonetheless frightened and irritated by it. In large packs by the thousands, over long nights, they howl at the roaring waves furiously fighting to the bitter end with this northern sea.

The melancholic course of the rivers of northwest France, the vast sands of the Midi, or the heaths of Brittany, act as the Ocean's vestibule, a natural introduction that prepares us for its impact. This intermediate region that heralds the sea strikes anyone approaching by these routes. Along these rivers, is an infinite wasteland of bulrushes, willows and other plants, which with the intermingling of increasingly brackish water, eventually become marine plants. Before reaching the sea, the heath acts as a preliminary sea of low rough grasses, ferns and heather. At a distance of one or two leagues, you notice scrawny, sickly, grimacing trees that herald by their bearing— I am tempted to say by their strange gestures—the proximity of the great tyrant and its oppressive breath. If their roots didn't hold them down, it is obvious that they would flee. They look down at the ground and turn their back to the enemy. On the verge of retreat, they seem disconcerted and frenzied. They bend down, bowing to the ground, and for lack of a better solution, as they stand fixed there, they contort themselves in the stormy winds. Still elsewhere, tree trunks become small and they endlessly extend their branches horizontally. On the beaches trees are overcome and engulfed by the fine dust given off by fragmented shells. Their pores close up. They lack air. They suffocate but conserve their form and remain there as trees of stone, as ghosts of trees, as gloomy ever-present shadows, as captives even in death.

Well before catching sight of the sea, one hears her and therefore begins to imagine this formidable character. At first, it is a far-off sound, muted and unchanging. Then little by little all other noises yield to it and are subsumed. Soon, one notices the solemn alternating and unvarying return of the same loud and deep note, which increasingly rumbles and roars. In comparison, the oscillation of a clock's pendulum measuring out time is not as regular. And yet, there is nothing monotonously mechanical about this pendulum. In the case of the sea, we feel or we believe that we feel the vibrant intonations of life. In fact, at high tide when one wave—immense and electric—rises above another, the sound of shells and of thousands of diverse creatures brought in with the tide mixes with the stormy rumble of the waters. A murmur at ebb tide makes it clear that, along with the sands, the waves are reclaiming a world of loyal tribes that the sea gathers to her breast.

And the sea has still other voices! When she is emotional, the sea's moan and deep sighs contrast with the silence of the mournful shore. In fact, the shore seems to be quietly meditating, in order to better hear the threats coming from the one who just yesterday was flattering it with a caressing wave. What will the sea be telling the shore next? I don't want to predict. I do not want to speak here of the frightful concerts that the sea may give, of her duets with the rocks, of the basses and the muffled thunder that she produces deep inside the caves, nor the astonishing cries in which one thinks one hears: "Rescue me!"... No, let's examine the sea in her solemn days, when she is strong but not violent. It should come as no surprise that, when confronting this sphinx, both children and ignoramuses have always exhibited a stunned admiration—not so much pleasure but fear. As for the rest of us, from many perspectives, the sea is still a great enigma.

What is her true size? It is greater than that of the earth, we are certain of that. On the surface of the globe, water is the rule, land is the exception. But what is their relative proportion? Water makes up four-fifths of the globe. This is the most probable theory. Others have suggested two-thirds or three-fourths. It is difficult to say for certain. Landmass increases and decreases. It is a work in progress. This part rises and that one sinks down. Certain polar lands that had been discovered and mapped by one sailor can no longer be found on the following trip. Elsewhere, countless islands, immense reefs of madrepores and coral are formed, rise up and upset our sense of geography.

The depth of the sea is even more of an unknown than its area. The first few soundings, which have only recently been attempted, have proved unreliable.

The small and daring liberties that we take on the surface of this indomitable element—our boldness in sailing over this deep unknown—do not amount to much, and can do nothing to diminish the sea's rightful pride. In fact, she remains inscrutable and impenetrable. We are just now beginning to learn for certain about what we imagine is a prodigious world, filled with life, war, love and varied works moving within her. But the moment we penetrate the sea, we can hardly wait to get out of this foreign element. If we need the sea, it has no need for us. It manages perfectly well without Man. Nature does not seem to care to have us as a witness. This is God's exclusive domain.

This element, which we perceive as fluid, ever moving, and capricious, does not really change. It is the embodiment of regularity. Man is the one who is constantly changing. Tomorrow, man's body—which, according to the Swedish chemist Jöns Jacob Berzelius, is four-fifths water—will have evaporated. In the presence of the great immutable powers of nature, Man's ephemeral apparition has every reason to dream. No matter his well-founded hope that his immortal soul will live in eternity, he is nonetheless saddened by his frequent deaths and by the crises which break at each moment of life. The sea seems to prevail over him. Each time that we approach the sea, it seems that she says from the depth of her immutability: "Tomorrow you pass away but I never will. Your bones will be in the ground, and, over the centuries, they will decompose. Majestic and indifferent, I will continue the great, perfectly-balanced life which hour after hour, reconciles me harmoniously with the life of far-away worlds."

On the violent beaches where the sea, twice daily, snatches stones away from the cliffs, then throws them back, dragging them along with a sinister sound like a ball and chain, this humiliating contrast is exposed in a deeply distressing and scornful way. At first, every young imagination pictures the sea as a war or a battle, and is frightened. But then, having observed that this fury has limits beyond which it may not venture, the reassured child feels hate rather than fear for this wild and seemingly resentful entity. And, in turn, the child throws stones at this great roaring enemy.

I observed this duel in Le Havre in July of 1831.[*] A young girl that I had brought there in the presence of the sea summoned up her young courage, becoming indignant at such defiance. She met the sea head on. This lopsided struggle between the delicate hand of a fragile creature and the frightful force that hardly noticed her made me smile. But the laughter did not last, when I realized what a short life this beloved child would have and when contemplating her ephemeral weakness, in the presence of this tireless eternity which will recapture us all. This was one of my first times gazing at the seas. These were my reveries that were marred by the all-too accurate omen that this struggle between the sea that I am gazing upon again today and that child that I can no longer behold inspired.

---

[*] This is a reference to a scene recorded in Michelet's Journal, in August of 1831, with Adèle Michelet, the author's daughter who died on July 15, 1855 at the age of 31.   —*Translator's note.*

CHAPTER 2

Beaches, Shores and Cliffs

The Ocean can be seen from everywhere. And from everywhere it appears imposing and formidable. It is thus around the capes that look out onto the Ocean in all directions. It is thus, or sometimes even more frightful, in the vast but contained sites where the framework of the shore constrains and infuriates it, where it enters violently with fast-flowing currents, which strike the reefs. One doesn't see it as being infinite, but one feels it, hears it, imagines it as infinite and the impression is no less profound.

That was the feeling that I had in Granville—where Normandy ends and Brittany begins—on that turbulent beach, with its great waves and strong wind. The rich, friendly and sometimes slightly vulgar gaiety of the beautiful Norman countryside disappears and through Granville, and through the dangerous Mont-Saint-Michel, we enter into a totally different world. Granville is Norman by race, but Breton in appearance. It proudly counters the horrific assault of the waves with its rocky coast. At times, these waves bring the discordant wrath of the Channel's northern currents. At other times, they roll from the West in a flow that is constantly intensifying along its thousand-league course, and that strikes with all the Atlantic's accumulated might.

I like this small, singular and somewhat sad town, which lives on the most perilous type of distant fishing. Families know that their food comes from this dangerous gamble with life and death. This real-ization adds a harmonic gravity to the already stern character of this coast. Quite often, I savored the evening's melancholy, either when strolling near the lower town on the already darkened shore or when, from the upper town perched on the rocky coast, I saw the sun setting through the slight mist on the horizon. Its enormous globe, often severely lined with black and red stripes, sunk without stopping to indulge the sky in the whimsical landscapes of light, which else-where often enliven the view. In August it was already autumn. Twilight hardly lasted. Scarcely had the sun disappeared, when the wind would freshen and the rapid green and dark waves would flow. One could only make out the outlines of a few women in their white-lined black cloaks. Above the shore at eighty or one hundred feet, the sheep that had lingered on the glacis' meager pastures, made the scene even bleaker with their plaintive bleating. The small upper-part of town built up its northern side, which faces the great sea, right on the edge of the cold and dark abyss that is beaten by an eternal wind. This is where the poorest dwellings are located. I was brought there to the home of a fellow who produced seashell paintings. Having climbed up some sort of a ladder into a dark little room, I saw his tragic view framed in a narrow window. This was as gripping as had been the view—also captured in a window frame and come upon quite by surprise— of the Grindelwald glacier in Switzerland. The glacier exposed an enormous monster of sharp ice that was making its way towards me. And now, through this window, I saw the sea of Granville—an enemy army of waves that were joined together in their assault.

Although he was not old, my man was sickly and feverish. Despite the fact that we were in August he had his window sealed shut against the draft. While looking at the paintings and talking with him, I noticed that he was a bit feeble-minded. His intellect had been weakened by a family tragedy. His brother had perished on that shore in a painful event. For him, the sea remained sinister. She seemed to harbor ill will against him. In the winter, she tirelessly whipped his windowpane with snow or icy winds. The sea did not let him sleep. Through long nights, she struck the rocks beneath him unceasingly and without respite. During the summer, she presented him with colossal storms and lightning from another world. At spring-tide, it was even worse. The sea would rise to sixty feet and its raging foam, jumping still higher, came rapping arrogantly at his window. He could not be sure that the sea would always stop there. In her moments of hostility, she could betray him. He maintained that he did not have the means to move but perhaps he was also held there, unwittingly, by some sort of magnetism. He would not have dared to make a complete break with this dreadful enchantress. He had a certain respect for her. He rarely spoke of the sea, and mostly he would refer to her without speaking her name, like the Icelander who, when at sea, does not dare name Orca out of fear that she might hear and come to him. I can still see his pallid face as he looked out over the shore and said: "That frightens me."

Was he crazy? Not at all. He was displaying good common sense. He seemed to me to be distinguished and interesting. Although agitated, he was quite methodical—too much so to have such impressions.

The sea drives many men crazy. The celebrated explorer David Livingston had brought an intelligent and brave man back from Africa. However, this man, who had defied lions, had never seen the sea. Upon boarding a ship, he was astonished by not only the unknown technology but also by this formidable element. It was too much for his brain. He went mad. Despite all that was done, he found a way to escape and threw himself blindly into the very waves that both terrified and captivated him.

Moreover, the sea has this same hold on the men who have entrusted their lives to her—those who have lived with her intimately and can never leave her. In a small port, I saw old pilots who, having become too weak, relinquished their positions. And yet, they were inconsolable. They hung about pitifully and their minds started to wander.

At the highest point of the Mont-Saint-Michel, one can see a platform called the Madman's Terrace. I know of no place more apt to drive someone crazy than this vertiginous structure. Imagine being surrounded by a vast secluded plain of what looks like white ash— dubious sand whose misleading smoothness is its most dangerous trap. It is land and yet it's not. It is the sea and yet again, not. It's not fresh water either although beneath the sands rivers constantly burrow through the ground. Rarely, and only for short amounts of time, a boat will venture forth. And, if passing by when the water is receding, you are likely to be swallowed up. I speak from experience. I myself was almost engulfed. A very light carriage which I was in, disappeared in two minutes time with its horse. Miraculously I escaped. But, as I walked away, even I was sinking down into the sand. With every step I felt a dreadful lapping, like the beckoning of the abyss that was softly calling me, inviting me, drawing me in and grabbing hold from below. And yet, I reached the rocks, the gigantic abbey, the cloister, the fortress and prison whose atrocious sublimeness is truly suited to the landscape. This is not the place to describe such a monument. On a great granite block, it rises up, climbs and then climbs even further without stopping, like a gigantic and useless babel—a monumental heap of rock upon rock, century upon century and always dungeon upon dungeon. At its lowest level, there is the monk's prison, higher up the iron jail built by Louis XI; higher yet the one constructed by Louis XIV; and beyond those, the current prison. All of this in a whirlwind, a gale, and never-ending turbulence. It is a sepulchre but one that knows no peace.

Is it the sea's fault if this beach is so treacherous? Not at all. The sea arrives there, as she does elsewhere, noisy and strong but loyal. The true fault lies with the land whose cunning immobility always seems so innocent, and who, below the beach, is filtering stream water—a sugary and whitish mixture that undermines solidity. It is especially man's fault, because of his ignorance and neglect. During the long barbarian ages, while he thought only of legends and establishing this great place of pilgrimage dedicated to the archangel, who had vanquished the devil, the devil took possession of that neglected plain. The sea is quite innocent. On the contrary, far from doing harm, this madwoman carries in her menacing waves a treasure of fertile salt. Superior to the Nile's silt, it enriches the area's cultivated fields and is the source of the charming beauty of Dol's former marshlands, which today have been transformed into gardens. Although, a slightly violent mother, she is a mother nonetheless. Overflowing with fish, she heaps millions and even billions of oysters upon Cancale, which is across from the Mont-Saint-Michel, as well as upon still other shoals. And with their broken shells she gives birth to the fertile life that turns into grass and fruit and covers the meadows with flowers.

One must attempt to truly understand the sea and not yield to the misguided ideas put forth by the neighboring land. Moreover, one cannot be fooled by the tremendous illusions that she herself creates, by the immensity of her wonders or by what on the surface appears to be moments of fury that are often in fact acts of kindness.

CHAPTER 3

Beaches, Shores and Cliffs (continued)

Beaches, shores and cliffs expose the sea from three different and always beneficial perspectives. They explain, translate and link us to this great power, which at first seems savage but is in fact divine, and therefore welcoming.

The advantage of the cliffs is that at the foot of these high walls one can gauge, more appreciably than elsewhere, the tide—that breath or shall we say that pulse of the sea. This pulse, which is imperceptible in the Mediterranean, is distinct in the Ocean. The Ocean breathes just as I do. It corresponds to my inner movement and to the one from above. It constantly forces me to reckon with it, to assess days and hours and to consult the sky. It calls me back to myself and to the world.

For example, as I am sitting upon the cliffs of Cap d'Antifer, I see this immense spectacle. The sea, which just a moment ago seemed lifeless, starts to shudder.

She is trembling. This is the initial sign of the great movement to come. The tide has passed Cherbourg and Barfleur and turned violently there at the lighthouse point. Its divided waters have flowed passed the Calvados region. They rise up at Le Havre. And from there, they come towards me, and on to Étretat, Fécamp and Dieppe where despite northern currents, they penetrate the canal. I must take care and closely observe the Ocean's time. Its height equals that of the dunes and sandy hills that can be scaled all along the shore, and here, at the foot of the cliffs, it commands our attention. This thirty-league long wall of granite does not have many stairs leading up from the beach. Its narrow openings, which offer us small safe-havens, are spaced apart at great distances from one another.

Even more intriguing—at low tide, one can observe the layered strata from which the history of the earth can be read in gigantic registers where the accumulated centuries provide a wide-opened book of time. Each year consumes another page. It is a world under demolition that the sea unceasingly ravages from below, but that the rains and the frosts attack much more effectively from above. The rising tide breaks up the limestone. It takes. It brings back. It constantly rolls the flint, smoothing it into pebbles. This hard work makes this coast, whose land is so rich, a veritable maritime desert. So very few marine plants survive the eternal grinding of the crushed stone. Molluscs and scallops fear it. Even fish keep their distance. Such a great contrast between the gentle countryside, which has been so humanized, and the sea, which is so inhospitable.

One sees it only from above. Below, the harsh reality of walking on the crumbling, moving ground with the rockslide makes the narrow beach impossible and even the slightest stroll requires strenuous exertion. One must remain above where splendid houses, beautiful woods, magnificent fields, wheat and gardens advance up to the edge of the great wall and look out without restraint onto that majestic street full of small boats and ships —the Channel— which separates the two shores and the world's two greatest Empires.

The land and the sea! What more does one need? Here, at this spot, both are charming. However, the person who loves the sea for herself—her friend, her lover—will more likely go seek her out in a less variable location. In order to enter into a steady relationship with the sea, large sandy beaches—where the sand is not too soft—are better suited. They allow you to dream and stroll without limit. Between man and the sea, they endure mysterious outpourings. I have never complained about these vast and free sands that others find dreadfully dull. I don't feel alone there. I come, I go, and I feel her presence. She is there, the great companion. If she is not too agitated—in a foul mood—I take the liberty of speaking to her and she is not averse to answering back. What things we have said to each other during the peaceful months when the crowds have left the never-ending beaches of Scheveningen and Ostend, those of Royan and Saint-Georges! This is where in a long tête-à-tête, some sort of intimacy is established. It is as if we acquire a sixth sense in order to understand this great language.

The Ocean can seem sad, when from the towers of Amsterdam, the Zuider Zee with its leaden rising tide appears or when on the dunes of Scheveningen you see the overhanging waters of the North Sea, always on the verge of flowing over the dyke. This battle fascinates me. I am fond of this land, with its severity. Here is man's effort, creativity and inventiveness. I also like the sea there because of the treasury of fertile life that I know lies in her bosom. This is one of the most populated seas on earth. When Midsummer's Night comes and fishing begins, you will see emerge from the depths the ascent of another sea—the herring's sea. The unlimited plane of water will not be large enough to hold this living deluge, which is one of the most triumphant revelations of the boundless fertility of nature. That is my immediate reaction in this place, and it is the same one I have in front of the paintings where great masters have portrayed the profound nature of the sea. I have always been drawn to Jacob van Ruysdael's dark *Pier* more than to any other painting in the Louvre. Why? Because in the reddish shades of its electrified waters, I don't feel the North Sea's coldness at all. On the contrary, I feel fermentation and the flux of life.

Nevertheless, if you were to ask me which Ocean coast makes the greatest impression, I would say: Brittany's coast, especially on the wild and sublime granite promontories where the Old World ends, at this bold point that defies storms and dominates the Atlantic. Nowhere did I feel the noble and extreme sadness, which leaves the most lasting impressions of the sea more intensely. Let me explain.

There is sadness and there is sadness: the sadness of women; that of the powerful; the sadness of those with highly sensitive souls who bemoan their fate; and that of the selfless souls, who accept their fate, give thanks to nature, and yet still feel the evils of the world and draw from this sadness itself the strength to act or to create. How often do we need to renew our souls by immersing ourselves in this state that can only be called heroic melancholy!

Nearly thirty years ago, when I visited this area, I did not realize how deeply attracted I would be to it. In the end, it comes down to its great harmony. Elsewhere, inexplicably, you can feel the discord between the land and its inhabitants. In the cantons where the truly beautiful Normand race is at its purest—where it has maintained that singular type of ginger coloring, that Scandinavian red hair—it has no relation to the land that it occupies by chance. On the contrary, in Brittany, on this geological land, which is the most ancient on earth, on its granite and limestone, walks its primitive race, a people who are also of granite. This is a severe race with great nobility, with the sharpness of stone. Whereas Normandy progresses, Brittany is in a state of decadence. Imaginative and spiritual, it is fond of the absurd, the impossible and the lost cause. However, despite Brittany's deficiencies one thing still remains, the rarest of things—character.

If you are tired of insipid anglicisms and want to escape the type of vulgarity that masquerades as pragmatism, as well as superficial pleasures, which are in fact quite unsavory, go sit instead on those rocks at the bay of Bouarnenez, on the Penmark headland. Or, if the wind is too strong, go sit in a small boat off the low islands of the Morbihan. The sea's warm rising tide comes in without a sound. Where Brittany is gentle it is very gentle. Its archipelagos' waters are deathly still. Where Brittany is rough, it is sublime.

In 1831, I only experienced Brittany's sadness. That sadness passed into my history. I did not know then the true nature of this sea. It is in the most solitary coves, between its most savage rocks, that Brittany is truly gay, by which I mean joyful and full of life. You will find the out-layers of the rocks gray and rough, but this surface is in fact living beings. There, a whole world thrives and at ebb-tide when the water drains away and the rocks are left to dry, it closes up upon itself. When the good sea, its wet nurse, brings its needed nourishment it opens up its little windows. This is where, the respectable population of tiny stoneworkers— the sea urchins, who have been observed and so well described by the naturalist Frédéric Caillaud—toil in great number. This world's perspective is diametrically opposed to ours. Beautiful Normandy frightens these creatures. The rough pebbles by the cliffs, which could easily crush them, are terrifying. The crumbling limestone of Saintonge, with its friendly beaches, does not reassure them. They would take care not to settle in a place that could collapse at any moment. On the contrary, they are happy to feel beneath them the immovable ground of Brittany's rocks.

Let us learn from them not to go by appearances, but rather by the truth. Charming shores with the most seductive flora are those which marine life avoid. They are rich but only in fossils. They are intriguing for the geologist. With the bones of the dead they educate him. The harsh granite, on the other hand, sees below it the sea brimming with fish. On these rocks there are still other forms of life such as the fascinating, modest nation of working molluscs—those poor tiny laborers whose industrious lives give the sea her serious charm and morality.

A woman's heart says: "And yet the silence is profound. These boundless workers are quiet. They say nothing to me. Their life flows from them to themselves and has no connection to me. For me the sea is death. It is solitude! Great and sad solitude!...It worries me."

How wrong! Everything here is friendly. These small creatures do not speak to the world, but they work for it. They rely on their sublime mother, the Ocean, to speak in their place. They express themselves through her great voice.

Between the silent land and the mute tribes of the sea, the Ocean carries on the great, loud, serious and sympathetic dialogue—the harmonic concordance of the great I with itself, the beautiful debate that is none other than Love.

CHAPTER 4

The Sea's Rivers:
The Circle of Water and the Circle of Fire

The earth had barely become aware of its existence when, casting a glance upwards, it compared itself favorably to the sky. The young science of Geology let out a Titanic cry against its elder, Astrology, the proud queen of the sciences. "Our mountains," said Geology "are not *cast down in a haphazard way, like the stars in the sky*. The mountains form systems that follow a common layout, which celestial constellations seem to lack." These are the bold and passionate words of a man who is as modest as he is illustrious — the geologist Mr. Elie de Beaumont.

Not only have we yet to decipher the great order that undoubtedly reigns in the apparent confusion of the Milky Way, but even the more visible organization of the earth's surface—the result of unfathomable revolutions within its interior—is now, and will continue to be a source of obscurity and mystery even for this most ingenious of sciences.

Although the formations of that great mountain, which rises from the water and which we commonly call *land*, seem to present a variety of symmetrical patterns, currently these patterns have not been reduced to an overall system. These dry and elevated areas appear more or less depending on sea level. Acting as a border, the sea, in fact, shapes the continents. All geography books should therefore begin with the sea.

Moreover, in recent years an important fact has come to light. Whereas the earth has seemingly discordant characteristics—the New World extends from North to South, for example, while the Old World stretches from East to West—the sea, on the contrary, displays great harmony and even an exact conformity between the two hemispheres. Thus, true consistency exists in this fluid region that was thought to be ever-changing. The most well-ordered process on the globe, the most symmetrical, is the one that at first seems the freest—the process of circulation. Even today, we do not completely comprehend the distinctive features of the great animal's skeleton and spinal column. But its vital movement—salt water creating fresh water, which in turn quickly becomes water vapor which is then reconverted back into salt water—that which creates the sea's currents, is an admirable mechanism as perfect as the circulation of blood in the most advanced animals. Nothing more closely resembles the constant transformation of our venous and arterial blood.

* * *

We would understand the surface of the globe in a completely different way, if rather than classifying regions by mountain ranges we classified them *by maritime basins*.

Southern Spain resembles Morocco more than it resembles Navarre. Provence resembles Algeria more than the Dauphiné region. Senegambia resembles the Amazon more than the Red Sea, and the Amazon resembles the rainforests of Africa more than it does its neighbors Chile and Peru.

The symmetry of the Atlantic is even more striking in its underlying currents, in its surface winds and breezes. Their action helps a great deal in creating these analogies and in forming what we can call: the fraternity of shores. The classifying element of any principle of geographic unity will increasingly be sought in *maritime basins*, where those faithful messengers—water and wind—create a relationship and assimilation between opposing shores. The key to geographical unity will no longer be exclusively found in the mountains whose two faces often are in contradiction with one another, with absolutely inconsistent plant and animal populations at the same altitudes, and where, depending on the exposure, on one side there is constant summer, and a stone's throw away eternal winter. Mountains rarely provide unity to an area. On the contrary, they most often expose its duality, its irreconcilability and its lack of harmony.

This brilliant insight belongs to Jean Baptiste Bory de Saint-Vincent, whose theories are confirmed a thousand times over by Matthew Fontaine Maury's discoveries as well as the laws that he has laid out in his *Physical Geography of the Sea*.

In the sea's immense valley, under the twin mountains of two continents, there are strictly speaking only two basins: the Atlantic basin; and the great basin of the Indian and the Pacific oceans. The unknown belt of the enormous Austral Ocean cannot be called a basin. It has no limits, no shore, and only in the North does it wrap around the Indian and Pacific Oceans as well as the Coral Sea.

The Austral Ocean alone is bigger than any other sea. It covers almost half the surface of the globe. Apparently, its depth matches its area. Whereas recent soundings of the Atlantic Ocean indicate 10 to 12,000 feet, in the Austral Ocean, the English explorer James Clark Ross and Denham found 14,000, 27,000 and up to 46,000 feet. Add to that the mass of the Antarctic ice floes, which are infinitely vaster than our Northern ones. We are not far from the truth, when we simply say: the Southern Hemisphere is the world of water and the Northern Hemisphere is the world of land.

Anyone, who wants to cross the Atlantic from Europe, must successfully leave our ports, which too often are closed by Western winds. It is only after having passed the variable zone of our changeable seas, that one soon enters the fine weather and eternal serenity, created on the sea and in the sky, by the northeast winds, the gentle trade winds. All is right here. There are no worries. However, as one approaches the Equator, the invigorating sea breeze ceases, the air becomes stifling. Here, below the equator, the doldrums predominate and create a sharp contrast between the trade winds of our Boreal Hemisphere and those of the Southern Hemisphere. The clouds weigh heavy. Driving rain pours down at every moment. You become sad and grumble. But, without this dark curtain, the sun would strike weakened heads like fiery arrows on the Atlantic's glassy waters! Without these downpours that assail the other side of the earth on the Indian Ocean and the Coral Sea, the extent of fermentation in their old volcanic craters would be unimaginable! The black mass of clouds, which was once a terror, a barrier to navigation, this sudden night stretching out over the water, happens to be the salvation, the protective facility, which makes passing through this region comfortable, and allows you to quickly rediscover the beautiful sun and pure sky of the South as well as the gentleness of steady winds.

The warmth of the Equator causes water to rise quite naturally into water vapor, which forms this dark band.

An observer looking down at the earth from another planet would see floating above it a ring of clouds, a bit like we see Saturn's rings. If he wondered about its purpose, a response could be: "By alternately absorbing and releasing, this ring acts as a regulator. It balances evaporation and precipitation, distributes rain and dew, modifies the temperature in each area and exchanges the water vapor of the two worlds by borrowing from the Southern world that which is needed to create the rivers and streams of our Northern world. What marvelous solidarity! The respiration of South America's forests condenses into clouds that fraternally water the flowers and fruits of Europe. The air, which renews us, is the tribute that one hundred islands of Asia— the powerful flora of Java or Ceylon—exhale and entrust to great messenger-clouds that roll with the earth and pour life out to it.

Set yourself down (in spirit I mean) upon one of the volcanic islands that the Pacific Ocean offers in such great numbers and look southward. Beyond New Holland you will see the Austral Ocean hemming in the two extremes of the Old and the New Continents with its circular current. In the Antarctic world, explorers note the location of a small island or so-called polar land-mass, only to see these pieces of land, which are most probably ice fields, disappear. Endless water, always water!

From this very same observation point where I have placed you, as you look towards the Arctic Hemisphere, in the East in contrast to the circle of Antarctic waters, you can see what Ritter called the circle of fire. In fact, it is a slack ring, a loose chain, formed by the volcanoes, starting in the Cordillera on the Western coast of South America, then in the heights of Asia, and finally in the countless basaltic islands that abound in the Oriental Ocean.

The first group of volcanoes, those of America, offers a series of sixty gigantic beacons, whose constant irruptions dominate the steep coastline and far-off waters over a thousand-league stretch. The other group that go from New Zealand to the Philippines has eighty still-active beacons, and many more that are now extinct. If one goes north (from Japan to Kamchatka), the glow of fifty blazing craters casts light as far away as the Aleutian Islands and the dark arctic seas. (See the works of Leopold von Buch, Carl Ritter and Alexander von Humboldt.) In all, three hundred active volcanoes dominate and encircle the eastern world.

On the other side of the globe, our Atlantic Ocean used to offer an analogous sight before the revolutions, which extinguished most of Europe's volcanoes, while also annihilating the continent of Atlantis. Humboldt believes that this great ruin, attested to so vigorously in legends, really existed. I dare to add that, given the overall symmetry of the world, the existence of this continent was only logical so that one side of the earth could be in harmony with the other. Along with Tenerife's volcano, which still survives, and with our extinct volcanoes of Auvergne, the Rhine and Hereford, rose up those that must have destroyed Atlantis. Together they constituted a counterpart to the Caribbean volcanoes as well as other American craters.

In India and the West Indies, from the Cuban as well as the Java Sea, these active or extinct volcanoes are the source of two enormous streams of hot water that flow north bringing warmth. We could call them the globes two aortae. Along side or below them are their counter-currents from the North, which bring cold water thereby creating a balance by compensating for the flow of hot water.

The cold currents apply a mass of relatively freshwater to the salty waters of the two hot currents. This fresh water returns to the Equator to the great electric furnace that in turns heats and salts it.

These streams of hot water, which are at first only some twenty leagues wide, manage to maintain their vigor and their powerful identity for quite a distance. But little by little, they come apart, become more temperate and yet expand and take on a width of a thousand leagues. Maury believes that the flow that goes from the West Indies and pushes North towards us displaces and modifies a quarter of the Atlantic's water.

These great traces of sea life, which have only recently been observed, were nonetheless as visible as the continents themselves. The very color of our great artery the Atlantic and her sister the Indian artery make their existence evident. On both sides, there is a great blue torrent, which runs over the green waters. It is a deep blue, an indigo that is so dark that the Japanese call it the *Black River*.

Ours visibly rises up between Cuba and Florida. When it leaves its boiler, the Gulf of Mexico, it is burning hot. It runs, hot, salty and quite distinct between its two green walls. No matter how hard the Ocean tries—it squeezes tight, it compresses— it cannot penetrate this stream. I have no idea what intrinsic density, what molecular attraction binds the blue waters together to the point that rather than allowing through green water, the blue water accumulates and forms a sort of spine or roof-shape, which slopes down to the right and left. Any object thrown into these waters goes adrift and sloughs off, since this stream is higher than the Ocean.

Rapid and strong, it runs first to the North, following the United States' coastline. But when it arrives at the point of the great banks of Newfoundland, its left branch dives down and as an undersea current, goes off to console the North Pole by creating the warm water sea (by this I mean a sea whose water is not ice-cold) that has just been discovered there. As for the right branch, when it arrives in Europe, tired and weakened, it is spread over an immense expanse. It comes upon Ireland and England, which redivide these waters that had previously been divided at Newfoundland. Faltering, lost at sea, it warms Norway a bit after having managed to carry to the Icelandic coast American wood, without which the poor snowy island, under its volcano, would die.

These two brothers, the Indian and the American, have this in common—having left the Equator, from the electric furnace of the globe, they carry with them prodigious powers of creation and agitation. On the one hand, they seem to be the deep womb to a world of living beings, their warm and gentle cradle. On the other hand, they are the center and the vehicle of storms. Winds and waterspouts travel along their surface. Such gentleness, such fury, is this not a contradiction? No, this merely proves that the fury only disturbs the exterior, the shallow surface layers. Nothing is felt in its depths. The weakest creatures, shelled atomies, microscopic medusae, fluid creatures that the slightest thing can bring to an end, take advantage of the same current, sailing peacefully below the storm.

Few arrive at our shores. They go as far as Newfoundland, where the cold current of the North Pole reaches them, then seizes and kills them. Newfoundland is none other than the great ossuary of these travelers struck down by cold. The lightest ones although dead stay suspended for some time but eventually rain down, like snow, onto the Ocean floor. They lay down those beds of microscopic shellfish, which can be found all along the bottom of the sea from Ireland to America.

Maury calls these two rivers of hot water—the Indian and the American—the two Milky Ways of the sea.

With their similar temperature, color and direction (precisely describing the same curved line), they do not share the same fate. The American first enters a rough sea—the Atlantic—that opens up towards the North and unleashes and propels against it a floating army of drift ice from the North Pole. This is where it expends its heat. The Indian current, in contrast, which at first moves through the islands, arrives at a sea, which is closed-in and better protected to the North. It can maintain itself—warm, electric and creative—for quite some time. And it can trace on the globe an enormous trail of life.

At its core is the apogee of terrestrial energy with its treasure-trove of plant life, its monsters, its spices and its fish. From secondary currents, which escape from it and go south, another world results—the world of the Coral Sea. There, in an expanse, which as Maury says, is *the size of four continents*, polyps conscientiously build their thousands of islands, banks and reefs which crisscross this sea. These dangerous reefs, which today are cursed by sailors, continue to rise and eventually will create a continent and who knows, in a cataclysm this might well be a refuge for the human race.

CHAPTER 5

The Sea's Pulse

As the writer Jean Reynaud observed in his fine article in the *Encyclopédie nouvelle*, our earth is not alone. The infinitely complicated curved-line that it describes is a manifestation of the forces and other influences that act upon it, a testament to its connections and interactions with the great nations of the heavens.

Its hierarchical relationships are particularly apparent with its superior the sun. And despite being the earth's handmaiden, even the moon commands a great deal of power over it. Like the flowers that it transports on its surface, the earth itself turns towards the sun and longs for it. In its most moveable parts—its fluid mass—it rises up as a sign of its feelings of attraction. It bursts its banks, it rises (as best it can) and twice a day, with a heaving bosom it offers up, at the very least, a sigh towards the friendly stars. Does the sea feel such an attraction towards other celestial bodies? Do the sun and moon solely control its tides?

The scientific world said so and navigators believed it, relying exclusively on Laplace's very incomplete findings. And for that reason terrible mistakes were made that resulted in shipwrecks. For Saint-Malo's dangerous shoal, calculations were off by 18 feet. In 1839, Rémi Chazallon, who almost died as a result of such errors, began to discover and calculate the secondary, and yet quite considerable undulations that alter the tide by influencing it in a variety of ways. Less dominant stars than the sun and the moon no doubt contribute to the back and forth motion of the earth's water.

According to which laws? Chazallon says: "The undulation of the tide in a port follows the same laws as vibrating chords." This important remark greatly impacts our understanding of the mutual relationship between the stars, which is similar to the mathematical relationship of celestial music as it was described in ancient times.

Through its spring and neap tides, the earth speaks to its sisters, the planets. Do they answer back? Undoubtedly. Their fluid elements—sensitive to the earth's momentum—must also rise. Throughout the heavens this mutual attraction, this tendency by which every star emerges from its self-centeredness must create sublime dialogues. Unfortunately, the human ear can decipher very little of this.

Another point worth considering is that the sea does not yield immediately to her dominant star. She does not exhibit the overzealousness of slavish obedience. She needs time in order to absorb and act on the emotional shock. She must call forth sluggish waters and conquer their inertia. She must attract and carry along those that are the furthest away. Because of the earth's incredibly rapid rotation these points of attraction are constantly shifting. Moreover, the overall movement of the legion of waves has to contend with all the inconveniences of natural obstacles such as islands, capes and straits as well as the ever-so varied shorelines, and the no less resistant obstacles such as winds and currents. There is also the rivalry with the earth's rivers, which, depending on the thaw and hundreds of other unforeseen events, are swept along the slippery slopes of mountains and are thrown into the sea thereby altering her well-regulated motion with this horrific clash. The Ocean does not yield. The force deployed by the rivers cannot intimidate her. The sea rebuffs these waters that are thrust upon her. They are gathered up into a heaping mound and rolled toward Rouen and Bordeaux with such great violence that it would appear that they might be pushed back to their mountain tops.

This diversity of obstacles produces apparent irregularities in the tides that are striking and bewildering. Nothing is more surprising than the inconsistencies of times between neighboring ports. For example, according to Chazallon, Baron Jean-Jacques Baude and others, there is one tide at Le Havre for every two at Dieppe. It is a tribute to human ingenuity to have been able to calculate such complex phenomena.

But below this surface motion, the sea has another movement within—a flow of currents that crisscross her at various depths. These hot currents and counter-currents, whether superimposed at various depths or flowing side-by-side in opposite directions carry out the sea's circulation—the exchange of salt and fresh water and the resulting alternating pulsation. The hot current pulses from the equator to the pole, the cold one from the pole to the equator.

Is this to say, as it has been in the past, that these rather distinct and separate currents are exactly analogous to the vessels, veins, and arteries in higher-order animals? Not really. But they do resemble the less determinate circulation that naturalists have recently found in certain lower species such as molluscs and annelids. This lacunar circulation, where the blood pours out in currents before entering specific canals, replaces and prepares the way for vascular circulation.

The sea is thus. It seems like a great animal halted at this first stage of organization.

Who brought to light the currents and regular fluctuations of this abyss into which we have never descended? Who taught us about the geography of these dark waters? Those who live and float there— the animals and plants.

We will see how the whale, the shelled atomies called Foraminifera, and the American wood transported as far as Iceland, all conspired to reveal the river of hot water that goes from the West Indies to Europe, as well as the cold counter-current that joins it at Newfoundland and passes along side or under it, its drift ice resolving into a far-reaching mist.

The thick red cloud of animalcules, transported from the Orinoco to France by a storm, explains the great Southwest air current, which refreshes our Europe with the rains of the Cordilleras.

Without the constant exchange of water that occurs through currents in her lowest depths, in certain places the sea would fill up with salt and refuse. It would be like the Dead Sea, which, with no discharge and no movement, has shores laden with salt and plants incrusted with crystals. By simply passing over it, winds become scorching, arid and carry in them famine and death.

So many scattered observations on both air and water currents, the seasons, winds and storms that remained alive through the memory of fishermen and sailors were often lost and died with them. It seemed fruitless and, to many, impossible to try to establish a non-centralized science of meteorology—that nautical guide.

The illustrious naturalist Jean-Baptiste Biot called for an explanation in order to justify why this science had produced so little. However, on both the European and American shores of the Atlantic certain perseverant men were founding this repudiated science on the basis of observation.

The latest and most celebrated, the American Maury, courageously took on a task that would have made an entire administration retreat—the analysis and organization of countless logbooks, those sketchy and often unfinished documents that ship captains bring back with them. As a result, the excerpts put in the form of tables, where matching data are highlighted, provided rules and generalities. A congress of sailors from all over the world meeting in Brussels decided that the observations, which henceforth would be noted with greater care, would be centralized in a single facility—the Washington Observatory.

This is Europe's noble tribute to a young America, to the patient and ingenious Maury, the learned poet of the sea, who summarized its laws, and still more. For, by his great heart and his love of nature, as well as by his positive results, he has won over the world. The Republic of the United States generously gave his maps and his first book (with a run of 150,000 copies) to sailors of every nation. Many eminent men in France and in Holland such as Jansen, Tricault, Julien, Margollé, Zurcher and others have become the spokesmen and eloquent missionaries of this apostle of the sea.

Why has America done more in this realm than us? Because America is desire. It is young and burns with the desire to create relations with the rest of the world. In the midst of its superb continent and despite its many states, it feels nonetheless isolated. So far from its mother, Europe, it looks towards this center of civilization, just as the earth looks towards the sun, and anything that brings it closer to this great luminary makes it quiver. For proof of this, one need only recall the euphoria and touching celebrations that occurred after the installation of the submarine telegraph that brought the two shores together and held forth the promise of dialogue and response within minutes, so that the two worlds would always be as one!

With true genius, Maury has proven the harmony that exists between air and water. The maritime ocean is exactly like the aerial ocean. Its alternating motion and its exchange of elements are completely analogous. It distributes heat over the world and causes either dryness or humidity. The latter comes from the seas, from the infinite central ocean, and especially from those great heating tubes of the universal furnace—the tropics. Arid conditions come, on the contrary, by passing over the scorched deserts, the great continents, the glaciers (the true intermediate poles of the earth) that soak up every last drop of moisture. By alternating the density and lightness of the vapor, the heat of the Equator and the cold of the poles, cause it to travel in horizontal currents and counter-currents, which are constantly being exchanged. Below the Equator, the heat lightens the vapor causing it to rise and creating currents that move from top to bottom. Before spreading out, they float in this dark reservoir, which, as we have said, is like a ring of clouds around the globe.

Along with the pulsating tide, these currents are the very pulse of the sea and air. The beating tide, imparted on us by the stars, comes from beyond. But the pulse of these different currents is intrinsic to the earth; it is its very life.

I feel that Maury's stroke of genius is to have seen that "the most obvious factor in marine circulation— heat—would not be sufficient. There is another, no less important factor (in fact one that is even more essential)—salt."

Salt is so abundant in the sea that if it were collected all together it could cover all of America in a mound that was 4,500 feet tall.

Salinity of the sea, which varies little, increases or diminishes nonetheless, depending on location, currents, or the proximity of the equator and the poles. Desalination and resalination are the factors that determine whether the sea is heavy or light, whether it is mobile or not. This continual mix, with all its variations, causes water to run more or less quickly, in other words it *produces currents*—horizontal currents within the sea and vertical currents between the sea of water and the sea of air.

A Frenchman, Joseph Lartigue, astutely noted some gaps and inaccuracies in Maury's geography book. But the American author, anticipating such criticism, does not hide that the current state of knowledge in this domain is still incomplete. On certain points, he asserts that he can only speculate. At times he is clearly uncertain, baffled and perplexed. His honest and trustworthy book allows us to glimpse his inner struggle with two opposing schools of thought. The first is *biblical literalism* that conceives of the sea as a thing, which, once created by God, is little more than a piece of machinery under His control. The second and more modern school of thought is the *sympathy of nature* that perceives the sea as animate, as a life force and almost as a person, in which the world's loving soul still continues to create.

It is intriguing to see this author being irresistibly drawn to this second point of view. He first attempts to explain everything mechanically or physically—by gravity, temperature, density, etc. But that is not enough. In certain cases, he adds in some sort of molecular attraction or magnetic effect. And even this is not enough. It is then that he boldly turns to the physiological laws that regulate life. He gives the sea a pulse, arteries and even a heart. Are these merely stylistic or comparative forms? Not at all. He has—and this is where his genius lays—a compelling and irresistible feeling for the sea's character.

This is the secret of his power. This is what thrills his readers. Before Maury, for so many sailors who traveled across her waters, the sea was but a thing. With his book, the sea has become a person. They all feel she is a violent and formidable mistress that they want to tame.

He loves. He loves the sea. But on the other hand he constantly stops and restrains himself, for fear of venturing too far beyond his limited framework. Like Swammerdam, Bonnet and so many other illustrious scientists with religious souls, he fears that explaining nature too thoroughly in its own right is an act against God. This timidity is unreasonable. The more it becomes evident that life is present everywhere, the more conscious we become of the existence of a great Soul worthy of adoration—that unity of being through which all is generated and created. Where is the danger, if the sea, with its constant aspirations towards organized existence, were found to be the most energetic form of the same eternal Desire, which long ago gave birth to and still continues to create life on Earth?

The sea is as salty as blood. It has a circulatory system, a pulse and a heart (as Maury has dubbed the equator) where it exchanges its two types of blood. Can we be certain that a being with all these characteristics is a thing, an inorganic element?

It is a great clock, a great steam engine that imitates exactly the movement of vital forces. Is nature trying to trick us? Or must we conclude that within those masses animality exists.

Maury also lays out, although secondarily and tangentially, the crucial factor of the sea's living immensity. These billions and billions of beings that she continuously creates and then does away with absorb her life's milk—the spume mixed in with her water—extract from it the many salts of which they and their shells are made etc., etc. From there, they produce desalinated water, which is lighter and therefore moves and flows more easily. In the Indian Ocean and the Coral Sea—those powerful laboratories of animal organization—this force, which is less noticeable elsewhere, can be seen in all its immensity.

"Each one of these imperceptible creatures," says Maury, "changes the balance of the Ocean; they bring harmony and act as its compensators." Is this going far enough? Are they not the sea's essential driving force, which created her great currents and set the machinery into motion? Who knows whether this vital *circulus* of sea animality is not the starting point of all physical *circulus*? Who knows whether the animalized sea doesn't set into motion for eternity, the animalization of the as-of-yet unorganized sea, a sea that wants nothing more than to be organized as she ferments with future life?

CHAPTER 6

Storms

Matthew Maury has written: "Periodically great upheavals occur in the sea, which seem to insure that the various stages of its work will be carried out. These can be considered sea spasms."

The author is referring most notably to sudden turbulence that seems to come from below, and which in the Asian seas are akin to full-scale storms. He attributes various causes to them. Firstly, the violent encounter between two tides or two currents. Secondly, the sudden overabundance of rain water on the surface. And finally, the breaking up and rapid thaw of ice. Others suggest the possibility of electric activity or volcanic upheaval that occur at the bottom of the sea.

And yet, it is likely that the bottom of the Ocean and in fact the majority of her waters are rather calm. Otherwise, the sea would be unfit to fulfill its crucial role as mother and wet nurse to living beings. At one point, Maury calls the sea a great nursery. A world of delicate beings, more fragile than those that live on earth, are cradled and suckled by her waters. This presents us with a very gentle conception of the sea's inner-world and leads us to believe that her rough violence is the exception rather than the rule.

By nature, the sea is generally steady and subject to powerful regular and periodic movement. Storms are merely transient acts of violence committed by winds, electric forces or certain intensely critical moments of evaporation. These are crises that occur at the surface and they do not bring to light the true and mysterious character of the sea.

It would be ridiculous to judge a person's temperament based on a few bouts of fever. This is all the more true when it comes to judging the sea based on momentary external turbulence, which seems to affect only a few hundred feet at its surface!

Deep below the surface, the sea's stable, perfectly balanced, calm and fertile life, completely devoted to giving birth, continues. She does not even notice these minor events occurring at the surface. Her great legions of children—who, contrary to what was once believed to be true, thrive in the depths of her peaceful darkness and only rise to the surface towards the light and storms once a year, at most—must love their extraordinary wet-nurse as much as harmony itself.

Be that as it may, these upheavals are too important in the life of man for him not to go to great lengths in order to observe them. This is not an easy task. It is hard to keep a cool head. Even the most reliable descriptions provide only vague and general traits but little of what gives each storm its originality or identity as an unforeseen consequence of a thousand obscure circumstances that are impossible to sort out. The observer watching from the security of the shore can see more clearly since he isn't concerned about his own safety. But can he judge its entirety as well as someone who is in the eye of the storm and has the benefit of this perspective to see all aspects of its frightful panorama?

We, men of the land owe seamen the respect of putting greater stock in their eyewitness accounts—in what they saw and suffered through. I find the thoughtless skepticism shown by scientists in the comfort of their studies towards what sailors tell us, for example, about the height of waves, to be misplaced. They ridicule sailors who describe waves as high as one hundred feet. Engineers believed that they could take measurements during a storm and calculate precisely that water could go no higher than twenty feet. An excellent observer assures us, on the contrary, that from the safety of the shore he distinctly saw wave upon wave that was taller than the tower of Notre Dame and even higher than Montmartre.

It is quite clear that we are speaking of different things. And the contradictions stem from that fact. If we are referring to what we could consider the storm's field, its lower bed, in other words, if we are talking about the long lines of waves which break in rows and even as they rage, maintain some sort of orderliness, the engineers' evaluation is correct. With their rounded crests and alternating valleys that follow one after another, they break at most at a height of twenty or twenty-five feet. However, waves that are impeded and do not move in unison rise up to quite different heights. When they clash their ability to climb increases prodigiously. They propel themselves and crash down with an incredible force capable of knocking over, shattering or sinking a ship. Nothing is heavier than seawater. The seamen are referring to the spray of those battling waves and their frightful fallout. These are phenomena whose true scale cannot be assessed.

Once, not on a stormy day, but rather on a day of high-emotion, when the Ocean was preluding with wild gaiety, I was quietly sitting on a lovely promontory of about eighty feet. I was enjoying watching the Ocean over a stretch of a quarter of a league, attacking my rock and rounding out the green mane of its long waves as I urged it on as if I were at a race. The sea struck valiantly and made the promontory shake. I felt thunder under my feet. But this orderliness suddenly came to an end. A wave from the West came out of nowhere outrageously striking my great, steady southerly wave from the side. In the struggle, the sun was suddenly blocked out on my high-perched promontory. And instead of the iridescent vapor of light foam, a large black wave leapt up and crashed down heavily enveloping and soaking me. I was thoroughly drenched. I would have very much liked to have had those honorable academicians and engineers who measure the Ocean's battles with such precision by my side.

One must not, from the comfort of an armchair, frivolously put into doubt the veracity of so many intrepid, hardened and resigned men who have come face to face with death too often to have the childish conceit of exaggerating the danger to which they have been exposed. Nor must one compare the calm accounts of ordinary sailors who travel great, well-known routes to the sometimes-emotional narratives of those daring explorers who were the first to visit, discover and describe the reefs. For the latter are as scrupulous in their desire to see and study danger from close up as the common sailor on the roll-on-roll-off ship is in his attempts to avoid it. Explorers like James Cook, François Péron and Jules Dumont d'Urville ran very real dangers in the less traveled waters of the Coral Sea and of Australia. They had to confront constantly changing banks, and clashing currents that crisscrossed each other thereby producing terrible resistance within narrow passageways.

"With no storm, but rather by the rolling of the sea alone and with the wind coming directly from behind, a wave came from the side causing jolts that were so strong that the ship's bell started ringing by itself and if these great rolling waves would have continued their jerking motion, the ship would have been destroyed, dismembered and demolished. At the shore of the Aiguilles Banks also known as the D'Urville Banks the waves reached heights of eighty to one hundred feet. I had never seen such a monstrous sea. Luckily, only the crests of the waves were breaking on us otherwise the corvette would have been engulfed.... In this terrible struggle, it remained immobile, not knowing what to do. At times, the sailors on deck were submerged. There was awful chaos that lasted no less than four hours that evening...a century that was enough to turn your hair white!... –This is what southern storms are like, so horrible that even on land the natives that can sense their arrival are horrified by them in advance and hide in their caves."

No matter how exact and interesting these descriptions are I take care not to copy them. Moreover, I would not dare imagine, or alter things that I have never observed first-hand. At least, I believe that I have grasped the differing characteristics that distinguish the Ocean from the Mediterranean.

During the six months that I spent in Nervi, two leagues away from Genoa, on the most beautiful and most sheltered sea in the world, I only witnessed a minor freak storm that did not last very long but which, in that short time, raged with a singular fury. Since I could not observe it well from my window, I went outside and walked through the winding little streets along palazzi. I ventured down, not to the beach (there is none there) but onto a ledge of black volcanic stone that lines the coast. This is a narrow trail that at times is no more than three feet wide. As the path ascends and descends it often overhangs the sea, dominating it by thirty and sometimes as much as forty or sixty feet. Visibility was poor. Continual whirlwinds acted as screens. It was difficult to see anything and what view there was, was limited and dreadful. The harshness of that stony coast, its sharp angles, its points and peaks, its rough and unexpected crevices forced the storm to jump, to bound, to make great efforts and go through hellish agony. The sea's white foam gnashed and smiled wretchedly at the ferocity of the lava which smashed it without pity. The sounds were unbelievable, absurd. None of them were consistent. There was grating thunder and whistling like steam engines so shrill you had to cover your ears. Dazed by this spectacle that stunned all of my senses, I tried to recover. As I leaned against a wall, which was set back and protected me from the madwoman's grasp,

I could better understand the uproar. The surf was low and rough. The worst of the battle raged along this strange and sharply ragged coast with those harsh twists and turns that jutted out into the storm and tore at the waves. The ledge plunged down into its thundering depths.

The eye as well as the ear was offended by the diabolical contrast between the dazzling snow-white foam that was being whipped into that pitch-black lava. All in all, I felt it was the sea much less than the land that made this a frightening experience. The contrary is true of the Ocean.

CHAPTER 7

The Storm of October 1859

The storm that I was best able to observe is the one that raged on the Western coast of France on October 24th or 25th of 1859 and which resumed with more furor in an expanded form on Friday October 28th. It lasted the 29th, 30th and 31st. It was relentless, unflagging, for six days and six nights with only one short respite. The entire coast was strewn with shipwrecks. Before and after, very serious barometric disturbances occurred. Telegraph wires snapped or were distorted. Communication was severed. Several warm years preceded it. However, a quite different sequence of cold and rainy weather began with this storm. Up until this very day when I am writing these words, the year 1860 itself has been persistently drowned in Westerly and Southerly winds that seem determined to thrust upon us all the rains of the Atlantic and the great Southern Ocean.

I observed this storm from a friendly and peaceful place whose gentle character made such an event unexpected. I am speaking of the small port town of Saint-Georges, near Royan at the mouth of the Gironde. I had just spent five months there in great tranquility, collecting my thoughts, looking deeply into my heart and searching for an answer to the very delicate and serious subject I was dealing with in 1859. Memories of the place and my book, *La Femme*, are pleasantly intermingled in my mind. Could I have written it elsewhere? I do not know. What is certain is that the wild fragrance of the region, its unadorned gentleness, the fragrance of invigorating bitterness with which its moors are enchanted, the flora of the moors and dunes did much for that book and will always be a part of it.

The population of the region corresponds well with the natural landscape. No crudeness. No coarseness. The farmers are serious, with solemn ways. The seamen are pilots and a small Protestant clan that escaped persecution. A primitive honesty (locks are unknown in this village). No noise. A rare modesty for men of the sea, discretion and tact that are not necessarily found in the upper classes. Well thought of and accepted by them, I nevertheless had the peace and quiet necessary for work. Moreover, I took an interest in these men and the risks they faced. Everyday, although unspoken, my best wishes would go with them in their heroic work. I worried about the weather, and often wondered, while observing the dangerous pass whether the sea, which for so long had been beautiful and gentle, would not suddenly take a cruel turn.

This place of danger is not at all sad. Every morning from my window, I would see the white sails— slightly rosy from the dawn— of the many trading ships that were awaiting the wind in order to leave. The Gironde, at this location is no wider than three leagues. With the solemnity of the great American rivers it has the gaiety of Bordeaux. Royan is a pleasant place where people come from all over this region of Gascogne. Its bay as well as Saint-George's are treated free of charge to the spectacle of porpoises playfully frolicking as their adventurous hunting expeditions bring them as far as the river and even among the bathers there. They leap and propel themselves in the air five or six feet above the water. They seem to be quite aware of the fact that no one engages in fishing at this spot where at every moment the concern is with navigating and rescuing ships and where hardly any thought is given to the pursuit of porpoise oil.

To this joyfulness of the water, add the beautiful and unique harmony of the two banks. The rich vineyards of the Médoc look out over the harvests of Saintonge with its varied agriculture. The sky does not have that sometimes slightly monotone, unchanging beauty of the Mediterranean. Rather, here it changes constantly.

Iridescent clouds rise up from both seawater and freshwater, casting back strange colors of light green, pink and purple onto the mirrors from which they came.

Fantastic creations, which are glimpsed momentarily, only to become mere memories, adorn this gateway to the Ocean with bizarre monuments, daring arcades, sublime bridges and sometimes even triumphal arches.

Saint-Georges and Royan's two semi-circular beaches with their fine sand offer even the most delicate feet the gentlest strolls that can be extended without fear of over-exertion in the midst of the fragrant pine trees that brighten up the dunes with their youthful greenery. The two promontories that separate the beaches from the inland moors send forth salubrious emanations even from afar. The scent that predominates the dunes is not very medicinal. It is the honeydew odor of immortelles in which all the sun and warmth of the sands are concentrated. In the moors, the bitters bloom with a penetrating charm that awakens the brain and revives the heart. These are thyme and wild thyme, tender marjoram, sage blessed by our fathers because of its many virtues. Peppery mint and especially the little wild pinks, exude the fragrances of the finest spices from the Orient.

It seemed to me that on these moors the birds sang more beautifully than elsewhere. I have never encountered a lark like the one I heard in July on the Vallière promontory. It rose up in the spirit of the flowers, golden from the sun setting over the Ocean. Its voice, which came from so high above (it was perhaps at a thousand feet), despite being so powerful, was no less modest and sweet. With its rustic and sublime song, it was clearly addressing its nest, in a humble furrow, and its young who were watching. It was as if the bird was interpreting in harmony the beautiful sun, the glory in which it was soaring without pride, encouraging them and saying: "Rise up, my children."

From all this—songs and fragrances, the fresh air and the sea made fresh from the water of the beautiful river—emanated an infinitely pleasant harmony, although one that lacked radiance. The moon seemed luminous to me and yet without a vivid brightness. The stars were clearly visible but did not sparkle. The climate was cheerful, very human and would have been voluptuous if it were not for the presence of something that makes one think, something that banishes daydreams and reduces one to thought.

Why? Is it the quick sand, the shifting dunes, the crumbling limestone full of fossils that make you aware of mutability on a universal scale? Is it the silent but not forgotten memory of the Protestant persecutions? Perhaps more than anything else it is the solemn pass, the frequent shipwrecks and the proximity of the most frightful of seas that make the inland serious.

A great mystery occurs at this solemn point, a treaty, a marriage that is much more important than any royal union. Admittedly, it is a marriage of reason with two ill-matched partners. The lady of the water of the South-West—coupled with the Tarn and the Dordogne Rivers, pushed forward by her violent brothers the mountain streams of the Pyrenees—the loving and sovereign Gironde River comes to offer herself to her imposing spouse, the old Ocean. Nowhere is he harsher or more surly. The dreary barrier of the Charente's mud and the long line of sand that stops him over 50 leagues, cause his ill humor. When he is not unleashing his fury against the towns of Bayonne and Saint-Jean-de-Luz he beats the poor Gironde. She does not emerge, like the Seine does, protected on several sides. She arrives abruptly in front of the unlimited Ocean. More often than not he puts her in her place. She retreats. She throws herself to the right and to the left. She hides in the marshes of Saintonge as well as under the vineyards of the Médoc, transmitting to its wines the sober and cold qualities that characterize her waters.

Now, imagine men who are brave enough to throw themselves into the great debate between these two spouses. Men who get into a ship, confronting the blows that the two of them direct at one another, and who go fetch the timid vessels that are waiting at the mouth of the river, not daring to venture any further. This is the life of my pilots. It is modest but so glorious when it is recounted properly.

It is easy to understand that the old king of ship-wrecks, the ancient hoarder of so many submerged goods, has nothing but ill will for those that come to vie for his prey. If sometimes, he lets them do as they please, often, he is also malicious and underhanded. He reaches up at them, taking his revenge and delights more in being able to drown a single pilot than in engulfing two ships.

And yet, there was a time when there were no accidents to speak of. During the very hot summer of 1859 besides one small boat that was destroyed in June no disasters occurred in these waters. But some sort of uneasiness foretold of misfortune. September came and then October. The dazzling crowds of visitors who only want to see the Ocean smiling had already slipped away. I stayed tied there by my unfinished work and also by my strange attraction towards those intermediary seasons.

Shifting and bizarre winds, never usually seen, were noted in the area. An example—a scorching Easterly storm wind coming from a direction that was usually tranquil. The evenings were sometimes hot (more so in September than in August). They were sleepless, agitated, tense nights. The pulse was racing, affected, for no apparent reason, its mood erratic.

One day, when we were sitting in the pine grove that was being battered by the wind, and yet slightly protected by the dunes, we heard a young voice that was singularly clear and sharp with a fine and strong steely tone. And yet it came from a very young girl, who was quite small and had an austere profile. She was passing through with her mother and was singing at the top of her voice the words to an old song. We asked them to sit down and sing us the entire thing.

The little rustic poem marvelously portrayed the two spirits of the region. Saintonge is agricultural and her people love their homes. They are not like the Basques with their spirit of adventure. But despite their sedentary tastes, they have made themselves into a maritime people and expose themselves to danger. Why? The words to the song explain it all!

The King's beautiful daughter, who was pleasantly doing some washing like Nausicaa in the *Odyssey*, lost her ring in the sea. A son of the coast throws himself in the water to retrieve it but drowns. She cries and changes into rosemary on the shore, which is so bitter and fragrant.

This ballad of the drowning sung, at that critical time in that forest moaning from the imminent storm, moved and enchanted me and yet confirmed my innermost foreboding.

Every time I went to Royan, I could expect that during that short trip of a few hours I would get caught in a thunderstorm on the road when I was unprotected. It weighed upon me in the vineyards of Saint-Georges and the moor of the promontory that I had to climb to reach them. It weighed even heavier on the great circular beach of Royan that I walked along. Although it was October, the moor exuded all its wild fragrances and at times it seemed more penetrating than ever. On the still calm beach, the wind blew in my face, warm and gentle as was the sea that licked my feet with its duplicitous caresses. But I was not fooled. I suspected what they were up to.

As a prelude, after several lovely evenings, there were dreadful bursts of wind. This recurred several times, and most notably on the 26th. That night, I was certain that there had occurred great disasters. Our sailors were out. During the long fluctuations of the equinoctial crisis, at first they wait a bit, and then when the trouble lasts, duty and trade come to the fore. They carry on and venture forth at the risk of a sudden blow. It made a great impression on me. I told myself: "Someone has been lost at sea."

This was all too true.

On a pilot ship that, despite the threatening weather, was going to pull a vessel from the dangerous pass, a poor soul was washed away and the small boat, which was itself close to being destroyed, could not rescue him. He left behind three children and a pregnant wife. What made this loss all the more unfortunate was that this good man, in an act of loving generosity, which is not at all rare among sailors, had actually married a poor girl who was not able to work as a result of an accident in which her fingers had been cut off. It was a terrible situation; she was an invalid, pregnant and a widow.

Money was being collected and I went to Royan to offer my small contribution. A pilot whom I met spoke of the event with obvious pain: "That is what our trade is like, Sir. We especially have to go out when the sea is rough." The chief administrator of the Navy, who has the registers with the names of both the living and the dead on hand and knows better than anyone the fate of these families, appeared just as sad and worried to me. It was clear that this was just the beginning.

I started back, and as I went along the beach, I had the opportunity during this rather long journey to observe and study an area of clouds that I believed extended over 8 or 10 leagues in every direction. To my left, Saintonge along whose banks I was walking was waiting, dreary and passive. To my right, on the other side of the river, the Médoc was in a state of somber calm. Behind me, coming from the West, from the Ocean, rose a bank of black clouds. But, ahead of me, a land breeze was blowing into them from Bordeaux. This wind was coming down the Gironde, and one could only hope that the powerful river's protective current could push back that gloomy screen of clouds that the Ocean was whipping up.

Still unsure, I glanced behind me and checked the Cordouan lighthouse. Out on its reef it looked to me to be fantastically pale. Its tower seemed like a ghost that was saying "Woe, woe."

I was in a better position to assess the situation. I could clearly see that the land breeze would not only be overtaken, but it was actually aiding its enemy. That land breeze was blowing very low along the Gironde. It was crushing and cutting down all obstacles below, leveling the way for the high dark clouds that came from the direction of the Ocean. It was creating a sort of sliding track, on which those clouds could be transported even more quickly. In very little time, from the direction of the land everything was over. The winds ceased. Everything faded into shades of gray. Unobstructed, the superior winds reigned.

When I arrived at the vineyards of Vallière near Saint-Georges, many people were in the fields, quickly finishing what they had to do in the belief that it would be quite a while before they would be able to work again. The first drops of rain were falling, but soon it would be time to flee towards home.

I had seen thunderstorms before. I had read thousands of descriptions of storms and was ready for anything. But I never expected the impact of the long duration, sustained brutality, and implacable consistency of this particular storm. At least when there is an increase or a decrease, a break, even a *crescendo*, some sort of variation in a storm's activity, the soul and senses with their compelling need for change can relax and be distracted. But, in this case, for five days and five nights, it was the same fury— with nothing more or nothing less—and no change in the horror. No thunder, no clashing clouds, no wrenching sea. Immediately, an enormous gray tent obscured the horizon in every direction; it was like being blanketed in a dreary ash-gray shroud that didn't completely eclipse all light and allowed you to glimpse a chalky and leaden sea that was odious and wretched in its raging monotony. The sea emitted only a single note—the howl of a great seething boiler. No poetry of terror could have been as effective as this prose. Always, always the same sound: "Hu! Hu! Hu! or Oo! Oo! Oo!"

We lived on the beach. We were more than mere spectators of this scene; we were involved. At times the sea came as close as twenty paces. When she struck a blow the house trembled. Our windows were hit (luckily only obliquely) with the tremendous Southwest wind that brought forth not a flood but rather a deluge with this Ocean swollen by rain. From the first day, we had to hastily and with great difficulty, close all the shutters and light candles if we wanted to see in the middle of the day. In the rooms that looked out onto the countryside, the noise, the commotion was equally marked. I continued to work, curious to see whether this savage force would succeed in oppressing and shackling a free intellect. I kept my mind active, always in control. I wrote and I observed myself. In the end only fatigue and a lack of sleep upset what is my most delicate strength as a writer, my sense of rhythm. My phrasing was discordant. This, my instrument's most important string was broken.

The only variation in the great howling was the bizarre and fantastic voices of the wind relentlessly blowing around us. The house was an obstacle for it. It was a target that it attacked in a hundred different ways. Sometimes it was the abrupt blow of a master knocking at the door: jolts as if a powerful hand was trying to tear the shutters off; piercing howls that came down the chimney; grief at not being able to enter; threats if we did not let it in, and finally fits of rage and appalling attempts to take the roof off. And yet all these sounds were muffled by the great Hu! Hu! that was so tremendous, powerful and frightening! The wind seemed secondary to us. However, it succeeded in allowing the rain to penetrate. Our house (I almost said, our vessel) was taking on water. The attic, punched full of holes, was leaking profusely.

Even more serious, through its desperate efforts, the furor of the hurricane succeeded in loosening one of the shutters' hinges, which from that point on, despite still being closed, rattled, shook, and quivered. It had to be braced by tying it firmly to the hinge that was the most securely in place. In order to do this it was necessary to risk opening the window. The moment that I opened it, despite being protected by the shutters, I felt myself drawn into a whirlwind. The horrible force of a noise like a continuous canon blast that someone was firing in my ear without stopping was deafening. Through the slits, I caught sight of something that displayed the full measure of its incalculable forces. The waves, clashing and crashing against one another often were unable to come back down. The gusts, that came up from below, carried away these weighty masses like feathers, causing them to vanish somewhere over the countryside. What would it have been like if with our shutters having been torn away and our window having been smashed in, the wind would have transported into our home those great terrifying and agitated waves, that it was carrying across the fields?...

We had the peculiar fate of being shipwrecked on land. Our house, which was so close to this water, could have easily had its roof or perhaps even an entire floor torn off. The village residents worried about this every night, as they told us. We were advised to leave it. But we continued to believe that this storm that had lasted so long would eventually end and we kept saying: "Tomorrow."

The news we were receiving was dominated with stories of wrecks. On October 30th, quite near our home, a ship that was coming back from the Southern Ocean with thirty or so men went down in the pass itself. After having avoided the rocks and the reefs, it arrived in front of a small beach with fine sand, where the women bathe. Well, on that gentle beach, lifted up by the whirlwind to what was undoubtedly a great height, it came back down with an incredible weight, and was knocked over, pummeled, and destroyed. It remained there like a dead body. What had happened to the men? No trace was found of them. It was believed that they had all been swept from the deck.

This tragic event led us to believe there would be others, and we could only imagine misfortunes. The sea did not seem to have her fill of misfortune. Everyone was at their wits' end, not her. I saw our pilots venture behind a wall that blocked them out in the Southwest, keep watch anxiously, and shake their heads. No vessels, luckily for them, dared to attempt to enter and therefore none called for their help. Otherwise, they were there, ready to give their lives.

I too, watched that sea insatiably. I looked at her with hatred. Since I was in no real danger, I was all the more keenly aware of her dullness and gloominess. She was ugly and looked awful. Nothing was reminiscent of the superficial tableaux of poets. However, in a strange contrast, the less vital I felt, the more she, on the contrary seemed alive. All those waves electrified by such violent motion were full of life, as if animated by a fantastical soul. In the overall furor each wave expressed its own furor. In the total uniformity (a true although contradictory fact) there was a diabolical swarm. Were my eyes and my tired brain deceiving me? Or was it thus? The waves reminded me of frightful mob; a horrible rabble, not of men but of barking dogs, a million, a billion fierce or rather wild mastiffs... But what am I saying? Dogs? Mastiffs? That is not quite right. They were like abysmal and unnamed apparitions, creatures with no eyes or ears but only foaming mouths.

What do you monsters want? Are you not drunk from all the wrecks that I've heard so much about? What are you demanding?

—"Your death and death in general, the elimination of land and the return to chaos."

CHAPTER 8

Lighthouses

The Channel at the straits, where the flow of the Northern Ocean is absorbed, is wild. The Sea of Brittany, with its violent eddies along its coast's basaltic indentations, is fierce. But the Gulf of Gascogne from Cordouan to Biarritz is a sea full of contradiction—an enigma fraught with battles. To the south, it suddenly becomes an extraordinarily deep all-consuming watery abyss. A brilliant naturalist compares it to a gigantic sinkhole that is capable of absorbing seawater abruptly. The flow that escapes from it under amazing pressure rises to heights unknown in our seas.

The swell from the Northwest is the machine's engine. When it flows a bit to the North, it pushes towards the far end of the gulf and crushes Saint-Jean-de-Luz. However, when it moves more to the West, it forces the Gironde River to flow back and covers the unfortunate Cordouan lighthouse with frightful waves.

This respectable martyr of the seas is not well-known. Of all the lighthouses of Europe I believe it is the oldest. The only one that can claim such antiquity is the famous Lanterna of Genoa. But there is a great difference between them. The latter, high atop a fort that rests quite peacefully on good solid rock, can laugh off any storm. Cordouan is on a reef where water is ever-present. It truly took great audacity to build amid the flow—rather—amid the raging flow in the eternal battle between that river and that sea.

At every moment it receives either cutting lashes or heavy blows that thunder like canon fire. It is an eternal assault. Even the Gironde, pushed forth by land breezes and the streams of the Pyrenees, at times, also beats against this gatekeeper of the pass, as if it was responsible for the obstacles set up by the Ocean beyond.

However, it is the sole light in this sea. The seaman who misses Cordouan has much to fear. Pushed on by the North wind, he could go on to miss Archachon. This most dreadful of seas is also a sea of darkness. At night there are no guiding signs, no reference points.

During the six months we spent on that beach, the focus of our daily contemplation, I am almost tempted to say, our constant companion, was Cordouan. We fully appreciated that its position as the guardian of the seas, the dependable watchman of the strait transformed it into a person. Standing on the vast Western horizon, it appeared to us in a hundred different ways. At times, in moments of glory, it was triumphant under the sun. Sometimes, pale and indistinct, it floated in the fog and said nothing of use. At night, when it suddenly lit its red lantern and cast out its fiery gaze, it seemed like a zealous inspector, who earnest and concerned in his responsibilities, watched over the waters.

It was held responsible no matter what came from the sea. Even while it shed light on a storm and protected us from its dangers the lighthouse was implicated. Too often, this is how ignorance treats genius—by accusing it of the evils it is merely bringing to light. Even my wife and I were unfair. If it was late in lighting up, if bad weather came our way, we would cast blame, we would scold it: "Oh! Cordouan, Cordouan, you white ghost can you only bring us storms?"

And yet, I believe that during the October storm it saved our thirty men. The ship was demolished, but they all escaped.

It is bad enough to have a shipwreck, or to run aground in full daylight, knowing the location, circumstances and resources that remain. "Great God, if we must be lost at sea, let it be in daylight!"

When the ship carried from the high sea by this wild swell arrived near the coasts at night, it had a one in a thousand chance of entering the Gironde. On the right, the luminous Point de la Grave warned it to avoid the Médoc region. On its left, the little lighthouse of Saint-Palais shed light on the dangerous rocks of Grand'Caute on Saintonge's side. Between these two white and steady signals, on the central reef burst the red flash of Cordouan, which minute by minute showed the way.

In a desperate effort the boat, just barely made it through. The wind, waves and current overwhelmed it at Saint-Palais. The helpful trinity of the three lights reflected off each other; the thirty men saw where they were, that they were going to hit the sand and that they could save their lives if they could abandon the ship in time. They were ready to throw themselves in. They trusted in the hurricane and the furor of the wind itself. The storm treated them in fact precisely like those waves that it carried onto land without allowing them to return. Struck and bruised, who knew where they were going to end up, but when it was all over they were alive.

Who can say how many men and ships lighthouses save? The light, seen on those horribly confused nights, where even the bravest of men gets ruffled, not only shows the way, but it lifts the spirit and keeps the mind focused. It is a great comfort to be able to say to oneself, while in supreme danger: "Persist! One more try!...If the wind and the sea are against you, you are not alone. Mankind is there watching out for you."

Our ancestors, whose ships stayed close to the coasts and constantly observed them, needed to light them more than we do. It is said that the Etruscans began keeping nighttime fires on sacred stones. The lighthouse was an altar, a temple. It was a column and a tower. The Celts also erected some. Very large dolmens can actually be found at locations that are optimal for seeing fires. The Roman Empire illuminated the entire Mediterranean from promontory to promontory.

The great terror of northern pirates and the fearful trembling life of the dark Middle Ages extinguished all this. People worried about raids.

The sea was something to be feared. Any ship could be an enemy and if it ran aground it was an object of prey. Pillaging shipwrecks was every lord's retribution. It is the noble *droit of Admiralty*. We all know of the count of Léon who became rich from his reef with his "stones more precious than those that can be admired on any King's crown."

Nowadays, fishermen have often innocently caused shipwrecks by lighting fires on shore that could be seen from the sea. Lighthouses themselves have caused wrecks since one can easily be confused for another. One signal taken for a neighboring signal sometimes provokes horrible mistakes.

After its great wars, France was at the forefront of the new art of illumination and its application to the salvation of human life. Armed with the Fresnel lens (a lamp as bright as four thousand that could be seen from a distance of 12 leagues), France created a ring of these powerful flares with their intersecting lights penetrating one another. Darkness disappeared from our seacoasts.

For the sailor who was guided by the constellations, it was as if France had lowered a second sky. It had created at once planets, fixed stars as well as satellites and endowed these invented stars with the nuances and different characteristics of those above. The color, duration, and intensity of their scintillation were varied. Some were given a still light that was good enough for clear nights, others were given a moving revolving light like a fiery gaze piercing the four corners of the horizon. The latter, like those mysterious animals that illuminate the sea, exhibit the lively palpitation of a flame that blazes and grows dim that springs up and then dies out. On dark and stormy nights they are aroused. They seem to take part in the Ocean's convulsions and unrattled, they return fire on the lightning from the sky.

Keep in mind that at that time—1826—and even still in 1830 the whole sea was dark. There were few lighthouses in Europe. None in Africa except for the one at Cape Town. None in Asia except for in Bombay, Calcutta and Madras. Not a single one in the vast regions of South America. Since then, all nations have followed France's example and have imitated it. Little by little light is being shed.

At this point I would like to circumnavigate our Ocean between Dunkerque and Biarritz in order to review the important lighthouses. But this would take too long.

Calais, with its four lighthouses, all with different colored lights, that must be visible even in Dover, waves to England or to those who are merely passing by, with welcoming gestures. The beautiful gulf of the Seine between the Cape of la Hève and Barfleur, which is illuminated by friendly lighthouses, opens Le Havre onto America and receives it directly into France's hearth as well as into its heart.

France itself juts out into the sea, to take in ships lighting all of Brittany's points with admirable care. At the vanguard from Brest to Saint-Matthieu, to Penmark, to the île de Sein everything is crowned with fires—all flashes differing by minutes or seconds— that say to sailors: "Careful! Watch for those rocks... Avoid that reef...Turn here....Good! You've arrived at the point."

Please note that all these towers, erected in dangerous locations, often built on shoals and even during storms, demanded absolute solidity. Several rise up to great heights. Medieval architecture, of which so much is said, only built such tall structures by giving them outside supports, buttresses, flying buttresses and towards the tip of the towers, they no longer relied upon stone, but turned to less artistic iron cramps which joined the stone together. This practice is evident in Strasbourg's spire. Our builders scorn these methods. Héaux's lighthouse, which was recently built by Mr. Reynaud on Tréguier's dangerous reef des Epées, has the sublime simplicity of a gigantic sea plant. It has no need of buttresses. It drives its chiseled foundation into the rock. On a foundation of sixty feet wide rises a column of 24 feet in diameter. Its great granite stones are fit against each other. Moreover, for the lower sections, the foundation is joined by dies— also of granite—that penetrate the stacked stone. All this is cut so exactingly that cement is unnecessary. From top to bottom, with each stone biting into the next one, the lighthouse is no more than a solid block more unified than the rock it is built upon. The waves do not know what to do. They strike, rage and slide. In their great blasts of thunder, their only gain is that the lighthouse shakes and bows down a bit. But there is no need for alarm. Even the most ancient and most solid towers sway.

Therefore, instead of the sad bastions that threatened the sea in the past, like those I have seen that were erected against the Barbary pirates, modern civilization has built towers of peace and kindly hospitality. These are beautiful and noble monuments that are sometimes sublime from an artistic perspective, and always moving for the heart. Their signals of various colors, with glimpses of star-like gold and silver, offer a helpful firmament that human Providence organized on Earth. When no stars appear in the sky, the sailor can still see these and muster his courage, recognizing them as his own fraternal stars.

It is pleasant to sit by a lighthouse, under its friendly light. It is a true hearth of marine life. Some of them, and not necessarily the oldest, are already venerable for the men they have saved. Many a memory is tied to them; tales surround them, lovely but true legends. Two generations are all that is needed for them to become antique, consecrated by time. A mother will often tell her young family: "This one saved your grandfather, and without it, you would have never been born."

How many visits does it get from the anxious wife, watching for a returning ship? In the evening and even at night you will find her seated there, waiting and asking the helpful light shining above to bring back her missing love and to guide him back to port.

Our ancestors quite justifiably honored these sacred stones as altars to man's rescuer-gods. For the heart in the midst of a storm, that trembles and hopes, this has not changed. And in the obscurity of the night, that woman who is crying and praying sees it as the altar and the god itself.

BOOK II

The Genesis of the Sea

CHAPTER I

Fertility

During the Midsummer's Night (from June 24th to the 25th) at five minutes after midnight, herring fishing begins in the northern seas. Phosphorescent lights undulate or dance on the waves. "There's the herring's lightning." This is the traditional signal that can be heard from every boat. A living world has just risen from the depths to the surface following the lure of heat, desire and light. The pale and soft moonlight is pleasing to this timid race. It is the reassuring beacon that seems to embolden them at this great love feast. They rise, they rise all together, and not one of them stays behind. Sociability is the rule for this race. They are only ever seen together. Together they live buried in obscure depths. Together, they come in spring to take their small share of universal happiness, to see the day, experience pleasure, and die. Packed tightly, squeezed together, they can never get close enough to one another. They navigate in compact schools. The Flemish used to say, "It is as if our dunes just started floating." Between Scotland, Holland and Norway it seems that an immense island has risen up and that a continent is about to emerge. To the east, a branch detaches itself and enters the Sund, it fills the mouth of the Baltic Sea. In certain narrow passages rowing becomes impossible. The sea is solid. Millions of millions, billions of billions…who would dare to hazard a guess at this army's numbers. They say that long ago, near Le Havre, one morning a single fisherman found 800,000 of them in his nets. In a Scottish port, 11,000 barrels of them were caught in one night.

They move like a blind and fatal element, and no form of destruction discourages them. Men, fish, everything sweeps down on them. They move forward, they continue to sail on. This should come as no surprise: while they are sailing they love. The more of them that are killed the more they produce and multiply. Thick, deep columns float in the shared electricity, solely engaged in giving themselves up to happiness' great work. All this is set in motion by the water and electrical current. If you pick randomly within this mass, you will find fertile fish, some who were fertile and others who would like to be. In this world, that is not familiar with fixed unions, pleasure is an adventure. To love is to sail. All along the way, they pour out torrents of fertility.

At two or three fathoms deep, the water disappears under the incredible abundance of the maternal flow where the herring eggs bathe. At sunrise, it is a spectacle to behold for as far as the eye can see, for several leagues, the sea is white from the males' milt.

These are thick, oily and viscous waves, where life ferments in its very own leavening. Up and down over a hundred leagues, it is like a volcano of milk—of fertile milk—that erupted and flooded the sea.

Full of life at its surface, the sea would be overcrowded if this indescribable power of production were not violently combated by a fierce army, capable of all types of destruction. Consider that each herring has forty, fifty, as many as seventy thousand eggs! If violent death did not remedy this situation, with each one of them multiplying on average by fifty thousand, and each of these fifty thousand multiplying in turn at the same rate, in just a few generations they would overflow and solidify the Ocean, or they would putrefy it, eliminate any other race and turn the globe into a desert. Here, Life imperiously demands the assistance and the indispensable aid of its sister, Death. They wage a battle, an immense struggle, which is harmonious, and guarantees our salvation.

In the great universal hunt for the condemned race, those who are responsible for fleshing out and preventing the mass from dispersing, those who drive the mass towards the shore are the giants of the sea.

Whales and cetacea don't disdain this type of game. They follow it, dive into the schools, and enter the living thickness. With their immense mouths, they absorb tons of infinite prey, whose numbers do not diminish, and who flee towards the coasts. There, a quite different and even greater destruction occurs. First the smallest of the small fish, the tiniest fish swallow the herring spawn and eggs. They gorge themselves with milt; they eat the future. As for the present, for the full-grown herring, nature created a glutton who with his widely spaced eyes, scarcely sees. Despite this, he eats all the more; he is nothing but a stomach. He is part of the gluttonous tribe of gades: whiting, cod, etc. Whiting fills itself, stuffs itself with herring and becomes fat. Cod fills itself, stuffs itself with whiting and becomes fat. This goes on to the extent that the greatest danger to the sea— extreme fertility—reoccurs here to an even more frightful degree. Cod is quite another thing than herring. It produces up to nine million eggs! A fifty-pound codfish produces fourteen pounds of eggs! A third of her weight! Moreover, this creature, whose motherhood is formidable, can breed nine out of twelve months a year. *This* is the creature that could endanger the world. Help! Let's launch ships, let's commission fleets. England alone sends out twenty or thirty thousand sailors after them. How many are sent by America, and how many from France and Holland, from all over the earth? Cod alone has created colonies, established trading posts and cities. Its preparation is an art. And this art has a language, an entire technical idiom unique to those who fish cod.

But what can man do? Nature knows that our small efforts, our fleets and our fisheries are of no use towards its goals. It knows that cod will conquer man. It cannot rely on him. It calls upon forces of death that are far more energetic. From the river's depths to the sea, one of the most active ones arrives, one of the most determined eaters, the sturgeon. Having gone to the rivers in order to make love in peace, he emerges thin and fierce; he enters the sea's banquet with an immense appetite. It is a great pleasure for this famished creature to find the fat cod that has absorbed legions of herrings. It is an infinite joy for the fish to find substance concentrated there, to bite into brimming flesh. This valiant cod-eater, although less fertile, is still fecund. It has fifteen hundred thousand eggs. A fourteen hundred-pound sturgeon has one hundred pounds of milt, or four hundred pounds of eggs. The danger reemerges. Herring threatened with its tremendous fertility, cod threatened and sturgeon continues to threaten.

Nature has to invent a supreme devouring creature, an admirable consumer and a poor producer—one with immense digestive but stingy generative powers. A helpful and terrifying monster that cuts through this invincible flow of recurring fertility, absorbing with great effort. A creature who swallows all species with great indifference, the dead, the living—what am I saying?—everything he comes upon. Nature's *beautiful eater*, its patented eater: the shark.

But these terrifying destroyers are defeated in advance. No matter their fury for eating, they produce little. The sturgeon, as we saw, is less fertile than the cod, and the shark is sterile, in comparison to any other fish. It does not pour itself out as they do in torrents throughout the sea. As a member of the Vivipara, the young shark, its feudal heir, who is born terrifying and armed, develops in the mother's womb. In her fertile darkness, the sea can smile at the destroyers to whom she gives rise, since she is quite sure of continuing to give birth to even more life. Her essential richness defies all the rage of these devouring creatures; it is inaccessible to their reach. I am speaking of the infinite world of living atoms, of microscopic animals, the true abyss of life that ferments in her womb.

It has been said that the absence of solar light precludes life, and yet in the ultimate depths the ground is strewn with starfish. The waters are populated with infusoria and microscopic worms. Innumerable molluscs drag their shells there. Bronzed crabs, radiating sea anemones, snowy cowries, golden lampreys, wavy volutes, everything is alive and moving. Luminous animalcules, who when attracted to the surface appear there like streaks, like serpents of fire and shining garlands, proliferate in the sea. In its transparent thickness, the sea must be fortuitously illuminated by them. The sea herself has a certain radiance, a certain half-glow that can be seen on both living and dead fish. She is her own light, lantern, sky, moon and stars.

Anyone can see the fertility of the sea in our salt works. The waters that are concentrated there leave purple deposits that are none other than infusoria. Any sailor that has undertaken a journey of any length says that he only traveled through living waters. The French explorer Louis Freycinet saw sixty million square meters covered in a scarlet red. This was none other than a plant-animal, which was so small that a square meter contained forty million specimens. In the Gulf of Bengal, in 1854, Captain W.E. Kingman sailed for thirty nautical miles through an enormous white stain that gave the sea the appearance of a snow-covered plain. There was not a single cloud, and yet the sky was lead gray in contrast to the brilliant sea. When examined closely, this white water was gelatine, and when observed under a magnifying glass it was a mass of animalcules that produced bizarre luminous effects when they moved about.

François Péron also tells about sailing for twenty leagues through a sort of gray powder. Seen through a microscope, it was none other than a layer of eggs from an unknown species that covered and hid the waters over an immense area.

Off the desolate coasts of Greenland, where man could easily believe that nature has ceased to exist, the sea is enormously populated. One can sail over two hundred nautical miles in length and fifteen in width on waters that are dark brown, due to the presence of a microscopic medusa. According to the German botanist Jacob Schleiden, each square foot of this water contains more than one hundred ten thousand of them.

These nourishing waters are dense with all sorts of fatty atoms, that are well-suited to the soft nature of the fish, who lazily opens his mouth and sucks in, fed like an embryo in the communal mother's womb. Does he know that he is swallowing? Hardly. The microscopic food is like milk that comes to him. The great fate of the world, hunger, exists only for those on land. Here, it is averted, unknown. There is no effort to move, no search for food. Life must float like a dream. What need is there for strength? Any consumption of force is impossible. It is saved for love.

That is the true work of this great world of the sea: to love and to multiply. Love fills its fertile nights. It dives deep and seems even richer for those that are infinitely small. But who is the atom really? Just when you think that you hold the last one, the indivisible one, you see that he still loves and divides his existence in order to create another being. At the lowest degree of life where there are no other organisms to be found, you can already find all the possible forms of generation in place.

This is the sea. It would seem that she is the great female of the earth, who is tirelessly desiring, permanently conceiving and unendingly giving birth.

CHAPTER 2

The Sea of Milk

Even the purest seawater, taken from the open sea, far from any intermixture, is slightly whitish and a little viscous. It flows slowly through your fingers when cupped in your hand. Chemical analyses do not explain this characteristic. An organic substance exists in this water that such analyses cannot break down without destroying what makes it distinctive or reducing it to common elements.

Marine plants and animals don this substance, whose enveloping mucosity is like gelatin both solid and trembling. Thus, they appear to be draped in diaphanous clothing. And nothing contributes more to the fantastical illusions that the sea's world presents us with. It reflects light in unique and strangely iridescent ways. As is the case of fish scales, or molluscs that seem to draw the luxuriousness of their pearly shells from it.

This is what strikes a child when seeing a fish for the first time. I was quite young when it happened to me, but I clearly remember the strong impression it made. This shiny, slippery creature with its silvery scales astonished and thrilled me more than I can say. I tried to grab it but found it as difficult to hold on to as the water that escaped through my tiny fingers. It seemed to me that the fish was identical to the element in which it was swimming. I formed the muddled idea that it was none other than water, organic animal water.

Much later, as an adult, I was equally struck when, on a beach, I would see some sort of Radiata. Through its transparent body I could make out the pebbles and sand. Clear as glass, slightly thick, quivering when it was poked, it appeared to me, just as it had appeared to the Ancients and or later, in the 18th century, to René de Réaumur who simply called the creatures *gelatinized water*.

This impression is reinforced even more when we come across those yellowy-white ribbons in their earliest stages of formation with which the sea is trying out a soft form of its more substantial fucus. The laminariae, which eventually turn a darker brown, also become as leathery as skins or hides. But when they are still young, in their viscous state, in their elasticity, they have the consistency of a solidified stream, made all the stronger by its suppleness.

What we know today about generation and the complex organisms of lower order animals and plants does not allow us to form the same conclusions as the Ancients or Réaumur. But all this does not prevent us from returning to a question first posed by Bory de Saint-Vincent: "What is sea mucus, this slime which is generally present in water? Is it not the universal component of life?"

Preoccupied by these thoughts, I went to see an illustrious chemist, who has a pragmatic and solid intellect and is as prudent an innovator as he is bold. With no preamble, I asked him my question *ex abrupto*: "Sir, according to you what is this viscous, whitish element present in seawater?"

His response: "It is none other than life itself."

And then reconsidering this overly simplistic and unnuanced remark, he added: "I mean that it's partially organized matter, which is already completely organizable. In the case of certain waters we merely have a density of infusoria, in others we have something that will be or could become such a presence. Moreover, such a study remains to be done. It has yet to be seriously undertaken."

Upon leaving him, I went straight to a great physiologist, whose opinion is equally as influential, as far as I am concerned. I ask him the same question. His answer was quite long and beautiful. Here is the gist of it:

"We do not know the constitution of water anymore than we know that of blood. Our best guess as far as seawater *mucus* is concerned, is that it is as much an end as it is a beginning. Is it the result of the vast remnants of death, which are then donated to life? Undoubtedly yes, this is a law of nature. But in fact, in this sea world with its rapid rate of absorption most creatures are absorbed while still alive. Death is not a prolonged state for them, as often happens on land, where destruction is slower. The sea is an extremely pure element. War and death take care of everything and leave nothing behind."

"Without arriving at the point of supreme dissolution, life continually molts and secretes, thereby eliminating itself of unnecessary excess. We, terrestrial animals, constantly shed. This shedding of skin, which can be seen as a partial but daily death, fills the world of the seas with a gelatinous richness that instantly benefits nascent life. It finds the oily overabundance of this communal secretion, those still animate particles with live liquids, that haven't had the time to die floating in the water. Nothing descends to an inorganic state, but rather is quickly integrated into new organisms. Of all the theories, this is the most plausible. Without it, you are thrown into extremely difficult problems."

The ideas of these men, who are among today's most advanced and most serious thinkers, are easily reconciled with those put forth, thirty years ago by the naturalist Etienne Geoffroy Saint-Hilaire on common *mucus* from which it seems that nature draws all life. According to him: "It is a substance that can be animalized, namely the first stage of organic bodies. There is no animal or plant that does not absorb or produce it in the first stages of life no matter how weak they are. In fact, its abundance actually increases in conjunction with the organism's debility."

That last remark opens up a penetrating perspective on sea life. For the most part, her children seem like fœtuses in their gelatinous stage. They absorb and produce mucous matter filling the waters with it, thereby endowing the sea with a gentle fertility like that of an infinite womb where new children continually come to swim as if in warm milk.

Let us witness the divine work. Let us take a drop of seawater. In it we will see the original creation all over again. God does not act in one way today and another tomorrow. I have no doubt that my drop of water's transformation will tell me about the universe. Let's wait and observe.

Who can anticipate, who can guess the story of this drop of water? What will emerge from it first? An animal-like plant or a plant-like animal?

Will this drop become that primitive *monad*, the infusorium, which by moving about and vibrating is soon transformed into a vibrio and which by climbing from rung to rung—hydra, coral or pearl—will perhaps in ten thousand years attain the rank of insect?

From this drop, will there come that plant fiber, the thin, silky downy strand that one might not realize is a living creature but that is none other than the new born hair of a young goddess, a sensitive and lovely strand of hair so aptly called: *maidenhair*.

This is not a fable it is natural history. This hair with its dual nature—plant and animal—is life's eldest child.

Look at the bottom of a spring, at first you see nothing. Then you can make out some slightly murky beads. With a good field glass this murkiness appears to be perhaps a small gelatinous or fluffy cloud. Under a microscope, this particle becomes more complex, like a group of threads or small hairs. They seem a thousand times finer than the finest hair from a woman. This is life's first timid attempt at becoming organized. These conferva, as they are called, are universally found in freshwater and in very still salt water. They are at the start of two classes of plants— those that originated in the sea and those that became terrestrial when land emerged. Out of the water emerged families of countless mushrooms while in the water grew families of the conferva, algae and other analogous plants.

This is the primitive component that is indispensable to life and we find it already where life seems impossible. This light mucus and these tiny creatures that look like barely defined droplets but are in fact swaying and moving about can be found in dark martial water rich in iron as well as in extremely hot thermal waters. It matters little how they are categorized—that Augustin de Candolle honors them with the title of animal or that Félix Dujardin ranks them at the bottom rung of plants. They ask only to live and to begin through their modest existence the long sequence of beings, which are only possible because of them. Dead or alive these little ones are food for the rest and administer from below the gelatine of life that others constantly draw upon in the maternal water.

It is completely unrealistic to point to animal and complex plant fossils as representative of the original creation. These animals (the trilobites) already had superior senses such as eyes. The plants are gigantic and are endowed with advanced organization. It is infinitely more likely that much simpler beings preceded these but that their soft constitution left no trace. How is it possible that these weaker organisms could have continued to thrive when those with harder shells had been pulverized or dissolved? In the Southern Ocean, fish with sharp teeth have been seen grazing coral like sheep graze grass. The soft early attempts at life, the animated gelatine that is hardly solid yet, had melted millions of times before nature was able to produce its robust trilobite and its indestructible fern.

Let us restore these little ones—these conferva—these microscopic algae, these beings that float between two kingdoms, these still indistinct atoms that pass at times from the plant to the animal kingdom, or from the animal to the plant kingdom. Let us restore the primogeniture, which is, apparently theirs by rights.

A vast and wonderful marine flora began its rise from them and at their expense.

At this starting point, I cannot help expressing my tender feelings for them. I am eternally grateful to them for three reasons. Whether small or large, these plants have three endearing characteristics.

First of all, there is their innocence. Not one of them is deadly. There are no poisonous plants in the sea. Everything in marine plants is healthy and hygienic—a blessing of life.

These innocents ask only to nourish the animal kingdom. Several of them, like the laminaria, produce a sweet sugar. Several others have a beneficial bitterness (like the lovely purple and violet ceramie that is also called Corsican moss.) All of them are rich in nourishing mucilage especially, several fucuses, the ceramie of salanganes whose nests are eaten in China, and the maidenhair, which is the savior of those with weak chests. For all cases in which today iodine is recommended, in the past in England they made kelp preserves.

The third characteristic that is striking in this vegetation is that it is the most loving of plants. At least it is tempting to believe this upon seeing its strange metamorphoses at the moment of its union. Love is life's attempt to go beyond its being and to exceed its capabilities. This is evident from the fireflies and other tiny animals, who are excited to the point of blazing up, but it is no less obvious in plants such as conjugatae, those algae, which at the sacred moment leave their vegetal life to usurp a higher one and endeavor to become animals.

Where did these wonders begin? Where did the first versions of animal-life evolve? Where did organized life originally occur?

In the past this was intensely debated. However, today, scholarly European circles agree about these things. I could find the answer to these questions in any number of well-accepted and authoritative books, but I prefer to borrow from a paper that was recently awarded a prize by the Academy of Sciences and is therefore ratified by that institution's expertise.

Living beings exist in water that is between eighty and ninety degrees. It was when the earth's temperature cooled down to this temperature that life became possible. Then, water had in part absorbed the element of death, carbonic acid gas. Breathing became possible.

The seas at first were like those parts of the Pacific Ocean that are not very deep and are strewn with small low-lying islands. These small islets are the extinct craters of former volcanoes. Explorers have only become aware of them because their highest points, which have been built up over time by polyps, are above sea level. But the depths between these volcanoes are probably no less volcanic, and must have been the receptacles of life in the earliest attempts at an original creation.

For ages, popular tradition saw volcanoes as the protectors of underground treasures, which, at times, let the gold hidden in its depths escape. This is poetic fiction that has some truth to it. Volcanic regions contain the earth's treasure— powerful virtues of fertility. They endowed the sterile land. From the dust of their lava, and their still warm ashes life must have bloomed.

Everyone knows of the fertility of Vesuvius' slopes and Mount Aetna's valleys with the long roots that push all the way to the sea. Everyone knows of the paradise that the beautiful volcanic cirque of the Kashmir valley forms below the Himalayas. The same exact thing is repeated for the South Sea Islands.

In the least favorable circumstances, the area around the volcanoes and the hot current that exists there sustain animal life in the most desolate locations. Under the horror of the Antarctic pole, not far from the volcano of Mount Erebus, John Ross found live coral at a thousand fathoms below the icy sea.

In the early ages of the world, countless volcanoes had an underwater action that was much more powerful than today. Their cracks and their intermediary valleys allowed sea mucus to accumulate in certain areas and to become electrified by the current. Undoubtedly, that is where the gelatine thickened, set, became firm, where it worked itself and fermented with all its youthful strength.

The leavening in all of this was the attraction of matter to itself. Creative elements, originally dissolved in the sea, were combined—or should I say were married. Elementary lives appeared, at first only to dissolve away and then die. Others, enriched by the remains of their predecessors, persisted. These preparatory beings, these slow and patient underwater creators, from that moment on, began the eternal work of production, which they continue to perform under our very eyes to this day.

The sea, which was nourishing all of them, would supply to each one what it most needed. Each one decomposes the sea in its own way, to its own advantage. Some like the polyps, the madrepores and shellfish absorb limestone, others such as tunicates and rough horsetails concentrate silica. Their remains and their constructions draped the gloomy and bare virgin rocks, those daughters of a fire, which had torn them from the planetary core and thrown them out burning hot and sterile.

Our tiny creators provided quartz, basalt and porphyry as well as semi-vitrified stone with a more human outward appearance as well as the sweet and fertile elements drawn from the mother's milk—as I call sea mucus—that they developed and laid down in order to make the land inhabitable. In these more favorable environments, the improvement and ascent of primitive species could be fulfilled.

At first, this work must have been carried out between the volcanic islands, beneath their archipelagos, in those sinuous twists and turns, those peaceful labyrinths where the waves only penetrate quietly and that act as warm cradles for newborns.

But the blooming flower blossoms in all its glory in the deep hollows of the Indian gulfs, for example. There, the sea was a great artist. She gave the land the lovely, blessed shape in which love enjoys being created. With her assiduous caresses, eventually rounding out the shore, she gave the land maternal curves and I would almost say the visible tenderness of a woman's breast, which the child finds to be so tender—shelter, warmth, and peace.

CHAPTER 3

The Atom

One day a fisherman gave me three creatures from the dregs of his catch that were near death: a sea urchin; a starfish and a beautiful brittle star which was still moving the delicate arms that it would soon lose. I gave them seawater and for two days forgot them while preoccupied by other matters. When I returned to them, everything was dead. Nothing was recognizable. The whole scene had undergone a renewal.

A thick gelatinous film had formed on the surface. I took an atom with the tip of a needle and once under the microscope that atom showed me this: A swirl of short, strong, thickset and fiery animals—kolpods—came and went, drunk with life, I dare say thrilled to have been born and celebrating their birthdays with a strange bacchanal.

In the background was a swarm of tiny microscopic young snakes or eels that were not so much swimming as they were vibrating in order to shoot themselves forward. These are called vibrios.

Despite the fatigue of watching so much motion, my eye soon noticed that not everything was moving. There were vibrios that rather than vibrating remained stiff. There were some that were linked together in an embrace, clustered together in swarms that had not come apart and that seemed to be waiting to be set free. In the lovely ferment all around these still motionless beings, the disorderly mob of these large stocky kolpods dashed about madly, raging, foraging. They seemed to be grazing on them without limit, feasting with delight, growing fat.

Remember that this grand spectacle was unfolding within the confines of an atom taken from that filmy surface with the tip of a needle. How many similar scenes could this gelatinous ocean, which had appeared so quickly in that vessel of water, have provided! No time had been wasted! Those who were dying or already dead had immediately created a new world from their fleeting life. From three lost animals, I gained millions and these were so young and so lively, carried away by such an intense, all-absorbing movement—a true passion for life!

This infinite world—which is so intertwined with ours—was practically unknown until now. In the 17th century, Jan Swammerdam and others, who had glimpsed it, did not go beyond the first stages. Much later, in 1830, the magician Christian Ehrenberg conjured this world up, revealed it and organized it. He studied the faces of these invisible beings, their organisms and habits. He watched them absorb, digest, navigate, hunt and fight. Their method of reproduction remained obscure to him. What of their loves? Do they have loves? Does nature go to the trouble of creating a complex form of generation in these extremely elementary beings? Or are they born spontaneously, like certain plant mould or as the masses say "like mushrooms?"

This is an important question, which leaves many scholars smiling and shaking their heads. We are so sure of holding the mystery of the world in our hands, of having laid down the laws of life without exception! It is up to nature to obey them. When Réaumur was told, one hundred years ago, that the female silk worm could reproduce alone and without a male, he refused to believe it: "Nothing comes from nothing." That fact, which many still refute and many are still proving true, has finally been accepted, not only in the case of the silk worm, but for bees, certain butterflies and still other animals.

Throughout history, in all nations, both scholars and common people have agreed: "Death brings life". It was especially held to be true that the life of these imperceptible creatures emerged immediately from remains that were bequeathed to them by death. Even William Harvey, who was the first to formulate the law of generation, did not dare refute this ancient belief. When, he said: "Everything comes from the egg" he added, *or from the dissolved elements of a previous life.*"

This is exactly the theory that has been so brilliantly revived by the experiments of Felix Pouchet. He established that the fertile jelly, called the "proliferous membrane" which gives birth not to new beings but rather to the germs and ovules from which new beings will be born, is created from the remains of infusoria and other beings.

We live in an age of miracles. One has to accept it. This particular miracle is not so astonishing.

In the past, people would have laughed if someone had claimed that animals, in a blatant disregard of the established laws, took it upon themselves to breathe through their foot. However, the extraordinary work of the zoologist Henri Milne Edwards has brought them to light. Similarly, it has been said, that Georges Cuvier and Henri de Blainville had observed that certain beings lacking normal circulatory organs compensate by using their intestines. But these great naturalists found this fact so outrageous that they didn't dare report it. Today, Milne Edwards himself, Jean de Quatrefages and others have established that it is true.

No matter the theories about their birth, once our atoms are born they offer an infinitely and admirably varied world. They already honorably represent every form of life. If they are conscious of each other's existence then they must be convinced that their total harmony leaves nothing to be desired.

They are not dispersed species that were created separately. They obviously form a kingdom, in which the different genera have organized a great division of vital labor. They have collective beings like our polyps and our corals, still bound together, enduring the subjugation of communal living. They already have tiny molluscs that adorn themselves with adorable shells. They have agile fish and wriggling insects, proud crustaceans, miniature versions of future crabs that are also armed to the teeth—warrior atoms that hunt peaceful atoms.

All this in an enormously and frightfully rich universe, which puts the visible world to shame! We have not even mentioned the rhizopods, who with their tiny mantles did their share to build up the Apennines, and raise the Cordillera. The Foraminifera alone—this huge tribe of shelled atomies—number up to two thousand species according to Charles d'Orbigny. They are contemporary with every age of the Earth. They are represented in the various layers of our thirty crises of the globe, having varied very little in form persisting as a genus, always remaining the same witnesses of the planet's life. Today the Southern pole's cold current, which is divided in two at the tip of South America, haphazardly sends forty species towards la Plata, and forty towards Chile. But the great factory where they are created and organized seems to be the hot sea river that flows from the West Indies. The Northern currents kill them. The great paternal stream carries the dead to Newfoundland and over our Atlantic ocean, the bottom of which is carpeted with their remains.

When the illustrious father, rather the godfather of the atom, Ehrenberg baptized them, sponsored them, introduced them into science, he was accused of having a weak spot for them. It was said that he was putting too much emphasis on these tiny creatures. He claimed that they were complicated and had highly evolved organisms. Such was his generosity towards them that he went as far as to give them one hundred and twenty stomachs. The visible world was offended and in a brutal response, the naturalist Félix Dujardin reduced them to the most basic simplicity. According to him, these supposed organs were nothing of the sort. However, since he could not refute their capacity for absorption, he admitted that they had the ability, when necessary, to suddenly create a temporary stomach that was the exact size of whatever they were about to swallow. This point of view did not win over Pouchet (who is partial to Ehrenberg's point of view).

What is indisputable and admirable in these

creatures is the vigor with which they move.

Many of them have all the outward traits of nascent individuality. They do not remain enslaved to the communist and polypous life that weighs down their direct superiors, the true polyps. Many of these impulsive invisible beings are individuals, in other words, they are capable of coming and going on their own as they please. They are free citizens of the world who depend on no one but themselves as far as directing their movements is concerned.

The infusoria have already equaled and surpassed anything that could be imagined in the realm of locomotion, in the various ways of moving through the more advanced world above. The impetuous spin of a powerful star or of a sun that drags weaker bodies along its path as if they were its planets, the unsteady course of a wild comet that passes or breaks up over indistinct worlds along its way, the graceful undulation of the slender eel swimming along in the water or onto land; the oscillating boat easily making its turns drifting along; and finally the slow and circumspect crawl of our Edentata leaning upon and grabbing onto anything and everything—all these different speeds can be found in the world of the imperceptibles. But with such simplicity! This one is no more than a strand that shoots forward like a springy corkscrew. This other has only a swaying tail or little vibrating cilia to act as both his oars and rudder. Together, the charming vorticellae, like urns filled with flowers moor themselves to an island – a tiny plant or a tiny crab— and then they cut themselves free from the others by simply detaching their delicate peduncle.

What is even more striking than their organs of locomotion, is what we could call their expression, their demeanor, their primitive gestures of mood and temperament. There are apathetic beings, others still are restless and ready to wage war, others are attentive, and for no reason it seems are in a state of pointless agitation. At times, in the midst of a throng of calm and peaceful folks, a deaf and blind scatterbrain upsets or distracts everyone.

What an astounding spectacle! They seem to be rehearsing the drama that our world will be performing, our noble and serious world of large visible animals.

First and foremost among the infusoria, let us respectfully mention the majestic giants, the two leaders of the order, the high point of movement, with their deliberate but formidably well-armed strength.

Take moss from a roof, put it in water for a few days, and then look at it under a microscope. A powerful animal, which is admittedly the elephant, the whale of infusoria, moves about with the vigor and grace of young life not typically seen in these giants. A little respect, please! This is the king of the atoms, the rotifer, which got its name because on either side of its head are two wheels that are either organs of locomotion—they make him look like a steamship—or perhaps act as hunting weapons that help him capture his tiny prey.

Everything flees; everything yields. Only one other being puts up a resistance and fears nothing, relying on his own weapons. This is a monster, but one that is already endowed with superior senses. He has two big crimson eyes. Although he is not very mobile and a true Tardigrada, he nevertheless sees and he is armed. His strong appendages have very accentuated claws, which allowed him to dock when needed, and of course help him when fighting.

This is nature's powerful beginning and in its thriftiness with substance and matter, it starts with nothing and creates majestically! It is a sublime overture! These beings—no matter their size—have a colossal capacity for absorption and motion lacking in the enormous animals that are classified in much higher categories.

The oyster, fastened to his rock, the slug dragging along on its stomach are to rotifers what the Alps and Cordillera are to me—disproportionately big beings that can only be measured with the eyes, hardly with arithmetic and thought.

However, in those mountain-like animals what became of the nimbleness and the passion for life displayed by the rotifer? What a fall we take when ascending! ...My atoms were too lively, too animated they were dazzling while those gigantic creatures are struck with paralysis.

What would happen if the rotifer could conceive of those collective beings like the superb and colossal brittle star and sponge on display at the Museum of Natural History in Paris in which infinity lays dormant? The sponge is to the rotifers what the Earth with its nine thousand leagues in circumference is to man. Well, I am convinced that in this comparison, far from being humiliated the atom would burst with pride and would say: "I am great."

Oh rotifer, rotifer! Don't look down on anyone. I fully appreciate your advantages and your superiority. But who knows perhaps that captive life that you disdain is progress! Is your exhilarating liberty with its breakneck turbulence an end point? As its starting point, on its way towards a higher destiny, nature prefers to take the form of immobile charm. It enters the dark sepulchre of gloomy communism in which each individual component counts for very little. It learns to overcome individual anxiety and to concentrate matter in order to benefit higher orders.

It lays dormant there for some time, like Sleeping Beauty. But whether it is sleep, captivity or even charm, this state is not death. That rough sponge made of its felt-like flint lives. Without moving, without breathing, with no circulatory organs, with no sensory apparatus, it lives. How do we know?

The sponge gives birth twice a year. In its own way it knows love and in fact more lavishly than others do. On the appointed day, small spheres escape from the mother sponge that are armed with frail fins, which allow them some freedom of movement for a while. They quickly fasten themselves to a surface and appear as delicate fresh water sponges, which will in turn begin to grow.

Thus, in this mysterious enigma on the uncertain threshold of life, with its apparent lack of any senses or organization, reproduction reveals the opening of the visible world by which we will ascend. Nothing exists yet, but in this nothingness there is already motherhood. Just as with the Egyptian gods, Isis and Osiris who gave birth before they were born, Love is born before Being.

CHAPTER 4

Blood Flower

At the heart of the globe, in the hot waters of the Equator, in these water's volcanic depths, the sea abounds in life to the point that she seems almost incapable of keeping her creations in balance. She goes beyond plant life. Even her first offspring border on animated life.

But these animals adorn themselves in a strange botanical luxuriousness, with magnificent coats made of eccentric and luxuriant flora. For as far as the eye can see, there are what, in their form and color, appear to be flowers, plants and shrubs. And these plants ripple with movement. These shrubs are excitable, these flowers tremble with a budding sensitivity and a dawning will.

This oscillation is full of charm, these ambiguities quite graceful! At the boundary between two kingdoms, in the flowing form of this fantastical spectacle, the mind first awakens. This is a dawn. This is a new day. With its dazzling colors, its mother-of-pearl or enamel, it foretells the coming night's dream and the day's thought.

Thought! Do we dare use this word? No, it is still dreams and reverie that eventually become clearer like a daydream.

Already, North of Africa or in the South by Cape Town the plant-life that once reigned in the temperate zone encounters animated rivals that vegetate and flower—equaling and soon surpassing the plant life.

There, the great spectacle begins and intensifies as it creeps up towards the Equator.

Uniquely elegant shrubs like gorgonians and isidae stretch out their sumptuous fans. The coral grows red under the waves.

Next to the dazzling rainbow-colored flower-beds the stone plants begin, the madrepores where every branch, or should one say, where their hands and fingers display rosy white blossoms reminiscent of those on peach and apple trees. This magical illusion continues over seven hundred leagues before the Equator and seven hundred leagues beyond it.

There are uncertain beings, such as the corallines that all three kingdoms fight over. They look like animals, they look like minerals but in the end they have recently been awarded to the plant kingdom. Perhaps this is truly the point at which life rises obscurely from its stony sleep, without yet being able to detach itself from this rough starting point, as if to make us aware—we of the ternary fraternity, who are so proud and so highly placed—of the humble mineral's right to ascend and to become animate and of the deep yearning at Nature's core.

"Our prairies and forests on land," says Darwin "seem desolate and empty when compared to those of the sea." And, in fact, everyone who travels across the transparent Indian Ocean is struck by the phantasmagoria found on the ocean floor. What is particularly surprising is the singular exchange of natural emblems and appearance between plants and animals. The soft, gelatinous plants with well-rounded organs that don't resemble either stems or leaves, that assume the generous smooth curves of animals, seem to want to trick us into thinking that they are animals. The real animals seem to try hard to be and resemble plants. They imitate everything about the other kingdom. In some cases they take on the solidity, the quasi-eternity of trees. In others they bloom and then whither like flowers. Thus the sea anemone opens up like a pale pink daisy or like a garnet-colored aster embellished with azure eyes. But as soon as it has allowed a daughter, a new anemone, to escape from its corolla you can see it melt away and vanish.

The proteus of the seas, the alcyonium is varied in quite another way, by taking any form and any color.

It plays the part of a plant or fruit, it takes the shape of a fan, becomes a shrub-like hedge or rounds itself off into a charming basket. But all this is fleeting, ephemeral, its life is so timid that with the slightest ripple it all disappears and nothing remains. In a single moment it returns to the womb of the common mother. You can find something similar to a sensitive plant in one of the alcyonium's most delicate forms, which at the slightest touch closes in upon itself, withdraws into its bosom, like a delicate flower on a cool night.

When you examine the edge of a shoal, or a coral reef from above you can see the carpeted bottom, green with star-coral and organ-pipe coral, as well as mushroom coral that are shaped like snowballs and brain-coral historied with their little labyrinths whose valleys and hills are tinged in vivid colors. The green velvet sea-flowers or actinians with shades of orange at the tip of their limestone branches, fish for their tiny food by gently moving their luxurious golden stamens in the water.

Above, majestic gorgonians that are several feet tall and the miniature trees of the isidae form a forest that protects the bottom-dwellers from the sun as they undulate like willows and liana or sway like palm trees. In these trees the plumose anemones, entwine their feathery spirals that look like the tendrils of a vine, which are connected by their light and slender branches tinged in brilliant colors.

It's charming and disturbing. It is as dizzying as it is dream-like. The water—like a fairy's illusive mirages—adds to these colors a prism of fleeting hues, a marvelous mobility, a capricious inconstancy, hesitation and doubt.

Did I see? No, it wasn't... was that a living being or a reflection?... Yes those are living beings after all, for I see a real world that lives and unfolds there. The molluscs are unafraid and drag their pearly shells about. The crabs are unafraid as well. They run about and hunt. Strange fish, that are potbellied and short, dressed in gold and hundreds of other colors, move about lazily. Crimson and purple annelids meander and move about near the delicate stars, called brittle stars, which beneath the sun stretch out, roll and unroll their elegant arms one by one.

In this phantasmagoria, the arborescent madrepores display their much duller colors with great solemnity. Their beauty lies in their shape.

Above all, it lies in their unity, with the nobility of a shared city-state. The individual is small and the republic imposing. At times, they have the thick stratum of aloe and cactus plants. Elsewhere, they are like a stags' heads with their superb antler-like branches. Still elsewhere, they display the extension of the vigorous branches of cedars, which after having spread their arms out horizontally then stretch them upward.

When these forms are stripped of the thousands of living flowers that covered them and brought them to life, they can – in this serious state—be perhaps more intensely intriguing. I like looking at trees in winter, when their delicate branches freed of the cumbersome luxury of leaves, tell us what they truly are and delicately reveal to us their hidden personality. It's the same with these madrepores. In their current nudity, like paintings that have turned into more abstract sculptures, it seems that they can teach us the secret of the lower orders of which they are the monuments. Several of them seem to be communicating with us by way of strange signs. They interlace and intertwine in complex ways, which must obviously express something. Who can interpret these signs and what words could translate them?

It is clear that even in this state there is thought within them. You can't rid yourself of the idea. You return to it and remain there like a child learning to read, you sound out the words and think you grasp the meaning. And then, the glimmer of understanding vanishes and you smack your forehead.

How many beehives in their cold geometry are less significant! They are merely a product of life! But this, this is life itself. The stone was not simply the base and the shelter of this people, it was a former people, and the first generation took this form, after being eliminated by the young that came to live above them.

Therefore, all the activity of the past and the appearance of the original city are there—quite visibly and strikingly. They are a compelling truth, like any vivid detail at Herculaneum or Pompeii. But here it was all achieved without violence and without any catastrophe, but rather by a natural progression. There is a peaceful calm and a singular gentleness that is compelling.

Any sculptor would admire the forms of a marvelous art, which while exploring the same motifs found infinite variations to the point that their example could change and renew our entire ornamental arts. But there is much more than form to be considered here. The rich arborescence toiled over by these hard-working tribes, the ingenious labyrinths in need of Ariadne's thread, is a profoundly symbolic interplay of plant life with all other forms of life; it is the effort of thought or of captive liberty—its timid effort to find its way towards the promised light. It is the charming flash of a young soul engaged in a communal life, but which slowly, non-violently, and gracefully frees itself. At home, I have two of these little trees. Their species are analogous and yet they are quite different. No plant is comparable. One is an immaculate but dull white, like alabaster, with a tender luxuriousness. Each branch, which itself splits into new branches, produces many buds and small flowers without ever being able to say: "Enough." The other one is not as white or as dense and each one of its branches is a world unto itself. They are both charming in their similarities and differences, in their innocence and fraternity. Oh, who can explain to me the mystery of the childlike and charming soul who produced this enchanting spectacle! You can still feel this free and yet captive soul circulating within its beloved captivity—dreaming of liberty, while not truly wanting it.

The arts have not, up until now, been able to seize upon these wonders that would have been so useful to them. The beautiful statue of Nature at the gates of the Jardin des Plantes in Paris should have been wrapped in this material. Nature should only have been shown in this ever-present triumphal spectacle. By using all her gifts, by sparing nothing, the majestic throne on which she was seated should have been raised as high as a mountain. The madrepores, these first born, who were more than happy to be buried below, would have supplied the base, offering their alabaster branches, their meanders and their stars. Above them, their sisters with their swaying bodies and fine hair would have provided a soft living bed that would have gently embraced the divine Mother in her dream of eternal birth with their caressing love.

Painting has not been any more successful. It has painted these animate flowers as if they were merely flowers. In the end, their colors are extraordinarily different. The colored engravings with which we must content ourselves give a poor idea of what they look like. Despite their best efforts, the flat pale colors of these engravings can never accurately render their smooth gentleness, their suppleness, and their warm emotions. Enamelwork, like Palissy's, would still be too hard and cold. His work, which was admirable for its reptiles and fish scales, would be too shiny to render these soft tender creatures with no skin. The tiny exterior lungs that the annelids expose, the light nebulous fibers that float about certain polyps, the moving and sensitive hairs that ripple below jellyfish, are not only delicate objects but are endearing ones. They are subtle, delicate, vague and yet warm. They are like a breath made visible. You see in them a rainbow of colors that amuse the eyes. But for them, this is serious business, this is their blood, their frail life, translated into shimmering colors and tinges that come alive and fade away, that in turn inhale, then exhale.... Beware. Don't snuff out the tiny floating soul, which despite being mute tells you everything and reveals its intimate mystery through its exhilarating colors.

Those colors do not survive for long. Most of them fade and disappear. The madrepores leave their base behind as their sole remains—a base that was thought to be inorganic and which is in fact life itself in a condensed and solidified form.

Women, who sense these things much more keenly than men do, were not fooled. They vaguely sensed that one of these trees, corals, was a living thing. From this came a justifiable preference for it. Despite science's best attempts to prove that it was no more than a stone and later, that it was only a shrub, women sensed something else.

"Madam, why is it that you prefer this dull red tree to all other precious stones?"

"Sir, it complements my complexion. Rubies make me look pale. This, on the other hand, which is dull and less vivid, brings out the whiteness of my skin."

She is right. The two things are related. In coral, just like on her lips and her cheeks, color is the result of the presences of iron, according to Julius Vogel. It makes one red and the other pink.

"But Madam, these brilliant stones have an incomparable shine."

"Yes, but this one is soft. It is as soft as skin, and retains its warmth. As soon as I have worn it for a few minutes it becomes part of my flesh and part of me. And I can no longer differentiate between us."

"Madam, there are redder ones."

"Doctor, let me keep this one. I like it. Why? I don't know...or, one reason that is as good as any, is that its oriental name rings true—Blood flower."

CHAPTER 5

Makers of Worlds

Our Museum of Natural History in Paris in its overly confined space is a magical palace. Jean-Baptiste Lamarck and Geoffroy's spirit of metamorphoses seem to dwell throughout the place. In the dark downstairs hall, the madrepores silently lay the foundation for the increasingly lively world that rises above them. Above, there are the workers of the sea, who, having achieved their full organizational drive in higher order marine animals, are preparing for the lives to come on earth. On top, are the mammals and overhead, divine tribes of birds who spread their wings and seem to still be singing.

The crowds of visitors hardly glance at the first group. They move quickly past these elders of the globe. It is cold and damp where they reside. The crowd climbs towards the light towards so many brilliant things. Mother-of-pearl, butterfly wings, bird feathers—these are charming. As I linger below, I have often found myself completely alone in that dark little gallery.

I love the crypt in this great church. I can best appreciate the sacred souls and ever-present spirit of our masters, their great, sublime endeavors, as well as the immortal courage of those voyagers who left from this place. No matter where their bones currently rest, they themselves remain in the Museum through the treasures that they gave and that they paid for with their very lives.

The other day, on October 1st, while I was lingering there, I read the labels for several madrepores with some difficulty. One, which, was placed very close to the door, displayed the name "Lamarck".

A warm feeling shot through my heart, a religious impulse.

Such a great name and already antiquated! It was as if, among the tombs of Saint-Denis, one came upon the name of Clovis. The glory of Lamarck's successors, their royalty, their debates have caused this figure, thanks to whom we passed from one century to the next, to seem obscure and from a remote past. This blind Homer of the Museum, is the one who, by the instinct of his genius, created, organized and named something we hardly knew existed at the time—the class of the Invertebrates.

A class? No, rather a world. They are the abyss of soft and semi-organized life that is still lacking a vertebra, a centralized bone structure—that essential support of personality. Moreover, they are of interest because they obviously are the beginning of everything. These humble tribes that were so neglected until then! Réaumur had classified the crocodiles with the insects. The glorious comte de Buffon did not deign to know the names of this tiny rabble. He shut them out of the Olympian Versailles that he erected to Nature. This great, obscure and confused people, these exiles from science, who, despite it all, filled every space and prepared everything, had to wait for Lamarck. In fact it was nature's elders who had been barred from entering. If they had been taken into account those who had been admitted previously would have amounted to little. Based on their numbers, it could be said that those that had been excluded, forgotten, left at the door, were in fact Nature itself.

The genie of metamorphosis had just been emancipated in Botany and Chemistry. It was a bold but productive move to take Lamarck from his Museum appointment in Botany, where he had spent his life, and instead have him teach about animals. This passionate genius who had grown accustomed to miracles through the transformations of plants, and was full of faith in the unity of life, freed both animals and the greatest of all animals—the Earth—from the petrified state in which they were being held. He reestablished the circulation of spirit from one form to another. Half blind and groping his way around, he intrepidly touched upon a thousand things that those with perfect vision did not yet dare to approach. Or at the very least he threw his light upon them. Thus allowing Geoffroy, Cuvier and Blainville to then find them warm and full of life. He said: "Everything is alive or used to be. Everything is life, either present or past." His was a great revolutionary struggle against inert matter that would go as far as to eliminate the inorganic. Nothing was completely dead. What had once lived could be dormant and retained a latent form of life as well as a capacity to relive. Who is truly dead? No one.

These remarks filled the nineteenth century's sails, swelling them as if with a powerful wind. Whether dangerous or not, he pushed on to places to which we never would have gone. We started a search in which we asked each thing whether in history or natural history: "Who are you?"

—"I am life"

Death started to flee under the gaze of science. The mind went forward as a conqueror and forced it to retreat.

First among these resurrected beings, I see my madrepores. Once, they were dead stone and coarse limestone, now they took on the fascination evoked by life. When Lamarck brought them together and explained them to us at the Museum, they had just been caught by surprise in the midst of their mysterious activities and extraordinary creations. We had learned from them how a world is made. We started to understand that if the earth makes the animal, then the animal also makes the earth and that each aids the other in the act of creation.

The animal kingdom is present everywhere. It fills and populates everything. We even find its trace in minerals such as statuary marble or alabaster that have been subjected to the crucible of the most destructive fires. With every step we take in our understanding of our current world, we also discover the extensive animal life of the past. The day that optics allowed us to see an infusorium, we could see it make mountains and paving the Ocean floor. The hard flint found in tripoli stone is a mass of animalcules, a sponge is living flintstone. Our limestone is all composed of animals. Paris is built of infusoria. Part of Germany rests on a sea of coral, which today lies buried. Infusoria, coral, testacean are composed of lime and chalk. They constantly draw these from the sea. Fish devour coral, then excrete it in the form of chalk and return it to the water from which it initially came. Thus, the Coral Sea—as she labors to give birth, in her upheaval and movement, in her constructions that are endlessly rising up or being torn down, built, ruined, rebuilt—is an immense limestone factory that goes back and forth between two lives: today's life of action and potential life that will act tomorrow.

Georg Forster, who traveled with Cook in the Pacific, clearly understood (although his claim was denied quite falsely) that those circular islands are volcanic craters that were raised up by polyps. No opposing theory explains these islands' identical form. They are always a small ring of about one hundred paces in diameter, low lying, beaten on the outside by the waves, but with a calm basin within. Some three or four plant species create a ring of sparse greenery around this interior basin. The water is of the most beautiful shade of green. The ring of white sand— the residue of dissolved coral—contrasts with the deep blue of the Ocean. Under the salt water, our workers labor away. Depending on their species or their personalities the bold ones can be found in the breakers, and the good-hearted, timid folks stay on the more peaceful side.

This is a world with little variety. But wait. The winds and the currents work to make it richer. All that is needed is one good storm for a neighboring island to assure its good fortune. This is one of the most magnificent roles of a storm. The bigger, the more violent, the more turbulent it is, the more it uproots everything, the more fertile it is. A downpour passes over an island. The stream that it produces— loaded with silt, with the remains of dead plants or with living ones, sometimes with uprooted forests— this black muddy stream flows into the sea and as soon as it is pushed on by the waves this way and that, it distributes its gifts to the near-by islands.

A great messenger of life, and one of the more transportable ones, is the sturdy coconut. Not only does it travel, but when thrown onto the reefs, if it encounters the slightest bit of sand, it takes root and is quite satisfied where any other plant would perish. If it encounters briny water that no plant would care for, it acts as if it were fresh water, it thrives, burrows in. It germinates, grows and becomes a tree—a hardy coconut tree. As a tree, it soon turns into fresh water as well as debris and therefore soil. This leads to the creation of other trees and soon palm trees appear. Water vapor, which is trapped by these trees, creates a stream, which, in turn, as it flows from the center of the island maintains an opening in the white ring that the polyps—those inhabitants of salt water—respect.

We now know how very quickly polyps work. In Rio de Janeiro, fishing boats that had been unused for forty days disappeared under tubularians that had covered them over. A strait near Australia, which once had 26 small islands, now has 150 that have been reconnoitered. Moreover, the English Admiralty has announced that there are even more than that, and that in 20 years, along the strait's length of forty leagues, it will eventually become unnavigable.

Australia's eastern reef is 360 leagues long—127 leagues of which is uninterrupted. New Caledonia's is 145 leagues long. Groups of islands in the Pacific are 400 leagues long and 150 leagues wide. The Maldive Islands alone are almost 500,000 miles long. Add to this list the sandbank of the Isle of France, off the coast of Greenland, and shoals of the Red Sea that are constantly growing in size.

Timor and its surroundings present a completely animal world. Everything one comes across is a living thing. The rocks offer up so many bizarre forms and rich colors, that one is overcome. You see them over an area of several leagues in the shallow seawater (maybe one-foot deep) working away in silence, but actively continuing their trade as creators.

Cook's companion, Forster was the first insightful observer to find them at work. He caught them in the act, as they conspired, without the slightest sound, to create islands by the thousands, archipelagoes and eventually continents.

This went on before his very eyes as it had during the earth's first days. From the depths of the sea, the central fire pushes up a dome or a cone that having been cracked opened by its lava for a time leaves a circular crater. But the volcanic force wanes. This warm crater is crowned by a living, animal and polypous jelly, which, by continuously excreting its mucous, builds up this crater until it almost reaches the surface of the sea. These creatures go no higher, for beyond that point they would dry out, and yet they pushes towards the light. Even if they lack any specific organ to perceive light, it still penetrates them. The powerful sun of the tropics that passes right through their small transparent beings seems to have an invincible magnetic attraction for them. When the tide goes down and exposes them, they remain no less opened and drink in the bright light.

Dumont d'Urville, who knew their little islands well, said: "It is a strange form of torture to observe from up close the peace that reigns in their interior basins, to see all around beneath the shallow water advancing shoals where corals stretch out in complete safety, while you yourself are in the middle of a storm." This lovely reef world is dangerous. Touch it and you will cause a wreck. The transparent sea is showing you a sheer abyss, which plunges 100 fathoms deep. Do not rely on anchors. Contact will wear through and soon sever any mooring line. Anxiety is high during the long nights when the southern swell pushes you onto these sharp razors.

The innocent reef makers are not lacking for responses to these accusations. They say: "Give us time. These edges will eventually soften and become welcoming. Leave us to our work. Once these shoals are linked to neighboring ones they will no longer create those terrible eddies. We are making an alternative world for you in case yours should be destroyed. You will be eternally grateful if a cataclysm occurs, if as some would have it, the sea flows from one pole to another every ten thousand years. Then you will be quite happy to find our southern islands and the refuge we will have created."

"Let's admit it," they say, "even if some unfortunate boats will be lost, what we are doing here is useful. It is good and important. We can be proud of our improvised world. Not to mention the beauty of its triumphant colors that outshine those on land, or the graceful curves where we revel—we seem to have solved so many of the difficult problems that perplex you. The division of labor, a charming variety combined with an overall regularity, a geometrical order which nevertheless has the grace of budding liberty—where can you humans find this?"

"Our endless work to reduce salt in the water creates the magnificent currents that make it a source of life and health. We are the spirits of the sea; we give her movement."

"Of course, she is not ungrateful. She comes just at the right time to nourish us. And just as punctual, the warm light caresses us and adorns us in its rich colors. We are God's beloved ones, his favorite workers. He entrusted us with the job of starting his worlds. All the later generations of this earth need us. Our friend, the coconut palm, that giant, which ushers in terrestrial life on our island, thrives only by asking to draw from our dust. Plant life, in the end, is a legacy, a gift, a token of our generosity. Enriched by us, it will nourish a superior creation."

"But why have other animals? We are a complete, harmonic and self-sufficient world. The cycle of creation could end here. With us, God crowned his islands; on his former volcanoes of fire, he is making a volcano of life—better yet—a living paradise is in bloom. He has what he wanted and now will go rest."

Not quite yet. Another creation must ascend above yours, something that you must not fear. This rival is not the storm, which you easily brave, not fresh water, which you gladly build next to. It is not even land, which little by little invades and covers up your construction. Where is this other power? In you. No polyp is resigned to remaining a polyp. In your republic there exists a restless creature, who believes that this perfected vegetative life is not life and it dreams of separation. It dreams of going off and sailing alone, of seeing the unknown, the vast world, of creating, even at the risk of shipwreck. It dreams of something that will dawn within it, but remains unknown to you—a soul.

CHAPTER 6

Daughter of the Sea

I spent the first months of 1858 in the pleasant little town of Hyères, which looks out onto a distant sea, as well as onto the islands and the peninsula that shelter its coast. From that distance, the sea is perhaps even more alluring than from the shore. The footpaths that lead to it either take you by gardens bordered by hedges of jasmine and myrtle or they climb a bit passing olive trees and groves where pine trees and laurel mingle. Every so often, between the trees, you catch sight of the sea. For good reason this place is called Coste-Belle—the beautiful coast. Often, on lovely, warm winter days we used to come upon a very touching invalid, a young foreign princess who had traveled there from 500 leagues away in order to prolong her frail life if only for a little longer. This short life had been sad and difficult. She had only recently found happiness and now she was dieing. She moved along slowly supported in a loving embrace by the person who lived for her and didn't believe he would be able to survive her death. If wishes and prayers could prolong a life, she would have lived, since she had those of everyone and especially of the poor. But both spring and her end eventually came. One April day, when everything was being reborn, we saw those two departed souls, as pale as Virgil's Elysian heroes, passing through that grove.

We arrived at the gulf with our hearts filled with these thoughts. Between the rather sharp rocks, the pools, which the sea left behind, retained small creatures that were too slow and thus had been unable to follow the retreating tide. A few shellfish were there withdrawn into their shells suffering from a lack of water. Laying spread out there among them, with no shell and no shelter was that living umbrella that has the unfortunate name—*medusa*. Why such a horrible name for a creature that is so charming? I had never before paid attention to these castaways that are so common on the shore. This one was small, the size of my hand, but particularly beautiful with soft and delicate hues. She was opalescent with what resembled a muted circlet of fresh lilacs engulfed by a cloud. The wind had flipped her over. Her crown of lilac hair floated above and below, her delicate umbrella (her body) was against the rock. Her poor bruised body was hurt. Her fine hairs, which act as her organs for breathing, absorption and even loving, were torn. All this laid upside down, with the sun of Provence—harsh at dawn and made even harsher by the dry Mistral that at times combines with it—beating directly down upon her. Thus, this transparent creature was doubly pierced as if by a spear. Living in the sea, with that caressing touch, she does not armor herself with a resistant skin, in the way we land animals do. She is completely exposed.

Near this arid pool, other pools filled with water were connected to the sea. Salvation was only a step away. But for this creature that can only move with the help of her undulating hairs, that single step was insurmountable. Under that sun, it was reasonable to conclude that she would soon dissolve, be absorbed and disappear.

Nothing is more ephemeral, more fleeting than these daughters of the sea. There are those that are more elusive, like the slight azure bands called *Venus's girdles*, which upon emerging from the water, immediately dissipate and vanish. The medusa, is a bit more stable and has a more difficult death.

Was this creature dead or dieing? I have trouble conceiving death—I maintained that she was alive. Just in case, it was little trouble to remove her from where she lay and throw her into the neighboring pool. To tell the truth, I was reluctant to touch her. The delightful creature with her visible innocence and rainbow of soft colors was like trembling jelly. She was slick and slippery. However, I disregarded all this.

I slipped my hand underneath her and carefully lifted the immobile body whose hairs fell back into place as she returned to her natural swimming position. I placed her in the near-by water, like that. She sank into the water without giving any sign of life.

I strolled along the water's edge. But within ten minutes, I would see my medusa again. She undulated in the wind. In truth, she was moving and started to float. With singular grace, her elusive hairs that were swimming beneath her gently took her away from the rocks. She was not going very quickly but at least she was moving. Soon I saw her quite far off.

Perhaps she would soon capsize again. No other means of sailing is weaker or more dangerous. They fear the shore, where so many hard things could harm them. At sea, the wind continually turns them over on their back, and with their fin-like hairs on top, they float around haphazardly, becoming easy prey for fish and the delight of birds that take pleasure in snatching them up.

During the entire season that I spent on the banks of the Gironde, I saw them being fatally pushed through the pass, thrown onto the banks by the hundreds and left there pitifully to dry up. They were big, white and quite beautiful when they arrived, like great crystal chandeliers with lavish girandoles, into which the glistening sun set precious stones. Alas! They were in an entirely different state at the end of two days!

Fortunately, the sand covered them over and hid them.

They feed everyone and they themselves eat hardly anything other than the simplest organisms—those little organized, still indistinct atoms that are floating in the sea. They numb them; they etherize them, so to speak, and then suck on them without making them suffer. They do not have teeth, or other weapons—defenseless. Only certain species (and according to Edward Forbes, not all of them) can, when attacked, secrete a solution that stings a little like a nettle. The sting is so mild, moreover that the naturalist Diquemarre was not worried about getting stung in the eye, which he did with impunity.

These are creatures that are in constant danger and yet are not well protected. They are already of a higher order. They have senses and judging by their contractions, they have a notable susceptibility to pain. Unlike the polyps, they cannot be divided up with impunity. Whereas, polyps regenerate, they simply die. Like polyps, they are as gelatinous as embryos but these are embryos that have been cast out from the shared, mother's womb too soon. They have been torn away from their solid foundation, from the association that assures the polyps' safety and have been exposed to risk.

How did these reckless creatures take leave? How did they set forth from their safe haven with no sail, oar or rudder? From where did they depart?

In 1750, Ellis saw a small medusa emerge from the top of a polyp. Several contemporary observers have ascertained that the medusa is a type of polyp that has left the association. Simply stated, the medusa is an emancipated polyp.

"This comes as no surprise!" says the scholar Mr. Forbes, who has studied these creatures so closely. This merely means that at this stage the animal is still complying with the laws of plant-life. From the tree—a collective being—is born the individual, the detached fruit, which will in turn create another tree. A pear tree is a sort of polypary of the plant kingdom in which the pear (a free individual) can give us a pear tree.

In the *Annals of Natural History*, Forbes tells us that just as the branch of a plant that was going to be full of leaves stops developing, contracts and becomes an organ of love—I mean, a flower—the polypary contracts some of its polyps, transforms their contracted stomachs to create placenta and the eggs from which come its mobile flower—the young and graceful medusa.

All this should have been apparent from their uncertain grace, their naive frailty that fears nothing, that sets off without any sailing instruments and that trusts life too much. This is the new soul's first and most touching escape. They leave the security of communal life, without yet having any defenses, they try to be themselves, try to act and suffer on their own account. They are the soft prototype of a free nature; they are embryonic liberty.

To be oneself, to be a tiny but complete world onto oneself—this would be tempting for anyone! Its appeal is universally understood! This type of splendid madness is at the heart of every effort and of all the progress in the world! But in these first attempts, how unjustified it seems! It seems as if the medusa was made for the express purpose of capsizing.

Weighed down on top and unsteady below they are built quite differently from their relatives the Portuguese men-of-war. The latter have only a small float above water, an insubmersible bladder. Their long—infinitely long—tentacles, which can be twenty feet or longer, drag across the sea floor, stabilizing them, sweeping through the sea, striking fish into a torpor and delivering them. Light and carefree, inflating their nacreous float that is tinged with blue or crimson, their sinister azure hairs eject a subtle venom which when discharged strikes their prey dead.

Less formidable, Velella are not lost at sea either. They have the shape of a raft; their tiny organisms are already slightly sturdier. They can steer and shift their oblique sails in the wind. Porpitae, which resemble simple flowers such as daisies, have the advantage of lightness. They float even after their death. The same is true for so many other fantastic and almost aerial beings: garlands of golden bell-flowers or garlands of rosebuds such as Physophorae and Stephanomies; as well as Venus's girdles. They all swim and float invincibly. They only fear land. They sail at sea, far from the shore and no matter how rough the waves, they find their salvation there. The Porpitae and Velella are so unafraid of the Ocean that when very bad weather arises, since they know they will never sink, they attempt to dive down and hide in the depths.

However, this is not the case for the poor medusa. She must fear both the shore and storms. She could weigh herself down at will and descend, but the abyss is off limits to her. She can only live at the surface, in the full light and in complete danger. She sees and hears; her sense of touch is quite sensitive—in fact too much so for her own good. She cannot steer herself. Her more complicated organs weigh her down and cause her to lose balance too easily.

We are also inclined to believe that she regrets this terribly dangerous attempt at liberty, that she misses the lower state and the security of a communal life. The polypary makes the medusa and the medusa makes the polypary. She returns to the association. But this vegetative life is so dull that with the next generation, she frees herself again and strikes out haphazardly using her useless navigation system. There are strange alternating phases between which she perpetually floats.

When mobile, she dreams of rest. When inert she dreams of movement.

These strange metamorphoses, which in turn elevate and then lower these undecided beings and cause them to alternate between two very different lives, are in all likelihood, characteristic of lower species such as medusas that have not been able to definitely enter onto the irrevocable path of emancipation. For other species, it is easy to imagine that their charming diversity is a sign of the inner progress of life, the fun, the grace and the laughter of a new form of liberty. This admirable artist, liberty, creates an infinite number of lovely variations and a deluge of small wonders on the terribly simple theme of a floating disk or umbrella, or a delicate crystal chandelier upon which the sun places a glow.

All these beauties, each more lovely than the last, floating on the green mirror in their gay and gentle colors with the charm of an innocent child-like coquetry, have troubled science, which in order to find names for them had to rely on the queens of history and the goddesses of mythology. This one is the undulating Berenicida, whose lustrous hair flows in the waves. That one is the tiny Orithyia lutae, whose white and pure urn, blown here and there by her husband, the god of the winds, is unsteady and hardly strengthened by her delicate tangle of hair that she often twists below her. Over there, the weeping Diana seems like a full alabaster cup that allows her splendid tears to spill over in the form of crystalline threads. She reminds me of the weary and lazy waterfalls that I saw pouring out in Switzerland that after having made too many detours seemed to fall merely from fatigue or languor. In the grand spectacle of illumination that the sea produces on stormy nights, the medusa plays a singular role. She renders the electric phosphorous—in which she, like so many other creatures is bathed and which penetrates her— in a charming way that is all her own. When that phosphorous is not visible, the night can be frightfully dark at sea!

That darkness is vast and formidable! On land, the night is less dark. You can always find your way because of the variety of objects that can be touched or whose outlines can be sensed. These offer reference points. But the sea's vast night—what an infinite darkness! Nothing, nothing! A thousand possible and unknown dangers!

When you live facing the sea, you can sense this even from the shore. When the atmosphere becomes electric, what joy it brings, when a slight ribbon of pale fire appears in the distance. What is that? You've seen it before, at home, on dead fish, like a herring. In these huge waves and in the long, slimy trails they leave behind, it is alive and even more luminous. That brightness is in no sense unique to death. Is it a result of the heat? Not at all. You find it at both poles and in the Antarctic as well as the Siberian seas. It is found in our seas and in all the others.

This is the shared electricity, which these partially living waters give off during stormy weather. It is the innocent and peaceful lightning for which all sea creatures act as conductors. They breathe it in and out. In general, they render it when they die. The sea gives it and then takes it back. Along coasts and straits, the friction and swirls cause it to circulate a great deal. Every living being takes some. They seize more or less depending on their nature. Over here, immense fields of peaceful infusoria are like a milky sea giving off a soft white light that, as it becomes more animated turns a glowing sulfur yellow. Over there, cones of light pirouette or role like red cannonballs. A great fiery disk is produced—a pyrosoma—that goes from being an opaline yellow, to momentarily being tinged with green, then becomes irritated and bursts into red, orange and finally with its mood darkening, it turns azure. There is a pattern to these changes that seems to indicate a natural function—the contraction and expansion of a creature that is breathing fire.

However, on the horizon, enflamed serpents toss about over an infinite stretch—sometimes as long as twenty-five or thirty leagues. Biphores and salpae— those transparent creatures that both the sea and phosphorus pass through—perform this serpentine comedy. This amazing association of individuals leads to these unbridled dances and then, to separation. Once separated, their liberated members produce liberated offspring, who in turn, will generate dancing communities so that their fiery bacchanal can spill out over the sea.

Greater and more peaceful fleets flood the waves with their lights. At night velellas light up their small crafts. Triumphant beroes go forth like flames. But none are more magical than our medusas. Is it purely a physical reflex? Is it a result of respiration, as some would have it? Is it a whim, as with so many creatures that playfully throw off their sparks out of a pointless and fickle sense of joy? No, the noble and lovely medusas—like the crowned Oceanides or the charming Diane—seem to express more serious thoughts. Like a gloomy, vigilant lamp their luminous hairs give off a mysterious emerald light beneath them. And other colors, which flare up and then fade, reveal emotion and mystery. It is like the mind of the abyss that is contemplating its own secrets, like an impending soul or one that will live one day. Or else, we could see in them the melancholic dream of an impossible destiny that will never attain its goal. Or is it a call for love's happiness, which is the only thing that consoles us, here below?

We know, that on our land, our fireflies' fire is a signal—a lover's confession—with which she calls attention to herself, gives her hiding place away, and betrays herself. Does it have the same meaning for the medusas? We don't know. We are certain that they shed both their light and their life at the same time. Their fertile vigor, their reproductive virtue escapes and diminishes with every flash of light.

If you want to have the cruel pleasure of enhancing this magical spectacle, expose them to heat. With that they intensify, they become radiant and so beautiful... that the scene ends. All at once the light, love and life has vanished, has all flowed away.

CHAPTER 7

The Stone Workers

When the good Dr. Livingston entered the lands of the poor people of Africa, who have such trouble defending themselves against slave merchants and lions, the women who saw that he was armed with the protective know-how of Europe, appealed to him as a friendly savior with this touching phrase: "Give us sleep!"

This is a phrase that all living creatures, no matter their language, direct towards Nature. Every one of them dreams of and desires security. There is no doubting this fact when we see the elaborate efforts they all make in order to acquire it. These efforts have created arts. Man doesn't invent a single one, without finding that animals—inspired by that steady and strong instinct for survival—had already invented it before him.

They suffer, fear, they want to live. One shouldn't think that the least advanced embryonic creatures are any less sensitive. The contrary is true. In every embryo, the nervous system—in other words the ability to feel and to suffer—is the first to be developed. Pain is the motivating force that little by little stimulates foresight and urges a creature to work hard. Pleasure plays a hand in it as well, and you can already see this in those that were thought to be the most insensitive. In fact, it has been observed that the snail shows great happiness after his trying search for love, when he finds the object of his affections. The two of them caress each other intensely with a moving charm by swaying their swan-like necks. Who says so? The serious-minded and highly precise Blainville. But alas, how profuse is pain! Who hasn't sorrowfully watched the slow and painful efforts of a mollusk without a shell, dragging himself along on his stomach? Such a creature is the shocking but faithful likeness of a foetus that a cruel fate has torn from his mother only to be thrown to the ground naked and defenseless. The pitiful creature thickens his skin as much as possible, tries to smooth the rough patches along the way and make his path slick. But none of this matters. He must face all the obstacles, all the collisions, all the pointed stones, one by one. He is hardened, resigned and I can accept this. And yet, when he comes in contact with something he contorts, contracts and shows signs of being highly sensitive.

Despite all this pain, the great Soul of harmony, which is the unity of the world, loves. She loves and through alternating pleasure and pain she cultivates all living beings and forces them to progress.

But, in order to progress, in order to climb to a higher stage, they must first run the gauntlet of trials that cause pain, stimulate inventiveness, and spark instinctive creativity. It is even necessary for them to push their type to the extreme, in other words, for them to come up against excess, which, through conflict, brings out the real need for a completely different type. Progress is therefore achieved through a sort of oscillation between contrasting qualities, which in turn emerge and become incarnate in another life form.

Let's translate these divine things into a more familiar and human language that despite not being suited to their importance will make them easier to understand.

Nature, which for a long time took pleasure in making and unmaking the medusa, in unendingly varying this charming theme of nascent liberty, one morning slapped her forehead and said: "I was impulsive. It was charming, but I forgot to protect the life of this poor creature. She will only be able to survive through sheer numbers, by being excessively fertile. I now need a creature that is more prudent and less vulnerable. If necessary, let him be fearful. But above all, I want him to live!"

As soon as they appeared, these faint-hearted creatures completely devoted themselves, to the best of their abilities, to caution. They avoided daylight and shut themselves away. In order to preserve themselves from hard, sharp and cutting contact with stones they use the universally employed method of moulting. After moulting in their gelatinous stage, they secrete a membrane, a tube that extends as they move forward. This pitiful expedient, that keeps these miners, called shipworms, from coming into contact with light and air, acts as an enormous drain on their substance. Every step cost them dearly, costs them the price of an entire house. A being that expends so much, just to live can only vegetate miserably and is incapable of progress.

Burying or hiding in the sand during low tide only to emerge when the tide comes back in, is not much better. This is the behavior that can be observed in solens. Twice a day they lead an unsettled, uncertain, transient life full of constant worry. In these inferior beings, something that was still unclear, but that was going to change the world in the long run had begun to manifest itself. The simple starfish with five arms, had a certain amount of support, something like a framework with articulated parts as well as an exterior with a few spines, some suckers that could move forward and backwards at will. This is quite a humble animal, but being both timid and serious, it seems to have made the best of this crude stage.

I believe that he says to Nature: "I was born with no ambition. I don't ask for the brilliant gifts of the honorable mollusks. I won't produce either mother-of-pearl or pearls. I don't want brilliant colors or luxury that would set me apart from others. I am especially uninterested in having the gracefulness of your careless medusas since the undulating charm of their attractive fiery hairs only leads to attacks or capsizing. Oh, Mother! I only want one thing—to be...to be one, and not have these exterior appendages that compromise my safety...to be squat, strong and to have a rounded form because it is the least vulnerable...in a word, I want to be centralized."

"I don't have an instinct for traveling. It is enough for me to sometimes roll from high tide to low tide. Scrupulously stuck on my rock, I will solve the problem that your future darling—man—will search to resolve in vain: the problem of security. I want to keep enemies out at all costs, while letting in friends like water, air and light. I know that it will cost me dearly in work and in continual effort. Covered in moveable spines I will be avoided. Hedging my bets against my enemies and striving to survive like a street urchin—they call me *sea hedgehog* or *sea urchin*.

How superior this wise animal is in comparison to polyps bound to the stone that they themselves have created purely from secretions, without truly working, but which does not provide them with any safety! How superior does he seem in comparison to so many mollusks that have more varied senses, but don't have the stable unity of his first spinal attempts, nor the ingenious tools that spring from this attempt!

The wonder of it all is that he is at once himself—this poor rolling ball that looks like a spiny chestnut—*he is one; he is multiple. He is stable; he is mobile* consisting of two thousand four hundred parts that can be dismantled at any time.

Let's see how he was created.

It was in a narrow cove in the sea of Brittany. He didn't have a comfortable bed of soft polyps or seaweed like the sea urchins in the Indian Ocean, who are exempt from such labor. Like Ulysses in the Odyssey, who when thrown to sea and brought in by the tide tried to grab onto a rock with his bloody nails, this creature was faced with danger and a difficult challenge. For our small Ulysses each ebb and flow is like a mighty storm. But his great will, his powerful desire cause him to kiss the rock to such as extent that this constant kiss created a sucker that formed a vacuum and united him with the rock itself.

This is not all. One of his scraping spines, which wanted to hold on to the rock, subdivided into a three-pronged pincer that acts as an anchor—a veritable saving grace—assisting the sucker if it were badly applied onto a rough surface.

After having clamped on, sucked his rock mightily, and stabilized himself, he became increasingly aware that there were advantages to transforming the convex rock by making it concave—digging a small hole that was just the right size and making himself a nest. For, youth is not eternal. Strength does not last. How comforting it would be, if one day, the urchin emeritus could slightly relax his daily efforts to stay anchored!

Thus, he drilled. This is his life. Made of detachable parts he works with five spines, which by dint of always digging together, became fused and created an admirable pick that he could use to bore his way into the stone.

A delicate framework supports this pick with its five beautifully enamelled teeth. They slide into a type of sheathe, come out, go back in, playing perfectly. This elasticity allows them to avoid rough impacts. Moreover, they mend themselves if there are any serious mishaps.

They rarely sculpt soft stone, which they scorn. Rather, this labor hero prefers hard rock or granite. The more solid and resistant the rock the stronger they feel there. What does it matter to them, after all? Time is not a factor and he has centuries before him. If he dies tomorrow, as a result of having worn out his life and his instrument another will set himself up continuing his work in the exact same location. They don't communicate much during their lifetime, these solitary laborers but there exists a fraternity in death for them. The young urchin that arrives only to find that the work is only half done, takes pleasure and blesses the memory of the fine laborer that laid the ground work for him.

Don't think that his work consists in constantly hammering away. There is an art to it. Once he has sufficiently attacked what holds the rock together and has completely laid it bare, he bites into the rough edges of the rock as if with tiny pincers and roots out the flint stone. This labor requires much patience and long breaks in the work, in order to allow the water to act upon the areas that have been stripped. In this way he can go from the first layer to the second and by this slow and continuous process reach his goal.

Even in this uniform life, there are moments of crisis—just like in the life of any worker. The sea recedes from a particular shore. In the summer, a particular rock becomes unbearably hot. One needs two homes—one for summer, one for winter.

For a creature with no feet and who has spines all over, moving constitutes a great event. Frédéric Caillaud has observed and admired the urchin at just such times. The feeble and moveable sticks that play—advancing and retracting—are sensitive, although by secreting a little bit of soft jelly all around them, they are cushioned. Finally, when it can no longer be put off, he engages himself; he steadies himself on his tips, as if on crutches, and rolls his Diogenes' tub until he reaches his safe-haven as best he can.

Once there, well contained once again in his spiny cockle and in the little nest where almost always work has already begun he hunkers down with a sense of solitary pleasure and of joyful security. Let a thousand enemies prowl outside, let the waves thunder and roar. It is a pleasure for him. Let his stone tremble each time the sea strikes; he knows that he has nothing to fear, that it is only his loving wet-nurse making that noise. He rocks in his cradle; he dozes off and tells her: "Good night."

CHAPTER 8

Shells, Mother-of-pearl and Pearls

The sea urchin set a milestone for defensive genius. So that no enemy has an opening to attack his citadel, his armor, or if you prefer, his fort—made of moveable, resistant and yet sensitive, retractable and if necessary reparable parts—is invincibly applied and anchored to his rock or better yet to an excavated rock, housing his whole body. It is a complete system that will never be surpassed. No shell is comparable—nor for that matter is anything produced by human ingenuity.

The sea urchin is the culmination of circular and radiated creatures. Through him they have succeeded in achieving their highest possible level of development. The circle has few variations. It is the absolute shape. In the urchin's sphere, which is so simple and yet so complicated, the circle reaches a level of perfection that brings to an end an initial world.

The beauty of the next world will be the harmonious symmetry of duplicate forms, their balance and the gracefulness of their fluctuation. From this point on, starting with the mollusk up to man, every living being will consist of two connected halves. Beyond finding unity, in every animal, there will now be a *union*.

The masterpiece that is the sea urchin had surpassed all goals. The defensive miracle had created a prisoner, he had not only shut himself in, but he had buried himself; he had dug his own grave. His perfected isolation, had sequestered him, had set him apart and had deprived him of any of the relationships that lead to progress.

In order for progress to resume its steady ascent, it first has to descend very low to the level of the elementary embryo, which at first only moves as the elements do. This new being is the planet's serf to the point that while in his egg he spins like the globe, describing a dual circle—his own rotation and the rotation of the earth.

Even when he has been emancipated from the egg, as he grows and becomes an adult, he will remain an embryo. In fact, his very name—*mollusk* is derived from *mollus*, meaning soft. He will represent a sort of first stage in the advancement of superior life forms. He will be the foetus, the larva, the nymph, as in the case of insects, in which although tucked up inside and hidden away, one nevertheless finds the organs of the winged being that is to come.

I fear for such a weak creature. Polyps, which are no less soft, ran less of a risk. Since life was equally present throughout all parts of their body, injury or mutilation would not kill them. The centralized mollusk is far more vulnerable. Such an opened door to death!

Especially in their early stages, the mollusks possess even less of the unsteady motion that could at times by chance save the medusa. After molting, the only thing with which they are endowed is the ability to exude a jelly in order to create two walls, which replace the sea urchin's armor and rock. Mollusks benefit from being able to draw their means of protection from within. Two valves form a house. A slight and frail house—those who float have a transparent one. For those that want to tie themselves down, free-running, sticky mucus provides moorings that are called their byssus. This filament forms just as silk does from an element that is initially completely gelatinous. The gigantic tridacna—the church font—stays so solidly in place because of these moorings that madrepores are confused. They mistake this shellfish for an island and build upon him, covering him over and eventually suffocating him.

It is a passive life, an immobile life. The periodic visit of sun light is the only event, the only action is absorbing what approaches and secreting the jelly that produced the house and eventually will produce the rest. The attraction towards the light, which is always coming from the same direction, centralizes this mollusk's sight. That is their eye. That steadily uniform effort, secretion, creates an appendage, an organ that earlier was the mooring and later will become the foot—a shapeless, inarticulate mass that can be used for many purposes. It acts as a fin for those that float, a chisel for those that stay hidden and want to dig into the sand, and finally as a foot for those that crawl, a foot that is contractile and allows them to drag themselves along. Some will even attempt to bend it like a bow, which allows them to jump clumsily.

Poor overly exposed tribe, knocked about by the waves, dented by the rocks and pursued by all the other tribes. Those who are not capable of building a home, search for a living bed for their fragile tent. They seek shelter among the polyps; they disappear in the soft world of the floating alcyonarians. Aviculae seek out a bit of peace and quiet cupped by a sponge. The brittle pinna mollusk only dares to live in muddy grass. Piddocks burrow into rocks and revive the urchin's craft— but their inferior work leaves much to be desired! Instead of the admirable chisel that would be the envy of any stonecutter, they only have a small rough file and in order to dig out a shelter for their fragile shell, they use the shell itself as a tool.

With few exceptions, mollusks are frightened creatures that realize they are food for everyone else.

176

The cone shell is so aware of the fact that he is being watched, that he doesn't dare to come out of his shell and eventually dies inside it because of his fear of death. The volute and the cowrie slowly drag along their lovely houses and try to hide them as best they can. The helmet shell uses his foot, which is as tiny as that of a Chinese woman, to move his palace. He has practically given up walking.

Their houses are a reflection of their lives. No other type of creature displays such a strong similarity between the nest and its inhabitant. In this case, as a product of its very substance, the structure is an extension of its fleshy mantle, with the same shape and colors. The architect, living under this roof, is also the living stone from which it is built.

For the sedentary creatures the craft is quite simple. The inert oyster, to whom the sea delivers food, only wants a good box with hinges that can be left a bit ajar when the hermit is eating his meals and that can be slammed shut when he fears that he himself might become an over-eager neighbor's meal.

Things are more complicated for the traveling mollusk, who says to himself: "I have a foot, an organ made for walking therefore I must walk." He cannot come and go as he pleases from his abode. When walking, the house becomes even more of a necessity, because that is when he could be attacked. It must protect his most delicate parts—the branches of his respiratory system and those branches from which he draws life by way of his tiny roots, which feed and restore him. His head is less important. Many can lose them with no negative consequences. However, if his viscera were not under his shield at all times, if they were harmed, he would die.

Thus, prudent and armored he seeks out his quiet life. At the end of the day, will he be safe at night in a wide-opened dwelling? Won't busybodies throw curious glances his way? Who knows maybe they will even take a bite!... The hermit reflects upon these questions and uses all his ingenuity, but no tool, other than his foot to resolve all problems. From this foot, which wants to keep the entryway shut, a long and strong appendage develops over time, which acts as a door of sorts. He places it at the opening and he is sealed in.

And yet, the constant problem and the fundamental contradiction regarding his nature is that he must remain safe while at the same time being in contact with the outside world. Only his mentors— air and light— can strengthen such a soft body and help him develop organs. He must acquire the same guiding senses as the blind—hearing and smell. He must acquire the sense of sight. And finally, he must breathe.

Such an important function and so urgent! No one thinks of it when it comes easily. But if it stops even for a moment—what a terrible fright! How excessively agitated and anxious we become when our lungs are engorged or our larynx simply congested for a single night. We can't stand it and sometimes despite the great peril to our health we open all the windows. It is common knowledge that the torment is such for an asthmatic that since they can't use their natural organ, they create an additional way of breathing—Air! Air! Or else death!

When nature is left no alternative, it can be terribly inventive. It's no surprise that those poor shut-ins, suffocating under their own roof, have found thousands of devices, thousands of types of valves that bring them some small amount of relief. Some breathe through a row of gills around their foot, some through a sort of comb, a disk or a shield, and others through elongated threads. Some have pretty plumes on their sides or on their backs they have some lovely branches that tremble, come and go and breathe.

These extremely sensitive organs that are susceptible to harm, take on charming forms. It is as if they wanted to be pleasing and moving—as if they wanted to be looked upon with favor. As part of their innocent game they take on the appearance of others in nature, they take all possible shapes and colors. These mollusks, these little children of the sea, with their childlike charm for illusion and their rich hues, eternally celebrate their mother and are her jewels. No matter how stern she is feeling, she has to smile.

With all this, this life of fear is full of melancholy. It is hard to believe that the beauty of all beauties, the Haliotis, does not suffer from the strict seclusion. She has a foot and is able to drag herself along, but does not dare. "Who is stopping you?" "I am afraid...that crab is lying in wait. All I have to do is open up a little and he will be in my house. A world of voracious fish floats above my head. Man, my cruel admirer, punishes me for my beauty. I am pursued from the Indian Ocean to the waters of the poles and now even in California and I am collected by the boatful."

The unfortunate wretch, who doesn't dare stray outside, has found a subtle way of acquiring air and water. She has made miniscule windows in her house that go directly to her tiny lungs. Hunger, however, forces her to venture out. Towards evening time, she crawls around and grazes on a few plants—her only source of food.

Let us note here in passing that these marvelous shellfish—whether it is the Haliotis, the Black or the White Olive, or the Gold-mouth Turban with its golden nacre—are poor herbivores that eat only the most moderate of diets. They are a living refutation of those who believe that beauty is the daughter of death, blood, murder and a brutal accumulation of substance.

These creatures need little to sustain them. Their major source of nutrition is the light that they drink in, that penetrates them, and with which they tinge and irisate the interior of their apartments. Also within their retreat they conceal their solitary love.

Each of them is dual. In each one of them is the lover and the mistress. Just like palaces in the Orient that only show dreary walls to the outside world and hide their wonders within, here the exterior is unrefined whereas the interior dazzles the eye. The backdrop for the union is the glow of a small sea of mother-of-pearl, which by multiplying its reflections gives even this confined house the charm of a magical and mysterious twilight.

If it is not possible to have the sun, then it is at least a great consolation to have the moon to oneself, a paradise of gentle hues, which changes constantly without changing and provides this immobile life with the slight bit of variety that every living being needs.

Children, who work in the mines, don't ask visitors for food or money but for a source of light. The same is true for these children, our Haliotises. Everyday, despite their blindness, they sense the returning light. They eagerly open themselves up to it, take it in and contemplate it with every fiber of their transparent bodies. Once the light has faded, they conserve it within themselves, they nurture it with loving thoughts.

They wait for the light, they wish for it. They desire and hope for it with all their tiny hearts. There is no doubt that when it returns, they feel the same delight we do when waking. Perhaps they feel it more intensely than we, who are distracted by our multi-faceted and varied lives.

For them, all eternity is spent sensing and detecting, dreaming of and missing the great lover—the Sun. Although they cannot see it in the same way we do, they certainly perceive that this warmth, the luminous glory, comes from outside and from a greatly powerful and yet gentle center. They love this other Self, this great Self that caresses them, illuminates them with joy and floods them with life. If they could, they would no doubt rush out to meet these rays of light. At least, tied to their doorstep, like the meditation bell at the entrance of a pagoda, they silently offer it...what? The bliss that the light brings and that gentle movement towards it is the first manifestation of the instinctive cult of the Sun. It's already a form of love and of prayer, to utter the humble word that one saint preferred to any prayer—the Oh!—which satisfies the heavens. When the Indian utters it at dawn, he knows that this innocent world of mother-of-pearl, pearls and humble shellfish is united with him from the depths of the sea.

I fully comprehend what the ignorant and charming heart of a woman feels in the presence of a pearl. She dreams and is moved and does not know why. This pearl is not a person, and yet it is not a thing. It is destiny.

What a lovely whiteness! No, I mean naiveté.—
Virginal? No, better than that. Virgins and little girls
no matter how sweet they are, always have a little bit
of youthful boldness. The naiveté of the pearl is rather
like that of an innocent wife, so pure, but subdued by
love.

It does not aspire to shine. It tones down, in fact
practically extinguishes its glow. At first, we only see
a dull white. It is only with a second look that we start
to discover its mysterious rainbow and what we call
its *orient*.

Where did it live? Ask the deep Ocean. What did
it live on? Ask the sun. It lived off light and from the
light's love, just like a pure spirit.

What a great mystery!...And yet, it makes us
understand well enough. We sense that this extremely
gentle being lived without moving for a long time,
was resigned. It lived in the tranquility that makes
one "wait while waiting," not wanting to do anything,
not desiring anything other than what the loved one
wants.

The child of the sea had placed his beautiful dream
in his shell, and the shell placed its dream in its mother-
of-pearl and that mother-of-pearl placed it in its pearl,
which is merely a concentrated form of itself.

But, they say, that the pearl comes to be only as the
result of an injury, a permanent ill, an almost eternal
pain, which attracts and absorbs the entire being, while

putting an end to its common life and transforming it into divine poetry.

I have heard that the great ladies of the Orient and of the North, who were far more delicate than the unrefined nouveau riches, avoided the fires of diamonds and only allowed gentle pearls to touch their delicate skin.

In reality, the blaze of the diamond is contrary to the blaze of love. A necklace or two pearl bracelets are harmonious with a woman. They are a truly feminine ornament, which instead of amusing, touches and makes the emotional more emotive. It says: "Let us love! But without a sound!"

Pearls seem to be in love with women, and they with pearls. Once these Northern women had worn them, they never took them off. They wear them day and night, hiding them under their clothes. On rare occasions, the happy jewels—the inseparable necklace—can be seen through luxurious furs that were always lined with white satin.

It is like the much beloved silk tunic that an odalisque wears beneath her clothes. She does not take this favorite garment off until it becomes worn and torn beyond repair, seeing it as a talisman, an infallible motivating force of love.

It is the same for the pearls. Like silk, they become imbued with the most intimate things and drink up life. An unknown force passes through it—the virtue of the one we love. When they have slept so many nights on her bosom, in her warmth, when they have taken on the scent of her skin and her blond shades, which make the heart delirious, these jewels are no longer merely jewels, they become part of the person and must no longer be seen by an indifferent eye. Only one man has the right to know of them, and only he has the right to penetrate the mystery of his beloved wife, which can be found in this necklace.

CHAPTER 9

Pirates of the High Seas: Octopi, etc.

In general, medusas and molluscs were innocent almost childlike and I have lived with them in a lovely and peaceful world. There have been few carnivores to this point. And those who were forced to live in this way destroyed only out of need. Moreover, for the most part, they lived off those in the earliest stages of life, such as atomies and animal jelly that can't truly be considered organisms. Thus, there was no pain. There was no cruelty and no anger. Nevertheless, their tiny and gentle souls displayed a flash—their yearning for light, specifically the light that comes to us from the sky, their yearning for love's light. This is revealed in the form of a constantly changing flame, which at night is the sea's pride and joy.

Now, I must enter a world that is quite dark in comparison: a world of war and of murder. From the outset, I must admit that as soon as life appeared, so did violent death, swift purification, useful but cruel purification of any creature that was languishing, anything that was laying about or that might languish, the purification of slow and weak creatures whose fertility would have cluttered the globe.

In the most ancient ground, two murderous creatures can be found: those who *devour* and those who *suck* their victims to death. The former is revealed in the imprint of the Trilobite—a species that is now extinct—an extinct destroyer of extinct beings. The latter lives on in a terrifying remnant—a beak that is almost two feet long, which, according to Dujardin, belonged to a great sucking creature, a cuttlefish or octopus. If such a beak was in proportion to his size, such a monster would have had an enormous body, with perhaps horrifying twenty or thirty-foot long arms lined with suckers that made him look like some sort of tremendous spider.

How tragic! These creatures of death are the first to be found in the Earth's deepest layers. Could we therefore say that death came before life? No, but the soft animals that kept such creatures alive vanished without leaving a trace or an imprint.

Were the devourers and the devoured two separate people of different origins? The contrary is more likely. The excessive strength of the early world, with its magnificent excess and abundance of food soon must have drawn two forms of life from the indistinct form of the mollusk, whose substance was suited for anything—two life forms that were contrasting in appearance but that were moving towards the same goal. The mollusk was inflated, blown up like a balloon, becoming an absorbing bladder, which as a result of being increasingly swollen and increasingly famished—and without teeth at first—sucked its food. The same force also shaped the mollusk into a being with articulated appendages which formed their individual shells, thereby hardening this encrusted fuddy-duddy, hardening its claws most of all, its biting mandibles that grind up the hardest of objects.

In this chapter we will only speak of the first of these two life forms.

This sucking creature of the soft, gelatinous world is soft and gelatinous himself. While waging war on mollusks, he remains a mollusk, in other words, an embryo. If he weren't so frightening, he would be a strange and ridiculous caricature of a warrior-embryo, a cruel, furious, soft, transparent but agitated fœtus who breathes a murderous breath. For, he does not wage war solely to feed himself. He needs to destroy. Even when he is full, completely stuffed, he still destroys. Since he lacks defensive armor, despite his menacing roar, he is nonetheless worried. He maintains his security by attacking. He regards every creature as a potential enemy. Just in case, he throws his long arms, rather his long whips armed with suckers, around them. Also, before any battle, he ejects his paralyzing and numbing discharge—a type of magnetism that makes fighting unnecessary.

Dual strength. In addition to the mechanical power of his sucker-lined arms that twist around and immobilize a victim, he has the magical power of that mysterious thunderbolt as well as a keen ear and a sharp eye. You are frightened.

What must it have been like for them in the overflowing richness of the early world where they did not have to hunt, since they were continually immersed in a sea alive with food, a sea that would interminably fill these monsters with their elastic membranes that stretched as needed? They decreased in size. However, Rang asserts having seen one that was the size of a barrel. Péron encountered another in the South Sea that was just as big. He rolled, he roared in the waves making a commotion. His six or seven foot-long arms unfurled in every direction, as if he were miming a wild scene with horrific serpents.

Based on these reliable narratives, it seems that we should not have dismissed Denis de Montfort quite so quickly when he declared having seen an enormous octopus strike a mastiff with his electric whips, strangle and finally suffocate him despite the dog's bites, his struggle and his howls of pain.

According to D'Orbigny in the article on Cephalopods in his Natural History Dictionary, this terrifying machine, the octopus, can build up pressure like a steam engine, even overload himself with power, thereby taking on an incalculable elasticity—momentum that allows him to actually jump from the sea onto a ship. This also explains the miracle that led many to label sailors from ancient times as liars, when they said that they had encountered a giant octopus, which having jumped onto the upper deck, gripping the masts and cables with his prodigious arms, would have taken the ship and devoured its crew, if they hadn't hacked off his arms with axes. Only after having been mutilated in this way, did the creature fall back into the sea.

Some believed they had seen sixty-foot long arms on them. Others contended having seen a moving island in the Northern Seas that was half a league wide and that was in fact an octopus—the frightful kraken, that monster of all monsters, capable of restraining and absorbing a one hundred foot long whale.

These monsters, if they actually did exist, would have endangered nature. They would have sucked the Earth dry. On the one hand, however, the giant birds such as the Epiornis, were able to wage war against them and on the other hand, land, which was more orderly must have weakened and deflated the awful chimera by reducing the amount of eatable items and decreasing their food sources.

Thank God, the octopi of today are a little less formidable. Their elegant species such as paper nautiluses, those graceful swimmers in their undulating shells; squids those fine sailors; beautiful cuttlefish with their azure eyes all sail the Ocean and only attack small creatures.

An idea appears in them, a hint of a future spinal system—such as the cuttlefish bone that is given to birds. They shimmer with all sorts of colors; in fact their skin is constantly changing color. We could call them the chameleons of the sea. The cuttlefish has an exquisite fragrance; the gray amber that is found in whales is a result of the infinite number of cuttlefish that they absorb. Porpoises also destroy them in great numbers. Cuttlefish, which are social animals that travel in herds, come to the shore as a group during the month of May in order to lay their cluster of eggs. Porpoises wait for them there and feast on this splendid banquet. These fine gentlemen are so particular that they only eat their heads and eight arms—those extremely tender and easily digestible morsels. They leaved the hardest parts—the back end of the body. The entire beach of Royan, for example, is covered with thousands of these poor mutilated cuttlefish. The porpoises celebrate with amazing jumps at first in order to frighten their prey, then in order to chase after them, and finally after their meal, in order to engage in a beneficial form of exercise.

Even with their beaks, which give them a strange appearance, the cuttlefish still arouse our interest.

Every color of the most varied rainbow appears in succession only to fade away as the light plays upon them or as they breathe in and out. As they lay dieing, they look at you with their azure eyes and betray the final emotions of life with the fleeting tinges of color that rise to the surface, appear momentarily only to disappear.

Although it was of such great importance in earlier ages, the overall decline of this class, which is less striking for its sailors (such as the cuttlefish, etc.), is quite obvious for that sad dweller of our shores—the octopus. He does not have the cuttlefish's sturdiness, which is built upon an inner bone that allows him to get around. Unlike the paper nautilus, he does not have a tough exterior—a shell that protects the most vulnerable organs. He does not have that sort of sail that assists in navigation and eliminates the need to row. He paddles around a bit along the shore, where, at best, he could be compared to a coaster that follows along the coastline. Because of his inferiority, he is used to practicing perfidious acts of trickery or ambushes of timid daring, so to speak. He hides, keeps still in the rocks' clefts. The prey passes by and he quickly lashes out with his whip. Weak creatures are stunned, the strong extricate themselves. A man when struck in this way while swimming can hardly be upset in his struggle with such a pathetic enemy. Despite his distaste, he must grab the octopus and turn him inside out like a glove— this is done easily enough. The octopus collapses and drops back down.

It is shocking and irritating to have been frightened for a moment or at least to have been surprised. You must tell this warrior, who comes upon you huffing and puffing, roaring and swearing: "You fake. You act brave but there is nothing to it. You are more a mask than a living being. With no foundation and no stability your only personality trait is pride. You roar, steam engine, you roar and you are no more than a sac and when turned inside out, your soft and flabby skin, is nothing but a punctured bladder, a burst balloon. And tomorrow you will be a nameless something or other— evaporated seawater."

CHAPTER 10

Crustaceans: War and Intrigue

If after visiting our fine collections of medieval armor and contemplating these unwieldy iron objects in which our knights dressed themselves up, you immediately go to the Museum of Natural History to see the crustacean armors, you will take pity on man's abilities. Man's armors are ridiculously carnivalesque disguises, both cumbersome and oppressive that are designed to suffocate warriors and render them harmless, whereas those of the crustacean, especially the weapons of the terrifying decapod, are so frightening that if they were enlarged to a human scale no one would be able to bear the sight of them, even the bravest men would be disturbed and mesmerized with terror.

They are all there on display, stopped dead in their battlefield stances, beneath that fearsome offensive and defensive equipment, which they wore as if it were so light—those strong claws, their sharp spears, their iron piercing mandibles, their cuirass bristling with javelin-like stings that have only to brush you lightly in order to stab you a thousand times. We are thankful that nature only made them in that size. For who could have done battle with them otherwise? No firearm could have made a dent in them. Elephants would have hidden, tigers would have climbed trees and even the rhinoceros's skin would not have protected him.

You sense that the inner agent or the motor of this machine, whose form is centralized and almost always circular, had, by virtue of this fact alone, enormous strength. Man's slender elegance, his longitudinal shape that is divided into three parts with four large divergent appendages that are far away from his center, make of him—no matter what people may say—a very weak being. Even in these knight's armors, with arms as long as telegraph poles and heavy dangling legs, he looks pathetically like a decentralized power-less and unsteady being that the slightest hit would knock to the ground. Crustaceans' appendages, on the other hand, stay so close and lay so well against their round, short and squat mass that the slightest blow dealt by them is given with the power of their entire mass. When these animals pinched, stung or cut it was with their entire being, which even at the furthest tip of their weapon was endowed with all their energy.

He has two brains (in his head and in his trunk) but in order to stay tight so as to get this terrifying centralization, the animal chose not to have a neck and to have his head in his stomach. What marvelous simplicity. That head unifies the eyes, the palps, the pincers and the jaws. As soon as the sharp eye has seen something, the palps feel for it, the pincers grasp it, the jaws break into it, behind them with no intermediary, the stomach, which has its own apparatus for grinding, manipulates and breaks it up. In an instance it is all over, the prey has vanished and has been digested.

This creature is superior in every way.

His eyes can see from in front and from behind. Convex, multifaceted and set on the outside of his body, they are capable of taking in a good stretch of the horizon.

The palps or antennae are testing organs and warning mechanisms. They test in three areas—at their tip they have the sense of touch and at their base the senses of hearing and smelling. This is an enormous advantage that we don't have. How extraordinary it would be if the human hand could smell and hear? Our powers of observation would be so much more rapid and comprehensive! Split up between three senses that work separately, sensations are often imprecise or fade quickly for that reason alone.

Of the decapod's ten feet, not only are six hands, or tongs, but what's more, their extremities are respiratory organs. The warrior found a revolutionary expedient for the problem that so plagued the poor mollusk: "To breathe, despite the shell." His answer to this: "I will breathe through my foot and my hand. I have placed this weak spot where I am vulnerable to attack, in my weapon of war. Just try to attack it there!"

Their only formidable enemies are storms and rocks. Few travel the high seas; few dwell at the bottom. They are almost all on the shore, stalking their prey. Often, while waiting for an oyster to yawn so that they can eat it for lunch, the sea swells, takes them and rolls them. Their armor becomes a danger to them. Because it is hard with no elasticity, it gets hit hard, brutally and in a manner that is sure to cause breakage. Their pointed ends are crushed, shatter and break into pieces against the pointed rocks. They can only emerge mutilated. Luckily, like the urchin, they are easily repaired by substituting another limb for the broken one. They rely on this to such an extent that when their limbs are caught they will break off their own limb in order to free themselves.

It seems that nature has particularly favored such useful servants. Against her fertile immensity, nature has unleashed the crustacean's ability to absorb immensely. They are everywhere, on every beach and are as varied as the sea. The sea's vultures—sea gulls—share the crustacean's essential role as agents of salubrity. If a large animal washes up on the beach, birds land on it immediately, while the crabs work from below and within so as to make it disappear.

The miniscule jumping crab called a sandhopper, which could be mistaken for an insect, occupies sandy beaches and lives beneath the sand. When a great number of medusas or other bodies wash up on the shore, you see the sand ripple and move and then it is covered with hordes of these dancing undertakers, who gaily take over the beach, swarming and skipping, while attempting to sweep everything up before the tide rises again.

Large, robust and crafty, crabs are a warrior nation. Their war instincts are so keen that they even know how to use sound in order to frighten their enemies.

When they go off to battle, they strike an intimidating stance with their pincers held high as they click their claws. In this stance they approach a superior force warily. At low tide, high atop some rocks, I could see them. But, although I was quite high above them, as soon as they felt that they were being watched, the gathering beat a hasty retreat. In an instance, the warriors, running sidelong as they do, were each taking cover under their own sentry box. They are more like Hannibal than Achilles. As soon as they feel they have the advantage, they attack. They eat the living as well as the dead. Even injured men have much to fear. It is said that on a deserted island, they ate several of Drake's sailors who were attacked and overcome by their teeming legions.

No living creature can do battle with them on equal terms. The giant octopus who suffocates the smallest of crustaceans risks losing his tentacles. The most gluttonous fish hesitates to swallow such a spiny creature.

As soon as crustaceans get big, they become tyrants, the terrors of two elements. Their unassailable armor is capable of attacking everything. They would reproduce in excessive numbers and would destroy the balance of life, if their armor weren't their greatest obstacle and threat. Hard and permanent not suited to life's variations, it is a prison for them.

In order to open up a pathway for breathing through this wall, they had to place the opening in a fortuitous limb, their leg that they often lose. In order to accommodate growth and the progressive enlargement of their inner organs, the armor must—and this is such a dangerous thing!—at times soften and become flabby—it must be nothing more than skin. Such change is only possible by shedding, peeling and throwing off a part of themselves. Complete molting. The eyes and gills that substitute for lungs undergo the process just like all the rest.

It is quite a spectacle to see a crayfish turn upside down, thrash about, go through torment, in order to tear herself away from herself. The process is so violent that she sometimes breaks off her legs. She is left drained, weak and soft. In two or three days, the limestone reappears and hardens the skin. The crab does not get away as easy as this. He needs a great deal of time before he can go back to his carapace. And until that time, all creatures, even the weakest, make him their quarry. Justice and equality are restored with a vengeance. The victims have their revenge. The mighty are subjected to the reign of the meek, as the entire species descends to their level and they fall victim to death's great equilibrium.

If we only died but once here on earth, there would be less sadness. But every living being must die a little bit every day, in other words, must molt and must undergo the small and partial death that renews and gives life. This causes a state of weakness as well as of melancholy that is not easy to accept. But what can we do? The bird that changes plumage each season is sad. The poor grass snake is even sadder at the time when he changes his skin. The human being also sheds his skin completely month by month, day by day, moment by moment. He constantly and slowly loses a bit of himself. He is not worn out by this, merely weakened during this vague and dreamy time when the vital flame grows dim only to come back even brighter.

This is all the more awful for the creature where everything must change all at once, where the framework must be taken apart, where the unbending exterior must be prised open and torn apart! He is overcome, stunned, faltering, not himself and at the mercy of the first creature to come along.

There are some fresh water crustaceans that must die in this way twenty times over the course of two months. Others, such as sucking crustaceans, succumb to this fatigue and cannot recreate themselves in exactly the same way and instead are deformed and lose the ability to move. In other words, they tender their resignation as hunters. In a cowardly manner they seek out an idle and parasitic way of life by shamelessly finding shelter in the viscera of bigger animals that despite themselves nourish them, exhaust themselves for their benefit, charitably work and provide for them.

Insects in their chrysalis seem to lose themselves, to be unaware of themselves, to be uninvolved in the pain. Instead they seem to be taking pleasure in this relative death like a baby in a warm cradle. But the molting crustacean knows himself and sees himself as he truly is—suddenly thrown from the most energetic of lives into one of deplorable helplessness. He seems bewildered and distraught. He can only hide shuttering under a rock and wait. Having never before met either a serious enemy or any sort of obstacle, having been exempt from any need for ingenuity because of the superiority of his terrifying weapons, when the day comes where he no longer has them, he has nothing at all to fall back on. Alliances could protect him perhaps if molting didn't occur for all of them and if each one was not equally disarmed at the time. Since they are all sick they are in no condition to protect the infirm.

Although it has been said that in some species the male wants to defend his mate, he follows her and if she is caught, then the spouses are both caught.

This terrible burden of molting, along with the bitter pursuit of the creature who increasingly is the king of the shore—man—as well as the extinction of ancient species who were a rich source of food for them, must have brought about a certain decadence in the species.

The octopus that is of no practical use and is neither hunted nor eaten has of course decreased in size and in number. This is all the more true of crustaceans whose meat is so excellent and that all of nature craves and enjoys!

They seem to know it. We can't say that the weakest among them have dreamed up an art for protecting themselves, but we can say they have come up with crude evasion tactics. They are constantly striving and they intrigue. That is in fact the exact term—they are like plotting intriguers, like people who have lost their social status, who with no respectable trade, live by their wits and are beggars rather than choosers. Bastard factotums—neither fish nor fowl—they manage a little of everything: the dead; the dying; the living and even sometimes land animals. The oxystome creates a mask and a visor for himself and also steals at night. The coconut crab at nightfall leaves the sea and goes pilfering, even climbing up coconut palms and eating fruits if he doesn't find anything better. The dromia hide by dressing up in other's bodies. In order to better protect the soft portion of his shell, the Hermit crab, who cannot completely harden his carapace, has come up with the idea of becoming a false mollusk. He notices a shell that is just his size, eats the inhabitant; he adapts himself to this stolen home to the point that he carries it around with him. At night, in this disguise he goes out for supplies: you can hear and recognize this pilgrim by the sound that he can't help but make with his shell as he limps and stumbles along.

Finally, there are those more decent sorts, discouraged by the motion and the battles at sea, who are won over by the less war-like and less hectic life on land. In the winter and during most of the rest of the year, they live on land and dig burrows. Perhaps, if the sea did not remain as dear to them as a beloved motherland, they would change completely and form into insects. Just like once a year the twelve tribes of Israel went back to Jerusalem in order to celebrate the feast of the Tabernacles, you can see these faithful children of the sea on certain beaches setting off as a community to pay their respects and entrust this great and good wet-nurse with their dear eggs and to place their young in the care of the one who cradled their ancestors.

~~~
CHAPTER 11
~~~

The Fish

The sea, that free element eventually had to create a creature for us in her own image, a creature that is eminently free, elusive, undulating, fluid, that flows like the rising tide, but also a creature whose wonderful mobility comes from a still greater inner miracle—a centralized organism that is slender, strong and very supple in a way that no other creature has been until now.

The mollusk dragging itself along on its stomach was the glebe's poor serf. The octopus, with his pride, his swelled head, his roar, a poor swimmer and not a walker, is no less fate's serf. Without his power to numb he would not have survived. The bellicose crustacean who is alternately so high and so low, the terror and the laughing-stock of all, undergoes periodic deaths during which he is the slave, the prey and the plaything of even the weakest creature.

Great and dreadful constraints: how can we free ourselves from them?

Freedom is found in strength. From the beginning, as it groped around for strength, life seemed to be confusedly dreaming of creating, at some time in the future, a central axis that would make the living being whole, and would increase the vigor of motion tenfold. There was a sense of this future when the radiates and molluscs made their first attempts. But they were too distracted by the overwhelming problem of exterior defense. The outer layer, always the outer layer, is what persistently preoccupied these poor creatures. Under these constraints, they produced masterpieces—the spiny ball of the urchin, the haliotis's conch, which is at once opened and closed, and finally the crustacean's armor with its articulated parts, defensively perfect and offensively terrifying! What more could one need? What else could be added? Nothing, it seemed.

Nothing? No, everything. Let there be a creature that relies on movement, a creature with uninhibited daring, who scorns those others as if they were infirm or doddering, who considers the outer layer to be subordinate and concentrates strength within himself.

Crustaceans surround themselves in an outer skeleton of sorts. Fish produce this in the center, in their intimate interior, along the axis to which the nerves, muscles and every organ will be connected.

Although this innovation runs counter to common sense, it is fantastical. Placing the hard and solid parts precisely in the area that the flesh is protecting! Bones, which are so useful on the outside, are placed in the deepest parts where their solidity is of no use!

Crustaceans must have laughed when they saw a soft, fat and stocky fish like those in the Indian Ocean for the first time, as he went out on his first outings slipping and sinking with no shell, no armor and no defences. His strength resided within himself, solely protected by his slimy fluidity, the luxuriant mucus that surrounded him, which eventually stabilized to form supple scales. This is a soft armor that stretches and bends, that yields without completely giving way.

It was a revolution on the same scale as when Gustavus Adolphus relieved his soldiers of that burdensome iron armor so that their chests were no longer covered with anything other than a buff jerkin a strong skin that was both supple and lightweight.

This was a daring but wise revolution. Our fish, who unlike the crab, is no longer a captive of his armor, is at the same time liberated from the cruel condition that was a direct result of this armor—molting—and thus freed from the danger, weakness, effort, and enormous loss of strength that occurs at that time. He molts little and slowly, like man, and bigger animals. He stores up life, he hoards it, amassing a treasure trove in the form of a powerful nervous system with its many telegraphic wires that will ring, will resound in the backbone and in the brain. Even if bones are lacking or very soft or if the fish retains an embryonic appearance, he maintains his great harmony because of this rich tangle of nerve fiber.

In fish, we don't encounter the elegant weaknesses found in reptiles or insects that are so slender that it is possible to cut them like a thread in certain areas. Like them, fish are segmented but their segmentation is hidden away and protected below the surface. They use this in order to contract without exposing themselves to being as easily cut up as reptiles and insects.

Like crustaceans, fish choose strength over beauty and for that reason they have done away with their necks. Head and trunk— it is all a single unit. This is an admirable principle of strength that allows them to cut through such a divisible element as water by striking extremely hard, sometimes if they want to, a thousand times harder than necessary. Thus, they are like a line, an arrow, they have the speed of a lightning bolt.

The inner bone, which appeared in the cuttlefish as a single and uniform bone is in this case a great system—that is both *one and yet quite multiple*. It is one as it relates to the strength of unity and multiple in its elasticity and in the way it can conform to muscles, which when alternately contracted and relaxed created movement. This fish shape is a marvel, a true marvel—so compact (at least from the outside) and so capable of contracting from within. Just look at this carina with its slender and very flexible ribs, as found in herring and shad, where the motor muscles, which push out with alternating thrusts, connect. Moreover, fish only expose their auxiliary oars—those stubby fins that are fairly safe. These fins are strong, prickly and sticky and are capable of injuring, evading and escaping. How superior all of this is to the octopus and the medusa, who offered everyone that crossed their path their soft tentacles of flesh—a delightful morsel for crustaceans and porpoises.

All in all, this true son of the water, who is as mobile as his mother, slides through the water because of his mucus, cleaves it with his head, shocks it with his muscles (that are contracted on his vertebrae and on his slender and undulating ribs) and finally with his strong fins cuts through it, rows and navigates.

Anyone of these powers would suffice. And yet, he unites them all—he is the absolute embodiment of movement. Even birds are less mobile, in the sense that they have to *land*. They settle down for the night. Fish never do. Even asleep they are still floating.

Along with being so mobile, they are also extremely sturdy and lively. Wherever there is water, they can be found. They are the Earth's most ubiquitous beings. Fish alone persist in the solitary spaces such as the Cordellieras and the mountains of Asia where the air is so rarified and no other living beings exist. These gudgeons and goldfish have the glory of seeing the entire earth below them. Just as herring and cod live in the greatest depths, under the extraordinary weight of pressure. Forbes, who divides the sea into a dozen stacked levels or layers, found each one inhabited. In the lowest level that is thought to be quite dark, he found a fish endowed with admirable eyes, who can therefore see by finding enough light in what to us seems like pitch-dark.

Another form of freedom for fish is the number of species—salmon, shad, eel, sturgeon—that can stand either fresh water or sea water and alternate or regularly go from one to the other. Several families of fish have marine as well as fluviatile species, such as rays and bass.

Nevertheless a particular temperature, food or habit can cause them to settle in an area, and confine them within this extremely free element. Warm seas are like insurmountable walls for polar species. On the other hand, the cold currents of the Cape of Good Hope stop species from warm seas. Only two or three species of fish are known to be ubiquitous. Few frequent the open seas. Most are coastal and only favor particular shores. Those from the United States are not like those from Europe. Moreover, there are particularities in taste that may not enslave totally, but retain them. The ray paddles around in the mud and the sole on the sandy sea floor, bullheads crawl along the shoal, moray eels enjoy living among the rocks, whereas perch prefer the strand, and triggerfish the shallows or a bed of madrepores. Scorpion fish alternately swim and fly when pursued by fish; they soar up and sail through the air but when birds chase them they dive instantly back into the waves.

The common expression for describing contentment— "Like a fish in water"— rings true. In calm times, an air sac that can be inflated allows fish to make themselves more or less heavy, as well as navigate easily while they float between two waters. They move along peacefully, cradled and caressed by the waves, sometimes sleeping along the way. They are both embraced and isolated by the unctuous substance that makes their skin and scales slippery and water-proof. Their environment does not vary much; it is always more or less the same, not too cold and not too hot. What an unbearable difference there is between this comfortable life and the life that we land-dwellers have been dealt! Each step that we take brings us hardship and challenge. The harsh land places rocks in our way, exhausts us, wears us out by making us climb up and down hills over and over again. Air temperature varies according to the season and often quite severely. The cold rain falls, with no mercy over the course of several days and nights; water penetrates us, gives us a chill, sometimes it even freezes in our hair and as we shiver it pelts us with sharply pointed crystals from every direction.

The happy life of fish, their blissful fulfillment is expressed in the tropics through the luxuriousness of their colors and translates in the North into the vigorousness of their movement. In Oceania and the Indian Ocean, they do themselves up, wander and roam in the strangest forms and the most fantastical finery. They frolic joyfully among the coral and on the living flowers. Our fish in cold and temperate seas are great sailboats, powerful oarsmen, true sailors. Their long and slender shape makes them as swift as arrows. They could teach a lesson or two to any ship builder. Some have as many as ten fins, which can at times act as oars and at times as sails. These can be held completely opened or else partially folded up. Their tails, those wonderful rudders, are also the main oar. The best swimmers have a forked tail, their entire backbone ends there and by contracting their muscles the fish move forward.

Rays have two enormous fins, two great wings that beat the waves. Their long, supple and agile tail is a weapon used for striking. Like a whip it splits and cuts through the waves. Because they are slender and displace very little water, as they sail sidelong, they float with ease and therefore have no need for a bladder like those that support less slender fish. Thus all fish have apparatus that is suited to their environment. Sole are oval-shaped and flat, so that they can slide into the sand. Eels, so that they can roll in the mud, take on serpentine shapes and become a long ribbon. Anglerfish that must often live attached to rocks, have hand-like fins that are more reminiscent of something found on a frog than on a fish. In birds the most developed sense is vision, for fish it is the sense of smell. Hawks flying in the clouds have a gaze that penetrates space allowing them to see game that is practically invisible. The same is true of the ray. From the greatest depths of the sea they are alerted by the scent of tempting prey and rise towards the surface. In this semi-obscure world, with its uncertain and deceitful light, one relies on smell and sometimes on touch. Those, such as the sturgeon that dig through the mud have a refined sense of touch. Sharks, rays and cod (with their big widely spaced eyes), see very badly but sniff and smell. The sense of smell is so sensitive in rays that they have a veil whose express purpose is to occasionally block smells in order to neutralize their strength, which could undoubtedly disturb them and overtake their brains.

To that powerful means of hunting, add admirably sharp, sometimes saw-like teeth that in some are arranged in several rows, as if the mouth, the palate and the gullet were paved with them. Even their tongues are armed with teeth. These fine and therefore fragile teeth have others behind them, ready to replace them if the front ones break.

As we said at the beginning of this second part of the book, the sea had to create these terrifying creatures, these all-powerful destroyers in order to combat and cure the strange ill that afflicts her—an excess of fertility. Death, that helpful surgeon, relieves the sea of the excess that could otherwise drown her, by persistently bleeding that immense abundance. As a defense against the frightful torrent of reproduction that occurs— the deluge of herring, the billions of cod eggs, so many horrifying reproduction machines, which by increasing tenfold or a hundred fold would overfill the oceans and suffocate nature— the sea mostly uses her rapidly consuming death machine, that armed swimmer, the fish.

This is a beautiful spectacle, great and startling. The universal battle between Death and Love looks insignificant on land in comparison to what goes on at the bottom of the sea. In the sea there is an inconceivable grandeur that is frightening in its furor, but on closer inspection, it appears quite harmonious and surprisingly well-balanced. This furor is necessary. This exchange of matter, which is so rapid it dazzles, this lavish abundance of death, is a form of salvation.

There is nothing sad about this. In fact, a savage joy seems to reign over all of it. Wonderful health, incomparable purity as well as terrifying and sublime beauty emerge from this sea life, where two forces, which seemingly destroy one another, are bitterly intertwined. In the dead and in the living, the sea is equally triumphant. Without making much of a difference between them, she lends and then takes back electricity and light, she derives from the play of sparks and that infinite number of pale flashes of light that all the way up to the poles creates a sinister spectacle.

The sea's melancholy is not found in her lack of concern about multiplying death. It is in her inability to reconcile progress with excessive movement.

The sea is a hundred times, a thousand times richer than land and her fertility comes much faster. She even erects and builds. The increasing amount of land, as we saw through the example of coral, is due to the work of the sea. For the sea is none other than the earth at work, the earth actively giving birth. Her only obstacle is her speed. Her inferiority is apparent in the difficulty she has—she who is so rich in reproduction—in organizing Love.

It is sad to think that the billions upon billions of sea dwellers only know an uncertain sort of love, one that is elementary and impersonal. These people of the sea that rise to the surface, one group after another, in their pilgrimage towards happiness and light, give the waves the best part of themselves, their very life, all for an unknown opportunity. They love and yet they will never know the object of their love that is the embodiment of their dream and desire. They give birth, without ever knowing the bliss of rebirth that one feels towards one's offspring.

Few, very few of the most lively, the most warrior-like, the cruelest know our type of love. These terribly dangerous monsters, the shark and his she-shark are compelled to approach one another. Nature has forced upon them the danger of having to kiss each other. This is a terrifying and suspect kiss. Accustomed to devouring and swallowing everything up blindly—animals, wood, rocks, anything—this time, an admirable thing occurs, they refrain! No matter how appetizing they might be to one another, with impunity, they draw close to the saw—their lethal teeth. The female boldly allows herself to be cornered, overpowered, with the frightful grappling iron that he throws in order to get a hold on her. She is not devoured, after all. She absorbs him and takes off with him. Intertwined, these furious monsters roll about in this way for entire weeks, unable, despite being famished, to resign themselves to a divorce, unable to tear themselves apart and even in the midst of a storm, they are invincible and unswerving in their fierce embrace.

It is said that even when separated they follow each other out of love, that the faithful shark, who is attached to the sweet object stays with her until she gives birth, loves his presumptive heir, the sole fruit of this marriage, and never, ever eats him. He follows him and watches over him. Finally, if danger comes his way this excellent father swallows the sharkling up in his large mouth but not in order to digest him, rather to shelter him.

If life in the seas has a single dream, one wish, a vague desire, it is stability. The shark's violent and tyrannical methods, his iron grip, his firm hold on the female, the fury of their union, gives the impression of a sort of desperate love. Who knows in fact whether this inability to form a union, this endless fluctuation in an eternal voyage to nowhere, is not a source of sadness in other gentle species that are more apt to form families? These children of the sea become quite enamoured of land. Many swim upstream, accept the blandness of fresh water that is so poor in quality and in nourishment, in order to entrust their hopes for their posterity, far from the storms. At the very least, they approach the seashore, in search of some sort of sinuous cove. They even become industrious in their attempts to make small nests from sand, silt and grass. Touching effort. They are not equipped with anything that resembles the instruments of insects—those marvels of animal industry. They are lacking even in comparison to birds. By dint of perseverance—with no hands, no paws, no beak and only their poor body—they gather a bundle of grass, penetrate it, and pass over it repeatedly until they achieve a particular cohesiveness. How many obstacles get in their way!

The female, who is blind and gluttonous, disturbs the work and threatens the eggs. The male never leaves them; he defends them, protects them and is more a mother to them than their own mother.

Several species, especially the most humble, have the same instinct. Gudgeons, for example, are a small fish that are in no sense beautiful or good, they are so scorned, in fact, that no one fishes them and when caught, they are thrown back in. Well, this creature who is the lowest of the low, is a loving father to his family, a hard worker, who despite being so small, so weak and without resources, is nonetheless the ingenious architect, the craftsman who makes the nest and out of sheer will, out of his tender feelings sees the construction of this protective cradle through to the end.

It is a pity, however, to see such labor of the heart fall short of its goal and to see that this creature is halted at this first artistic impulse by the destiny of his nature. This makes us wonder. We sense that this world of water is not self-sufficient.

Great mother who began life, you cannot see it all the way through to the end. Allow you daughter, Land, to continue the work that you have started. You see it in your very womb, at the sacred moment, your children dream of Land and its stability; they approach her and pay homage to her.

Once again, it is your responsibility to begin a series of new beings, with an unexpected marvel—a grand first rendering of loving and warm life, of blood, of milk, of tenderness—which will be fully developed in terrestrial races.

CHAPTER 12

The Whale

"The fisherman who stayed out late in the North Sea's night, sees an island, a shoal, like the spine of an enormous mountain that is floating above the waves. He drops his anchor...The Island flees and carries him away. Leviathan was a shoal." (Milton)*

---

* In Book I of Milton's *Paradise Lost* we find:
"Thus Satan, talking to his nearest Mate,
With head uplift above the wave, and eyes
That sparkling blazed; his other parts besides
Prone on the flood, extended long and large,
Lay floating many a rood, in bulk as huge
As whom the fables name of monstrous size,
Titanian or Earth-born, that warred on Jove,
Briareos or Typhon, whom the den
By ancient Tarsus held, or that sea-beast
Leviathan, which God of all his works
Created hugest that swim the ocean-stream.
Him, haply slumbering on the Norway foam,
The pilot of some small night-foundered skiff,

Such an error is quite natural. Dumont d'Urville made this mistake. In the distance he saw breakers and eddies all around. As he moved closer, white spots seemed to indicate the presence of a rock. Above this shoal, swallows and those storm birds—petrels—played, frolicked and swirled. The rock was floating looking venerable due to its great age and made completely gray from the barnacles, shells and madrepores upon it. But the mass moved. Two enormous jets of water that came up from the front revealed the awakening whale.

An inhabitant from another planet who would approach ours in a balloon, from a great height, would observe the surface of the globe and wishing to know whether it was inhabited would say: "The only beings that I have discovered here are of a rather good size—of one hundred to two hundred feet long—their arms are only twenty-four feet long, but their superb tail, which is thirty feet long, thrashes the sea regally, masters it and allows them to move forward with great speed, with a majestic ease that makes it easy to identify them as the sovereigns of the planet."

And he would add: "It is unfortunate that the solid

Deeming some island, oft, as seamen tell,
With fixed anchor in his scaly rind,
Moors by his side under the lee, while night
Invests the sea, and wished morn delays."

part of this globe is deserted or that it is only inhabited by animalcules that are too small to be perceived. Only the sea is inhabited by a good and gentle race. Family is honored among them, mothers suckle their young with tenderness and although their arms are quite short, they manage in a storm to hold them closely against themselves so as to protect them."

They travel together happily. In the past we used to see them sailing two by two, sometimes as a family of ten or twelve in isolated seas. Nothing was more magnificent than these great fleets that were at times illuminated by their phosphorescence, sending up sprays of water thirty or forty feet high, which in polar seas give off steam. They approached ships peacefully, filled with curiosity, as if they were encountering a new species of brothers. They took pleasure in the arrival and gave the newcomers a warm reception. As part of their games, they would throw themselves straight up and fall headlong with a great crash creating a foaming chasm. Their familiarity went as far as touching the ship and its dinghies. Imprudent trust that was cruelly abused! In less than a single century that great species of whales is on the verge of extinction.

Their customs, the way they are organized are like those of our herbivores. Like ruminants they have a series of stomachs in which their food is elaborated. Teeth are of little use to them, so they have none. They comfortably graze the living prairies of the sea, by which I mean the gigantic sweet and gelatinous fuci or the beds of infusoria and schools of imperceptible atoms. Hunting is unnecessary for such food. Because they have no need to wage war, they were exempt from producing those horrible jaws and saw-like teeth, those instruments of death and torture that sharks and so many other weak creatures have acquired as a result of their murderous ways. They do not pursue, according to Pierre Boitard. Instead food comes to them on the waves. Innocent and peaceful, they swallow up a universe of life, which is hardly organized, dies before even having known life, and asleep passes into the crucible of universal change.

There is no relation between this gentle race of mammals, who like us have red blood and milk, and those monsters of the preceding age—those horrific stunted specimens that emerged from the primitive sludge. Whales, who are much more recent, found purified water, a free sea and a peaceful earth.

The Earth had dreamed its old disturbing dream about fish-lizards and flying dragons—the terrifying reign of the lizard. It was emerging from the sinister fog and entering into the pleasant dawn of harmonic conception. Our carnivores had not yet been born. There was a brief moment (a few hundred thousand years perhaps) of great gentleness and innocence, where excellent beings such as possums, appeared on land, creatures that love their families so much that they carry them around and if necessary have them return to their womb. In the water, the good-hearted giants appeared.

The sea abounded with milk and oil. Her warm animalized fat was fermenting to an unprecedented force and wanted to live. She swelled, became organized in the form of these colossuses, nature's spoilt children that she endowed with incomparable strength and more importantly with excellent passion-filled red blood. This was it first appearance.

This was the world's greatest achievement. All those selfish, languid and relatively vegetative pale-blooded creatures seem to have no heart, when compared to the generous life that bubbles in this crimson-colored royal dignity where rage and love flow. The strength of the superior world, its charm, its beauty is blood. A totally new type of youth begins in nature because of it. Passion's flame, love, the love of family, and race which as understood by man, will bring about the divine crowning achievement of life—Pity—all this is because of blood.

But, with this magnificent gift, nervous sensitivity increases infinitely. One is more vulnerable, much more capable of feeling pleasure and of suffering. The whale, who has hardly any of the hunter's instincts, —neither the sense of smell nor a well-developed sense of hearing—benefits completely from the sense of touch. The fat that protects them from the cold, does not guard against impacts. Their finely organized skin with its six distinct types of tissues quivers and vibrates at the slightest touch. The delicate papilla that are found on them are instruments that allow for a delicate touch. All of this is brought to life, invigorated by a rich flow of red blood, which even when taking the difference in size into account, infinitely surpasses in abundance that of terrestrial mammals. An injured whale floods the sea in an instant with her blood, turns it red over a great distance. Whereas our blood can be measured in drops, whales were lavished with streams of it.

The female whale carries for nine months. Her pleasant, slightly sugary milk has the warm sweetness of a woman's milk. But, as the whale must always cleave through the waves, breasts located in front on the chest would expose the infant to being hit. Thus, they moved a little further down, in a more peaceful area, closer to the womb from which he was born. The little one finds shelter there and benefits from not being hit directly by oncoming waves.

Because such a life form is inherently shaped like a ship, the mother's waist is narrow and this means that she cannot have the profuse waist of a woman— that adorable miracle of life on land, that stable and harmonic life, where everything disappears into tenderness. No matter how tender the whale—that great woman of the sea—is, she still must make everything dependent on her battle against the waves. Moreover, her organism is the same under this strange mask—the same shape, the same sensitivity. Fish on the surface, woman beneath it.

She is extremely timid. At times, a bird can frighten her and cause her to dive down so abruptly that she hits the sea floor.

Among the whales, love, which is subject to such difficult conditions, necessitates a site of profound calm. Just like the noble elephant, who fears being observed by the uninitiated, the whale only loves in the wilderness. The meeting place is near the poles, in the solitary coves of Greenland, in the fog of the Bering Strait, undoubtedly also in the warm sea that was discovered right by the North Pole. Will we ever rediscover that sea? The only way to get there is by way of the dreadful narrow passes that open up in the ice, only to close back up and change with every passing winter, as if to prevent man from returning. For the whales, it is thought that they pass under the ice fields, going from one sea to another by way of a dark route. This is a foolhardy voyage. They are exposing themselves to great dangers under this enormous layer that is barely perforated with a few air holes, because they have to come up for air every fifteen minutes—or with their air reserves a little longer. If they don't find the air holes in time, the ice is so hard and so thick that no force, no blow from the head can break it. It is as easy to drown there as it was for Leander at Hellespont. But since they do not know this story, they embark daringly and pass through.

Their solitude is great. This is a strange site of death and of silence for such a feast of passionate life. A polar bear, a seal, a blue fox are perhaps respectful, prudent witnesses but they observe from afar. There is no lack of chandeliers, girandoles, or fantastical mirrors. Bluish crystals, peaks, aigrettes of dazzling ice, virgin snow are all witnesses that surround and observe them.

What makes this union touching and solemn is that it necessitates an express will. They do not possess the shark's tyrannical weapon, those grips that subjugate the weaker of the two. On the contrary, their slippery sheaths keep them apart and at a distance. They elude and slip away from one another in spite of themselves because of this heartbreaking obstacle. At such a moment of accord, it looks more like a battle. Some whalers claim to have been privy to this unique spectacle. The lovers, in their burning desire are at time standing erect like Notre-Dame's two towers, bemoaning their short arms as they attempt to embrace. They fall back into the water with all their enormous weight.... The bear and man run away terrified by their sighs.

The solution is unknown. Those that have been proposed seem absurd. What is certain is that in every way—for love, for suckling their young and even for self-defense—the unfortunate whale suffers from the dual constraints of both its weight and its difficulty in breathing. They only breathe outside of water and if they stay under they suffocate. Therefore they are terrestrial animals and belong to the land? Not at all. If by chance, a whale washes up on shore, the enormous weight of his flesh and fat overwhelm him; his organs collapse. He suffocates in this case as well.

In the only element in which the whale can breathe, asphyxia comes just as it does in that unbreathable water in which he lives.

Thus, from the grandiose creation of a giant mammal emerged none other than an impossible being the first poetic burst of the creative force, which first set its sights on the sublime and then gradually reverted to what was possible and durable. The admirable animal had everything, size and strength, warm blood, sweet milk, a good heart. Nothing was missing except for a way to survive. The whale had been made with no regard for the general proportions of the globe, and no regard for the imperious laws of gravity. It did not help that, beneath it all, they had enormous bones. Their gigantic ribs are not sturdy enough to hold their chests sufficiently free and opened. As soon as they escape their enemy the water they find their enemy the land and their weighty lungs crush them.

Those magnificent blowholes, the superb waterspout

that they throw up thirty feet high, are signs, testimony of a still child-like and barbaric organization. By throwing it up towards the sky by this powerful effort, these blowers (as these animals are called) seem to say: "Oh, nature! Why did you make me a serf?"

Their lives were problematic and it did not seem that the splendid but flawed prototype could last. Such difficult and furtive love, suckling in the roll of the storms, between asphyxia and being cast ashore, the two great acts of life are almost impossible and are carried out by dint of heroic efforts and will! What living conditions!

The mother never has more than one young, and that is already enough. Three things plague her and her offspring: the labor of swimming; suckling; and the fatal need to resurface! The upbringing is a battle. Beaten, rolled about by the ocean, the infant takes milk only when he can seize the opportunity, as she continues to swim the mother can lay on her side. She is admirable in the efforts she makes in performing her motherly duty. She knows that in his meek attempts to suckle her offspring would let go. In this act in which a woman is passive and lets her infant do as he pleases, the whale is active. Taking advantage of the moment she squirts a barrelful of milk through her powerful valve.

The male rarely leaves her. Their predicament is painful when the bloodthirsty fisherman tries to attack them through their offspring. They harpoon the little one so that the parents will follow along; in fact they make incredible efforts to save him, to carry him away. They rise out of the water and expose themselves to the blows in order to bring him to the surface and get him some air. Even when he is dead, they still defend him. Although they could dive below and escape, they stay at the surface endangering themselves in order to follow the small floating body.

For two reasons they often wash up on the shore. Unlike fish, they cannot stay below in the lower and more peaceful levels during storms. And they want to stay together, so the fate of the strong is determined by the weak. They drown as a family.

In December 1723, at the mouth of the Elbe River, eight female whales were washed ashore and near their bodies their eight males were found. In March 1784, in Audierne in Brittany the same thing happened. First some fish and porpoises approached the shore in a state of alarm. Then came a strange and awful thundering noise. It was a large whale family, which the storm was pushing towards the shore, who was struggling, was overcome, did not want to die. In this case, again the males died with the females. Several of the females, who were pregnant and defenseless against relentless waves, were (along with the males) cast ashore and knocked out by the blow.

Two of them gave birth of the shore letting out piercing cries, just like women, and also with distressing moans of despair as if they were mourning for their children.

CHAPTER 13

Sirens

I land and here I am on solid ground. I have had enough of shipwrecks. I would like to see more durable races. Cetaceans will disappear. Let's reduce our design and with the exception of its size, let's retain everything about this gigantic poetic incarnation that is the first born of those with breasts, milk and warm blood.

Most of all, let's retain the gentleness, the affection, the loving family. Let's make certain to keep, these divine gifts in the more humble but good-hearted races to whom the two elements—sea and land—are going to jointly contribute their spirit.

The blessings of life on land can already be sensed. When leaving behind the existence of a fish, several things that were once impossible will become easier.

Thus, the whale, who was a loving mother, could hug and hold her child close, but she could not hold him against her breast. Her arm was too high up and the breast on this living ship could only be towards the rear. In the new beings who not only swim but who crawl on land—such as the walrus, the manatee and the seal—the breast moves up towards the chest so as not to drag along or hit against the ground. We see woman foreshadowed in the shape and graceful stance that can be deceptive from afar.

In fact, when seen up close, although it is not as white or as charming, it is very much a feminine breast—a globe that swells with love and with sweet need to suckle. And with each movement it duplicates every sigh of the heart that beats beneath. This breast calls out to carry a child, to give him sustenance and a place to rest. All this was denied the swimming mother. The mother who can land can have these joys. The stability of the family, the affection that is deeply felt and deepens everyday, and above all Society—all these great things begin as soon as a child can sleep on her breast.

But how was the passage from cetaceans to amphibians made? Let's try to understand.

First of all the relationship between them is obvious. To their great detriment, many amphibians are still dragging behind them the whale's heavy tail. And in at least one species, whales have hidden within their tail the first stage and the distinct beginnings of the two back feet that the higher-level amphibians will have.

In seas that are strewn with islands, and thus divided up by land, cetaceans were constantly forced to stop and had to modify their habits. Their reduced exertion and captive life style diminished their size and reduced them from a whale to an elephant. The elephant seal appeared. Having kept the memory of the extraordinary tusks that had armed certain large cetaceans that lived in the sea, he still displays big front teeth, although they are not offensive. Even the teeth they use for chewing are neither clearly those of herbivores nor those of carnivores; they are not really suited to either diet and work slowly.

Two things made whales lighter—their mass of oil that allowed them to float in water and that powerful tail whose alternating strokes, beating from side to side, pushed them forward. But all this is overwhelming for the amphibians that paddle in shallow waters and crawl on the rocks like heavy snails. Fish, with their great agility, laugh at such creatures that cannot catch them. They can hardly overtake mollusks that are as slow as they are. Little by little they get used to eating the abundant, gelatinous and nourishing fuci that fatten them up without providing them with the vigor of animal meat.

Thus, in the Red Sea, in the seas of the Malaysian Islands and those of Australia we can see that unusual colossus the dugong, crawling about with his chest and breast towering above the water. They are sometimes called the dugongs of the tabernacle; inert idols that stand out, but can hardly defend themselves and who will soon become extinct. Thus they will enter into the realm of legend, taking their place among those other true legends that we foolishly mock.

Who made this great change? Who created these land-dwelling cetaceans like the dugong and his brother the walrus? The comfort of land, which was truly peaceful before man, the attraction to plants as a food source and undoubtedly the attraction to love, which is so difficult for whales and so easy in the life of the terrestrial amphibian.

Love is no longer elusive and uncertain. The female is no longer that proud giant who had to be followed to the ends of the earth. This female lying on the undulating seaweed is submissive and ready to obey her lord and master. She makes life gentle and comfortable. There is little mystery. Amphibians live quite simply in the sun. The females, who are many in number are attentive and form a harem. From a state of wild poetry we fall into the bourgeois manners or if you prefer into the patriarchal mores that come with readily available pleasures. The good-hearted respectable patriarch with his large head, his mustache and tusks, sits imposingly on his throne between Agar and Sarah, Rebecca and Lia, whom he loves greatly just as he loves his children that form a veritable little herd. In his calm life, this red-blooded male's great strength is completely devoted to family affection. He envelops his loved-ones in a tender, proud and quick-tempered love. He is valiant, ready to die for them. Alas, his strength and furor are of little use to him! His corpulence makes him vulnerable to his enemies. He bellows, he crawls, wants to fight, but cannot—he is a gigantic undeveloped specimen, a failed experiment, living between two worlds, a poor disarmed Caliban!

Weight, which is fatal to the whale, is much more so for the dugong. Thus, let's reduce his size a little more, let's ease his stoutness, let's make the backbone more supple, and more importantly let's eliminate that tail or rather, let's split the fork of the tail into two fleshy appendages that will be much more useful. The new being, the seal—lighter, a good swimmer, a good fisherman, living off the sea, but loving on land (his little paradise), will devote his life to always returning to that land, in order to climb that rock from which his wife and children are calling him and to which he brings them fish. With his prey in his mouth, but without the tusks that the walrus uses for climbing, he uses his four limbs—both the front and the back ones—for grasping onto the kelp, stretching and straining each limb as best he can, so that eventually they ramify giving him five fingers.

What is particularly beautiful about a seal, what moves you as soon as you see his round head is his brain capacity. No being, except for man, has such a developed brain, according to Boitard. They make a strong impression—much more so than monkeys whose grimaces strike us as unpleasant. I will always remember the seals in the Amsterdam Zoo the charming museum that is so rich and so well organized and that is one of the world's most beautiful places. It was a 12th of July, after a rain storm and the air was humid. Two seals were trying to cool off in the deep water. They were swimming and leaping. When they rested, they looked at me, this voyager, gazing with their gentle velvety eyes that are so intelligent and friendly. Their expression was a bit sad. They lacked and I lacked a common language. You cannot take your eyes off them and regret having this perpetual barrier between one soul and another.

Land is their beloved home; they are born there, love there and when injured they go there to die. They bring their pregnant females on land, lay them down on seaweed and feed them fish. They are gentle, good neighbors and defend one another. Only during mating season (the time for love) do they become delirious and fight amongst each other. Each seal has three or four wives that he sets up on land on a mossy rock with enough space. This is his district. He does not tolerate being encroached upon and makes certain that his occupancy rights are respected. The females are gentle and defenseless. If they are hurt, they cry, they move about expressing their pain with looks of despair.

They carry for nine months and raise the child for five or six months, teaching him to swim, fish and choose the best food. They would keep them much longer if their husband were not so jealous. He chases them away, fearing that the overly weak mother will replace him with this rival.

Such a short upbringing has undoubtedly placed limits on the progress that the seal might have made. Motherhood is complete only in the case of the manatees—an excellent tribe in which the parents don't have the heart to send their children away. The mother keeps him for a very long time. Even when she is pregnant again and suckling a second child, we see her leading her eldest about. This is a young male that his father does not mistreat, who returns his father's love and whose father allows him to stay with his mother.

This extreme affection, which is characteristic of the Manatee, is expressed in their organization in the form of a physical advance. In the case of that great swimmer, the seal, or of the extremely heavy sea elephant, their arms are merely flippers. This flipper is drawn in and is close to the body; it cannot free itself. Finally, the female manatee, that loving amphibian-woman, *mama di l'eau* as our blacks say, performed the miracle. Anything can eventually become unbound through constant effort. Nature is driven by its obsession to caress children, to take them and hold them close. The ligaments yield, stretch and let the forearm go. And from this arm a webbed polyp radiates.... This is the hand.

Thus the manatee has the supreme joy—she embraces her child with her hand in order to hold him to her bosom. She takes him and places him against her heart.

There are two things that could lead this amphibian far:

Already the hand—that organ of industry and essential instrument for future work— is born in them. They need only become more supple and supplement the teeth, as in the Beaver, and art will begin, especially the art of sheltering one's family.

Moreover, bringing up offspring became possible. Because of the good-hearted father's willingness to keep his innocent rival around, the child, placed on the mother's heart slowly soaking up her life, stays near her for a long time, at an age when he has everything to learn. This is what brings about progress.

If we are to believe certain legends, that progress did continue. Amphibians developed and moved closer to the human form and had supposedly become half-man, men of the sea, Tritons and sirens. Except that unlike the melodious sirens of mythology, these sirens remained silent, incapable of creating a language for themselves, of communicating with man and evoking his pity. These races supposedly died off in the same way that today we are seeing the unfortunate Beaver, who cannot speak but who does cry, die off.

Some casually suggest that these strange figures were seals. But is such a mistake possible? Seals, in all their varieties, have been known for quite some time. Since the seventh century at the time of Saint Columban they have been fished, caught and eaten.

In the sixteenth century, men and women of the sea, were not just seen momentarily in the water, but were brought on land, displayed, fed in large cities such as Antwerp and Amsterdam, seen by Charles V and Phillip II as well as Vesalius and other early scientists. There is mention of a sea-woman who lived for many years dressed as a nun, in a convent where anyone was free to see her. She did not speak, but she worked and spun. However, she could not rid herself of the love of water or keep from returning to it.

Some will say, if these beings truly existed, why were they so rare? Alas, we don't have to look very far for an answer. It is because in general they were killed. It was a sin to allow them to live "because they were *monsters*." The ancient accounts state this categorically.

Anything that did not conform to known types of animals or, on the contrary, anything that came close to resembling man was considered a *monster* and done away with. A mother who had the misfortune to give birth to a malformed son could not protect him—he was suffocated between the mattresses. It was assumed that he was the son of the Devil, a mischievous invention with which to offend creation and to slander God. Moreover, these sirenia, too analogous to man, were even more likely to be thought of as a diabolical illusion. They were so horrified by such things in the Middle Ages that they were considered to be the dreadful miracles that God performs out of anger in order to strike sin down with terror. People hardly dared to name them aloud. They were anxious to make them disappear. The daring sixteenth century still thought of them as "devils in men's fur" and thought they should only be touched with a harpoon. They were becoming extremely rare at the time that certain infidels and speculators thought to keep them and put them on display.

Are there at least remains or some bones? We will only know the answer to this question when the museums of Europe start to completely display their immense holdings. I understand that space is lacking and it will always be lacking, if a palace is needed to expose these items. But the simplest, most inexpensive shelter with an immense roof would make it possible to lay out such sturdy objects. Until now we have only seen portions and selected items.

Let me add, that in order to be realistic when displaying these stuffed amphibians, these *monsters* that look too much like man, they must be presented in ways and in poses where the illusion is maintained. Give them this honor, they paid a high enough price for it. Let the mother Seal or the mother Manatee appear before me on a rock like a siren, with her hand and their breast as they were initially used—to hold their children against their bosom.

Does this mean that these beings would have been able to climb to our level? Does this mean that they were the authors, the ancestors of man? The eighteenth-century writer Benoît de Maillet thought so. I frankly do not think it is plausible.

Undoubtedly, the sea started everything. But the parallel series of landforms of which man is the crowning achievement did not emerge from the most superior marine animals. These were already too well established and too specialized to be the source of the indistinct prototype of such a different form of nature. They had pushed the fruitfulness of their type very far, almost too the point of exhaustion. Thus, the elders died off and it is at the bottom rungs among the most obscure and youngest beings of a related class that a new series that will climb even higher will emerge.

Man was not their son, but their brother—a cruelly hostile brother.

The strongest of the strong, the ingenious one, the active one, the cruel king of the world has finally arrived. My book is flooded with light. But what will it show? And how many sad things do I now have to bring into this light?

This creator, this tyrannical God was able to produce a second nature within nature. But what did he do to the other one, the original one, his wet-nurse and his mother? With the teeth that she gave him, he bit her breast.

So many animals, who were living peacefully, were becoming more human and initiating arts, today are bewildered, stupefied and are nothing more than beasts. The monkeys that were the kings of Ceylon, whose wisdom was celebrated in India, became horrifying savages. The Brahman of creation, the Elephant is hunted, enslaved and has been reduced to a beast of burden.

The freest of beings, who formerly brought joy to the sea, those good-hearted seals, the gentle whales, the peace-loving pride and joy of the Ocean, all have fled to the polar seas and to the awful world of the ice floe. But they cannot bear such a difficult life, and soon, they will completely disappear.

Polish peasants, an unfortunate race, could understand and deeply appreciate one of these silent exiles, who found refuge in the lakes of Lithuania. They say: "He who makes the Beaver cry will never succeed."

This artist has become a frightened beast, who no longer knows anything or can do anything. Those that still survive in America have retreated, are still fleeing and no longer have the strength to do anything. Long ago, a traveler found one quite far out towards the superior lakes. He was meekly returning to his trade and was cutting some wood because he wanted to build his family a home. When he saw the man, he let the wood drop. He did not even dare to flee. He simply burst into tears.

BOOK III

The Conquest of the Sea

CHAPTER I

The Harpoon

The Arctic explorer John Ross stated that, "The sailor who arrives within sight of Greenland has no pleasure in seeing this land." I find that easy to believe. First of all, it is a harsh, seemingly merciless coast where even the snow cannot stick to the steep black granite. The rest is nothing but ice. No vegetation. This desolate land that hides the pole from us seems like a land of death and famine.

During the very short period of time when the water is not frozen, you might be able to survive there. But it is frozen nine months out of twelve. What can you do during all that time? What can you eat? You can hardly find anything. Night lasts several months and it's sometimes so dark that the explorer Elisha Kane, although surrounded by his dogs, could only locate them when they breathed, by sensing their humid breath. In this long, terribly long darkness, on this hopelessly sterile land, draped in impenetrable ice, two solitary figures wander about who are determined to live in the horror of an impossible world. One of them is the fishing bear, the fierce prowler under his magnificent fur and thick layer of fat that allows him to survive for long periods of time without food. At a distance, the other strange figure looks like an ill-conceived and awkward fish with long hanging flippers standing straight up on his tail. This false fish is man. The two of them smell each other and seek each other out. Each one hungers for the other.

And yet sometimes the bear flees, refuses the fight, because he believes that the other is even more ferocious and more voracious.

A hungry man is a terrifying thing. Armed with a simple fish bone, he pursues this enormous beast. But he would have died a hundred times over, if he only had this formidable companion for food. He survived only by committing a crime. Since the land gave him nothing, he looked towards the sea and since the sea was closed off to him, his only solution was to kill his friend the seal. He found the fat of the sea concentrated in the seal in the form of the oil without which he would have died of cold even before dying of hunger.

The Greenlander's dream is that when he dies, he will pass over to the moon where there will be firewood, fire and the light of the hearth. Oil substitutes for all this down on earth. Consumed in large quantities, it keeps him warm.

There is a great contrast between man and the sleepy amphibians who even in this climate manage to live without much suffering. The seal's gentle eyes betray this quite clearly. As the sea's nursling, he is always in contact with her. There are always cracks in the ice that allow the excellent swimmer to provide for himself. Even though we may think he is heavy, he climbs a block of ice skillfully and allows it to carry him to his destination. The water that is thick with mollusks, rich in animated atoms, nourishes the fish that the seal will eat. And the seal, having eaten his fill, falls asleep on his rock, in a deep sleep that nothing can disturb.

Man's life is completely different. He seems to be there despite God. Accursed, everything is at war with him. On the photographs we have of the Eskimo, we read his dreadful fate in his intent gaze, in his steely black eyes that are dark as night. He seems petrified by a vision, by the daily spectacle of dismal infinity. This person, plagued by an eternal Terror, hides his quick, keen intelligence—full of expedients in a life of unforeseen danger—behind a harsh mask.

What could he have done? His family was hungry and his children were crying out. His pregnant wife was shivering with cold on the snow. The polar wind was unrelentingly heaping a deluge of frost—that swirl of sharp arrows that sting and penetrate, that daze and cause you to lose both your voice and senses. The sea is closed off—no more fish. But the seal is there. And how many fish are there in a single seal? What a wealth of accumulated oil! There he was, asleep and defenseless. Even awake, he doesn't flee. He can be approached and touched. Like the manatee, you have to beat him to get him to go away. Those that are caught when young follow you obstinately even after having been thrown back in the sea. Such easy opportunities must have disturbed man and given him pause, caused him to fight temptation. But in the end, the cold defeated him and he carried out this murder. Since that time, he has been rich and has thrived.

The flesh fed these starving people. The oil that was absorbed in great quantities kept them warm. The bones were used for thousands of domestic tasks. Ropes and nets were made with the seal's fibers. The sealskin, cut to the woman's size, covered her shivering body. They both wear the same clothes with the exception of the little shawl that she lengthens and stylishly trims with a thin red leather border so as to please him and so as to be loved. But what is much more useful is that through hard work, from pieces of skin that have been sewn together they make a light, yet strong device, which this bold man dares to climb into and that he calls a boat.

It is a pathetic and small vehicle—long and slender, weighing almost nothing. It is completely covered over, with the exception of a hole, where the rower sits, pulling the skin tightly around his waist. You would wager that it would capsize every time....But no. It flies on a wave like an arrow; it disappears and reappears, between the floating mountains, amidst the rough and choppy swirls created by the surrounding ice floes.

Man and boat are one. The combination is like an artificial fish. But how inferior to the real thing! It does not have the equipment, such as the air bladder that keeps the fish suspended and allows him to make himself lighter or heavier as needed. It does not have the oil that is lighter than water, and that causes the fish to float or go rise up to the surface. It especially does not have what gives the true fish the vigor of movement—the strong contraction of the backbone that allows him to strike strong blows with his tail. It only vaguely imitates the fins. Its oars that are not tight against its body, but rather moved from a distance by a long arm are quite soft in comparison and are more quickly fatigued. What compensates for all this? Man's tremendous energy, and beneath that steely mask, his lively reason, which in flashes, decides, invents, and at any moment finds solutions to the dangers of that floating skin, which is the only thing that stands between him and death.

Very often, it is impossible to pass through. Ice blocks the way. Then the roles change. The boat was carrying the man, but now he carries the boat, puts it on his shoulder, crosses the cracking ice, and then launches his ship once again, further away. At times, floating mountains come towards him, providing only narrow passages between them, which open up and then suddenly are blocked off. He can disappear in them, buried alive. At any moment, he can see the two bluish walls drawing closer, weighing down on his boat and on him with such an extraordinary amount of pressure that he can be reduced to the width of a hair. A large ship had this fate. It was broken in two; the two halves were crushed and flattened.

They claim that their fathers fished whales. At that time, they must not have been as poor, their land was less cold, they were more resourceful and no doubt had iron. Perhaps this came to them from Norway or Iceland. Whales have always been abundant in the seas of Greenland. They have been a great source of greed for those for whom oil is a primary necessity. Fish provide only drops of oil, seals supply it in streams, whales in mountains.

Man was the first to attempt such an endeavor. Ill equipped, poorly armed and with the sea roaring beneath his feet in the shadows amongst the ice floes, one on one he made contact with the colossus.

He trusted his strength and courage so much that he relied on the vigor of his arm, on the precise blow and the weight of the harpoon. He believed he could penetrate both the skin and the wall of fat, that thick flesh.

He believed that at the moment of his horrific awakening in the storm that the injured creature would create, with the whale's leaps and the blows from his tail, he would not be engulfed with the creature. The epitome of daring was that he tied a rope to his harpoon so as to be able to pursue his prey. He braved the dreadful jolts with no thought that the frightened beast could suddenly go below, escape into the depths, dive headfirst.

There was another sort of danger. Instead of the whale, he might find in its place the whale's enemy, the terror of the sea, the Sperm Whale. He is not big. He is only sixty to eighty feet long. His head alone is one third of his total size—twenty or twenty-five feet. In that case...woe to the fisherman! Because he will become the fish, he will become the monster's prey. The Sperm Whale has forty-eight enormous teeth and horrifying jaws capable of devouring everything— man and boat. He seems drunk with blood. His blind rage frightens all the cetaceans, who flee howling, even throwing themselves onto the shore, hiding in the sand and mud. Even when dead, they dread him, not daring to approach his corpse. The most savage of the

Sperm Whale species is the Killer Whale also known as the Physeter by the ancients, a creature that was so feared by Icelanders that they were afraid to say his name aloud when at sea for fear that he would hear it and approach them. They believed on the contrary that another whale species (the Humpback whale) loved them and protected them and would provoke the monster so as to save them.

Many say that the first men to face such a frightening experience had to be inflamed, eccentric and reckless. According to them, the whole thing was not begun by the wise men of the North, but by our frenzied heroes the Basques. They were the tremendous walkers and hunters of the Mont Perdu, and unrestrained fishermen that sailed their unpredictable sea—the Bay of Biscay—in small crafts. They fished tuna. They saw whales playing around them and began to run after them, just like they relentlessly chase after Pyrenees chamois in quagmires and chasms. This enormous game, enormously tempting because of its size, because of the opportunity and the danger it provides, was hunted to death everywhere and anywhere it led them. Without realizing it, they pressed on all the way to the pole.

There, the poor colossus thought he was safe and undoubtedly not thinking that anyone could be so crazy, he slept quietly, when our heroic scatterbrains approached without making a sound.

Tightening his red belt, the strongest of them all, the most agile, threw himself out of the boat and onto the immense back, with no thought to his life, and with a grunt, plunged the harpoon in.

CHAPTER 2

The Discovery of the Three Oceans

Who opened up navigation on a grand scale to man? Who revealed the sea and established its zones and routes? And finally who discovered the earth? The whale and the whaler.

All this occurred well before Columbus and the famous seekers of gold who, with great fanfare, received the glory for rediscovering what fishermen had already found.

The ocean crossing that was so celebrated in the 15th century had already often been accomplished with the narrow crossing between Iceland and Greenland. It had even been done in the open sea since the Basques used to travel to Newfoundland. The crossing was the least of the dangers for these men, who went to the ends of the earth to seek that supreme danger—the battle against the whale. Having gone off to the Northern Seas, to go hand to hand with the living mountain, in the middle of the night, and what's more, in the midst of a veritable shipwreck, with one foot on the whale and with a chasm below, those who undertook this had resilient enough hearts to approach the ordinary events in the sea with very little concern.

This was a noble war, a great school for courage. That hunt was not like hunting today—an easy carnage that is carried out cautiously and from afar with a machine: they used to strike with their hand and risk their lives. They used to kill few whales, but they gained a great deal in maritime ability, patience, wisdom and boldness. They brought back less oil but more glory.

Each nation demonstrated its own particular genius in this endeavor. They could be recognized by their appearance. There are a hundred forms of courage and their graded variations were like a heroic gamut. In the North, there were the Scandinavians, the red races (from Norway to Flanders) with their red-blooded fury. In the South, there were the Basques with the energetic impulse and lucid madness that so capably guided them around the world. In the center was Breton steadiness, silent and patient, but in the hour of danger sublimely eccentric. And finally Norman good sense, which is armed with communal spirit, fore-sight and calculated courage. It defies everything and accepts only success. Man's beauty was evident in this supreme manifestation of human courage.

We owe a great deal to the whale. Without them, fishermen would have remained close to the coast, since almost all fish stay along the shore. The whales emancipated them and led them all over. As they were carried along they ventured out into the open seas and gradually went so far, that while following the whales they found that they had unwittingly crossed over from one world to the other.

At that time, there was less ice and they maintained that they went as far as the pole (at least seven leagues away). Greenland did not appeal to them. They were not looking for land but rather for the sea alone and the whales' route. As for the whales, the entire Ocean is their home and they sail all around it, especially its breadth. Each species prefers to live at certain latitudes in a zone of water that is either more or less cold. This is how the major divisions in the Atlantic were traced.

The population of inferior whales with only one fin on their back (the fin whale) is located in the warmest and coldest zones below the Equator and in the polar seas.

In the large intermediate region the fierce sperm whale tends to go towards the South, devastating the warm waters.

The right whale, on the other hand, fears them— or at least used to fear them, since they are so rare today! Feeding especially on mollusks and other elementary forms of life, they used to seek them out in the temperate waters that were slightly to the North. They were never found in the South's hot current. That is what drew attention to the current and what brought about the essential discovery of the true route from America to Europe. From Europe to America, one is pushed along by the trade winds.

If the right whales detest warm waters and cannot cross the Equator, then they cannot go around America. How then is it possible that a whale wounded on our side, in the Atlantic, can sometimes be spotted on the other side between America and Asia? It is because a passage exists to the North. This was the second discovery, a bright light that was shone upon the shape of the Earth and the geography of the seas.

In the end, whales have led us everywhere. Because they are rare today they make us search the two poles, the furthest corner of the Pacific at the Bering Strait and the immensity of the Antarctic waters. There is even an enormous region, which no state or merchant vessel has ever crossed, that is a few degrees above the farthest points of America and Africa. Only whale ships go there.

They could have made the discoveries of the fifteenth century much earlier, if they had wanted to. All they had to do was look to the wanderers of the sea—the Basques, Icelanders or Norwegian and our Normans. For a variety of reasons, no one trusted them. The Portuguese only wanted to use their own men; from the school they had created. They were afraid of our Normans whom they chased from the African coast so as to take possession of it. Moreover, the kings of Castile were still very suspicious of their subjects, the Basques, who because of their privileges, were like a republic and were thought to be a dangerous and indomitable people. This is why these princes missed more than one opportunity. Let's only mention a single one—the Invincible Armada. Phillip II who had two older Basque admirals, placed a Castilian in command of it. They also did not follow the Basque's advice. Hence, the great disaster against England.

A terrible disease broke out in the fifteenth century—the hunger, the thirst, the absolute need for gold. People and kings all cried out for gold. There was no longer any means of balancing revenues and expenditures. Counterfeit money, cruel trials and awful wars, everything was used, but still no gold. Alchemists made promises, saying they were soon going to be able to produce gold—but everyone had to wait. Like a furiously hungry lion, the Treasury ate up Jews, ate up Moors and after such rich food, it had nothing left to eat.

The people were the same. Thin and having been sucked dry, they asked for, they begged for a miracle that would make gold fall from the skies.

We know the very lovely story of Sinbad in *The Thousand and One Nights* and its beginning—that eternal story that is constantly repeated. From the street, the poor worker Hindbad, loaded down with the wood that he is carrying on his back, hears concerts and galas that were occurring in the palace of Sinbad, who had become very rich as a result of his great travels. He compares their lot and envies him. But Sinbad tells him everything that he had to suffer through in order to acquire his gold. Hinbad is horrified by the tale. The overall result of this tale is to exaggerate the dangers as well as the benefits of travel—this great game of chance—while at the same time discouraging sedentary work.

In the fifteenth century, the legend that was clouding people's minds was a stale version of the fable of the Hesperides—an *Eldorado*. This land of gold that was said to be in the Indies and that was thought to be the location of Eden, was still thought to exist. It was merely a question of finding it. They took great care not to look for it in the North. This is why so little use was made of the discovery of Newfoundland and Greenland. In the South however, gold powder had already been found in Africa. This spurred them on.

The dreamers and scholars of this pedantic century accumulated and made commentary of texts. And the discovery, which in and of itself should not have been very difficult, became so by dint of reading, careful consideration and chimerical utopias. Was this land of gold actually heaven? Was it located in the Antipodes? Were there such a thing as Antipodes?...Upon hearing this word, the Doctors of the Church, the black robes, stopped the scholars and reminded them that the Church doctrine was formal on the fact that the heresy of the Antipodes had been categorically condemned.

This is a serious problem! They were stopped in their tracks!

Why would America, which had already been discovered, be so hard to discover? Because they both hoped to find it and feared what they might find.

The scholarly Italian bookseller, Columbus, was quite sure of his facts. He had gone to Iceland to gather the traditions, while the Basques told him everything they knew about Newfoundland. A Galician had been thrown overboard there and had lived there. Columbus' associates were pilots, established in Andalusia, named Pinzons, who are believed to be the same family as the French Pinçons of Dieppe.

This last point is quite probable. Our Normans and the Basques, who were Castilian subjects, were closely connected. There were those dubbed the *Castilians*, who under the command of the Norman Béthencourt, undertook the famous expedition to the Canary Islands, according to Navarrete. Our kings gave privileges to the *Castilians* who settled in Honfleur and Dieppe while those from Dieppe had trading posts in

Seville. It is not certain that a native of Dieppe found America four years before Columbus, but it is almost certain that these Pinçons from Andalusia were fleet owners from Normandy.

No Basque or Norman could have received permission from Castile in his own name. An able and eloquent Italian was necessary, a persistent Genovese who pursued the subject for fifteen years, who found the exact moment, grabbed the chance and was able to alleviate any qualms. The moment came at the time when destroying the Moors was costing Castile dearly and when there were more and more cries of "Gold!" The moment came when a victorious Spain was quaking from its war-like crusade and its Inquisition. The Italian seized this lever and became more of a staunch believer than the true believers. He acted through the Church itself. The moral consequence of leaving so many pagan nations in the oblivion of death was put forth to Isabella. It was clearly proved to her that discovering the land of gold was equivalent to exterminating the Turk and recapturing Jerusalem.

We know that of the three ships, the Pinçons provided two, which they themselves commanded. They went ahead. Although it is true that one of them went off course, the others, François Pinçon and his young brother Vincent—the pilot of the Nina—signaled Columbus to follow them to the southwest on October 12th 1492. Columbus, who was going due west, would have encountered the brunt of the warm current that goes from the West Indies to Europe. Crossing that liquid wall would have been quite difficult. He might have died or sailed so slowly that his crew would have mutinied. On the contrary, the Pinçons, perhaps basing themselves on tradition, navigated as if they were aware of that current. They did not confront it head on, but where its strength wanes in the south, thereby passing through it with no problem and landing at the very place where the trade winds push the waters from Africa towards America, in the waters of Haiti.

This is noted in Columbus' own journal, where he frankly admits that the Pinçons were leading him.

Who was the first to see America? One of the Pinçon's sailors, if we believe the royal inquiry of 1513.

Based on all of this it would seem that a good portion of the profits and of the glory should have gone to them. They pleaded their case. But the king found in favor of Columbus. Why? In all likelihood, because the Pinçons were Norman and that Spain preferred to recognize the groundless rights of a Genovese with no country than those of Frenchmen, from Spain's great rival nation—subjects of Louis XII and Francis I, who one day could have transferred their rights to their rulers. One of the Pinçons died of despair.

Besides, who had lifted the great obstacle of religious reluctance? Who was able to make a convincing case for the expedition with such eloquence, skill and persistence? Columbus and Columbus alone. He was the true creator of the enterprise, and he also executed it quite heroically. He deserves the glory that he has preserved in posterity.

Like the explorer Jules de Blosseville (a good-hearted man and an excellent judge in important matters) I believe that of all these discoveries, the only truly difficult one was the trip around the world, which Magellan undertook with his pilot, the Basque Sebastien des Cano.

The most dazzling and the easiest was the crossing of the Atlantic, guided by the trade winds and the encounter with America, which had long ago been discovered to the North.

The Portuguese did something even less impressive still when they took an entire century to discover the Western coast of Africa. Our Normans, had found half of it in no time at all. Despite what has been said about the Lisbon school and the praiseworthy perseverance of Prince Henry who created it, the Venetian Cadamosto shows the lack of skill in the Portuguese pilots in his account. As soon as they had one with real daring and genius, Barthelemy Diaz who rounded the Cape of Good Hope, he was replaced with Vasco da Gama, a great lord who was a member of the King's

House and who was above all a man of war. They were more concerned with making conquests and capturing treasures than they were with actual discoveries. Gama was admirable in his courage, but he followed his orders to not allow anyone else in the same sea all too strictly. A ship of pilgrims from Mecca, loaded with families, whose throats he cut in a barbaric way, exacerbated the feelings of hatred, intensified the loathing of the Christian name in the entire Orient and closed off more and more of Asia.

Is it true that Magellan had previously seen the Pacific indicated on a globe made by the German Behaim? No, that globe that still exists does not show it. Could he have seen a map belonging to his master, the King of Portugal that indicated it? It has been said, but not proven. It is much more likely that the explorers who had already been sailing about the American continent for some twenty years had really seen the Pacific sea, with their own eyes. This rumor that had been circulating coincided perfectly with calculations that a counterweight to the hemisphere in which we live was necessary in order to insure the balance of the globe.

No one had a more terrible life than Magellan's. Everything about it was a battle—distant sea travel, escapes and trials, shipwrecks, a failed assassination attempt, and finally his death among the barbarians. He fought in Africa. He fought in the Indies. He got married among the Malay—those very courageous and fierce people. He seems to have been just like them.

During his long stay in Asia, he gathered all the knowledge he could and prepared his great expedition where he would attempt to go by way of America directly to the Moluccas for spices. By going directly to the source, he would be sure to get them at a better price than had been possible until then when spices came by way of Western India. Thus originally the undertaking was purely commercial. A discount on pepper was the initial inspiration for this voyage that would be the most heroic one ever made on this planet.

Obsession with the royal court and intrigue dominated everything at that time in Portugal. Magellan, who was mistreated in Portugal, went over to Spain and Charles V in a magnificent gesture gave him five ships. But the king did not dare completely trust this Portuguese defector and forced him to take a Castilian associate. Magellan left with two threats hanging over him—Castilian malice and the vindictive Portuguese who were attempting to assassinate him. There was soon a revolt on board and he displayed tremendously indomitable and barbaric heroism. He put his associate in irons and declared himself sole commander. He had the rebels stabbed, flayed and he cut their throats. In the midst of all this there was a shipwreck and ships were lost. No one wanted to follow him anymore when they saw the terrifying tip of America, the desolate Tierra del Fuego and the bleak Cape Froward. This land that was torn away from the continent by violent upheavals by thousands of furiously bubbling volcanoes looks like granite in turmoil. Blistered and cracked by the sudden change in temperature, it is horrifying. There are sharp peaks, like eccentric bell-towers or black breasts, atrocious three-pointed teeth and all that lava and basalt, all that mass that has been melted down by fires is covered in gloomy snow.

They all had had enough. He said: "Further!" He searched and he sailed in circles, extricated himself from hundreds of islands, and entered onto an unending sea, which on that day was *pacific* and which was to keep that name.

He died in the Philippines. Four ships were lost at sea. The only surviving one, *Victory*, had only thirteen men in the end, but it had its great pilot the bold and indestructible Basque, Sebastien, who came back alone in 1521 as the first man to have gone around the world.

Nothing could be more important. The earth was henceforth certain of its sphericity. This marvel of physics—water that was uniformly spread over a globe to which it adhered without dropping away—this miracle, was proven true. Finally, the Pacific was discovered—that great and mysterious laboratory, where far from our gaze, nature works in depth on life, elaborates worlds and new continents.

This was a revelation with not only an immense material significance, but with an enormous moral impact as well. It increased man's boldness a hundred fold and launched him into another voyage, on the free ocean of science and into an effort, which was both foolhardy and fertile, to circumnavigate infinity.

CHAPTER 3

The Law of Storms

Only recently have we learned to build ships that were suited to sailing in southern waters, with their extremely long and strong waves, which in those limitless waters, roll and amass into veritable mountains. What can we say of those first men—such as Diaz and Magellan—who ventured into them with the heavy hulls of their day?

For the polar seas of the Arctic and Antarctic, specially made ships are necessary. Explorers like John Cabot, Willem Barentsz and Hugh Willoughby were courageous on their battered rowboats, sailing up icy torrents, confronting Spitsbergen, opening up Greenland by way of its gloomy entryway—Cape *Farewell*—penetrating as far as that area, where even recently, two hundred whaling ships were destroyed.

What made these earlier heroes sublime was their very ignorance, their blind courage and desperate resolve. They knew nothing about the sea, confronted frightening phenomena whose causes they could hardly have suspected. They did not know the sky any better. The compass was their only equipment. They had none of the instrumentation that guides us and speaks to us in a precise language. They went forward as if in the dark with their eyes closed. They themselves say that they were afraid, but they were undeterred.

For them the tragic dialogues between the ocean of the water and of air—storms at sea, whirlwinds, magnetic storms that we call aurora borealis, all this phantasmagoria—seemed like the fury of a troubled and irritated natural world, or perhaps, like struggling demons.

For three centuries progress came slowly. With Cook and Péron we can see how difficult, dangerous and uncertain sailing was even in the not too distant past.

Although Cook had great courage, he also had a vivid imagination and was affected by this knowledge as he writes in his journal: "The dangers are such that I dare say that no one will venture further than I did."

And yet, it is precisely since his time that voyages started with some regularity and that they pushed on to the furthest possible points.

The Titanic nineteenth century observed these phenomena dispassionately. It was the first to dare to look at storms head on, note their fury and in a manner of speaking take dictation from them. Their warning signs, their characteristics and their results were all recorded. Then they were explained and generalized. A system emerged under a bold title that would have seemed blasphemous in the past: "The Law of Storms."

Thus, what had been believed to be a whim was reduced to a law. These dreadful realities, now governed by certain regular properties, would lose a great part of their dizzying hold on us. Calm and strong, man in the midst of danger would now be informed as to whether equally regular means of defense could be used to resist them.

In a word, if we are able to have a *science* of storms, can we not also create an art of rescue, an art for avoiding hurricanes and even of benefiting from them?

This science could not take root as long as old ideas that attributed storms to the "wind's whim" were still held to be true. Through close observation it was learned that winds do not have whims, but rather that they are a contingent and sometimes are caused by the storm. The storm itself is usually an electrical phenomenon that is often unaccompanied by wind.

The Naval expert, Charles Romme, whose brother was a member of the French National Convention and the main author of the Revolutionary calendar, laid down the initial foundation. The English had noticed that during storms in Indian, they would sail for a long time without making headway and often found themselves back at the starting point. Romme collected all these observations, showed that the same was true for hurricanes in China, Africa and in the Caribbean Sea. He was the first to note that rectilinear gusts of wind are quite rare and that generally speaking a storm has a *circular character* and is a whirlwind.

The whirlwind storm that occurred in 1815 in the United States as well as one in 1821 (the same year as the great eruption of Mount Hecla in Iceland) where the winds blew from every direction towards a central point attracted the attention of Americans and of Europeans. Brande in Germany as well as Redfield in New York made the first advances after Romme. They established the law that a storm was usually an advancing whirlwind that moves forward while turning in on itself.

In 1838, the English engineer Sir William Reid, who had been sent to Barbados after the famous storm that killed fifteen hundred people there, clarified that two-fold rotating motion. But his most important discovery came when he observed and formulated that: "In our Northern Hemisphere storms spin from right to left." In other words, they go from the East, move to the North, turn to the West and then to the South to return to an Easterly direction. In the Southern Hemisphere storms spin from left to right.

This is an observation with great practical implications, which henceforth guided all maneuvers.

Reid, quite justifiably gave his book the grand title: "The Laws of Storms."

In his case it was the laws governing their movement, rather than the explanation of their causes. His book did not say what creates storms or what they are in and of themselves.

On this subject France reemerges. Jean Peltier, in his book *On The Causes of Whirlwinds*, demonstrated both with a great deal of data and his clever experiments, that whirlwinds on land and on sea are electrical phenomena, where winds play a secondary role. One hundred years ago, Giambatista Beccaria had suspected this. But it was left to Peltier to penetrate the subject by reproducing them and by creating miniature whirlwinds and storms.

Electrical whirlwinds readily appear near those vents of the underground world, called volcanoes; thus they are much more common in the seas of Asia than in ours.

The Atlantic, which is opened at both ends and crisscrossed by winds, must have fewer whirlwinds and more rectilinear winds. However, Henry Piddington refers to a limitless number of circular winds.

From 1840 to 1850 Piddington and Maury compiled vast amounts of information in Calcutta and in New York. Maury is very well known for his maps, his

Directions to accompany the wind and currents, his *Physical Geography of the Sea*, which are gospel to today's navy. Piddington is less of an artist but no less of a scholar. In his *Guide for Sailors*, an encyclopedia of storms, he provides the results of his infinite experience and the detailed means by which to calculate the distance of a hurricane or whirlwind, how to determine its speed, assess the curve of the wind and the nature of different sorts of waves. He corroborated Peltier's ideas, adopted the theory of the electrical cause and refuted the explanations for these phenomena that were based on the winds, believing that the effects were being taken for the cause.

The ancient art of augury, the science of omens, which is not in the least contemptible, is happily made new in this excellent book.

Sunsets are far from being immaterial. If they are red and impart blood-red waves to the sea that other ocean, the ocean of the air, is preparing a storm for you. A ring around the sun, a red glow within a pale circle, flickering stars that seem to be descending are all signs of threatening activity from above.

It is much worse if in a nasty looking sky, you see small clouds flying by like dark purple arrows, if dense forms start looking like strange buildings, like shattered rainbows, like bridges in ruin or hundreds of other types of passing fancies. You can be sure that the great drama has already started above. Everything is calm but on the horizon pale flashes of lightening quiver. Everything is calm and in the silence, at times a rolling sound that stops suddenly can be heard. The sea reaches the shore, plaintive and swollen with sighs. And at times from the depths, a muted sound rises.... In that case, pay attention, as the English say: "It is the call of the sea."

Birds are forewarned. If they are not too far from the coast, you see them—cormorants or sea gulls— returning to land as quickly as possible, looking for any opening in the rocks. In the open sea, they'll use your ship as an island and a resting-place. They fly around it and at times will quite openly ask you to take them in and will perch on your masts for a while. Soon the dark petrel—a bird with an evil-looking way of flying—skillfully places himself between the ship and the storm, putting the ship in danger.

Rejoice, if it is thundering. The electric discharge occurs above. There will be much less of a storm. This is an ancient observation that has been scientifically confirmed by Peltier and Piddington's experiments as well as by many others.

If the electricity, which has accumulated above, descends silently, if it does not rain, the discharge will occur below and will create circular currents. There will be both a whirlwind and a storm.

Sometimes a whirlwind will overtake you in a harbor. In 1698, Captain Langford in the harbor and well-anchored, saw a whirlwind coming and immediately left, seeking protection in the sea. More cautious vessels stayed and were damaged.

In Madras and Barbados, signals are given to warn ships lying at anchor. In Canada, the electric telegraph, which is even faster than the sky's electricity, circulates news of a storm from one port to others where it will hit.

For the sailor in the open sea, the barometer is a great advisor. Its flawless sensitivity reveals the precise extent to which the storm is weighing on it. Silent, at first, it seems to be sleeping. But a light blow has struck it, like a violinist's bow as he warms up. It is concerned. It responds, vibrates and oscillates; it withdraws, goes down. The supple atmosphere, under the heavy vapor, weighs down and then suddenly rebounds and climbs back up. The barometer has its own storm. Glimmers of pale light escape from its mercury at times and fill its tubes. (Péron observed this at Mauritius.) In gusts of wind it seems to breathe easily. "The water barometer breathed in and out like a wild animal when fluctuating," say Daniel and Barlow.

The hurricane moves forward nonetheless, and sometimes bears straight towards you, its immense darkness lighting up with all its electrical glimmers. At times, it announces its arrival with spurts or balls of fire. In 1772, during the great hurricane in the West Indies, where the sea rose by seventy feet, in the dark of night, the mounds on shore were lit up with flaming globes.

Its approach is more or less rapid. In the Indian Ocean, which is scattered with islands and obstacles, whirlwinds often only advance two nautical miles per hour, whereas in the warm current that comes our way from the West Indies, it hurries along at a rate of forty-three nautical miles. Its translation force would be incalculable if it weren't for the fact that within itself it has an oscillation that is battling against wind from inside and out.

Fast or slow its fury is the same. In 1789, it only took a moment and a single wave to damage all the ships in the harbor of Coringa, in India, and to throw them up onto the land. A second wave flooded the city and with a third it collapsed and twenty thousand inhabitants were crushed. In 1822, on the contrary, at the mouth of the bay of Bengal, a whirlwind could be seen for twenty four hours, sucking in air while water was being taken up accordingly and fifty thousand men were swallowed up.

It can look different. In Africa it is the *tornada*. In calm and clear weather, you can feel a weight on your chest. A black spot appears in the sky, like a vulture's wing. Then the vulture swoops down; it is immense. Everything disappears and starts to spin. It is over in fifteen minutes. Devastated land; upset sea. There is no news of the ship. Nature has already forgotten it.

Near Sumatra and in the Bay of Bengal, in the evening or at night—but never in the morning—you can see an arc form above. In an instant it grows, and from this black arc drab sheets of pale flashes of lightening fall upon a dull light. Woe to those who are hit with the first wind to come out of there! They could sink or be swallowed up.

But the usual form is that of a funnel. A sailor who was caught up in one said: "I found myself in what looked like the bottom of the crater of an enormous volcano. Around us there was nothing but darkness, whereas, above a gap and a little light." This is technically called the eye of the storm.

Once in its clutches, there is no way to extract oneself. It grasps onto you. Wild roars, plaintive howls, the cries and death rattles of drowning victims, the moans of the wretched ship that comes back to life, as if it were back in its forest, wails before dying—this whole awful chorus does not prevent you from hearing the sharp hissing of snakes in the rigging. Then suddenly a silence.... The center of the whirlwind passes into the terrible, deafening and blinding lightning.... You regain consciousness. It broke the masts without anyone having heard a thing.

According to Seymour, the crew sometimes has black nails and weaker eye sight for a long time after the incident. Then they remember with horror that at the moment that the whirlwind passed, sucking up water, it also sucked up the vessel, wanted to drink it in, held it suspended in the air and out of the water, only to loosen its grip and let it drop into the abyss.

According to Keu Woo seeing it fill to overflowing with water, swelling, absorbing both waves and ships, the Chinese imagine that it is a terrifying woman—mother Typhoon—who as she floats in the sky, choosing her victims, conceives, carries and becomes heavy with the many dead children—the whirlwinds of iron. Temples and altars have been erected to her. People pray to her, adore her in the hopes of humanizing her.

The good Piddington does not adore these phenomena. On the contrary, he speaks of them unceremoniously and compares them to a strong and sly pirate that takes advantage of his strength and that no one should be arrogant enough to do battle with. One should flee, and not make it a point of honor.

This treacherous enemy often lays a trap. It draws you in with a fair wind. It can't wait to embrace you.

Leave that fair wind behind and if possible, turn your back on it. Sail as far away as possible from this dangerous companion. Don't sail in convoy. It would take that opportunity to draw you into its dance, to overpower you and swallow you up.

I would like to follow all of this excellent man's fatherly advice. It would be of no use if the two adversaries—whirlwind and ship—encountered each other in a small confined space or a field of combat. But this rarely occurs. Most often, this swirling water and air is immense and occurs within a circle of ten, twenty or thirty leagues. This gives the ships a chance to observe and to maintain a respectable distance. The point is to know above all where this whirlwind's center of attraction is. After that, one needs to know its speed and the pace at which it is approaching you.

These two torches shed a fine light between which today's sailor can travel! On one side, his Maury teaches him the general laws of the atmosphere and the sea, the art of selecting and following currents, it steers him through plotted routes that are akin to Ocean streets. On the other side, his Piddington, in a small volume, summarizes and places in the palm of his hand, first-hand experiences of storms, what needs to be done to avoid them and at times to take advantage of them.

This explains and justifies the kind words of a Dutchman, Captain Jansen: "On the sea, your first impression is of being on the edge of an abyss, of infinity and of our own triviality. Even on the biggest of ships you always feel that you are in danger. But, when the mind's eye probes the space and the depth, the danger disappears for man. He elevates himself and understands. Guided by astronomy, aware of these watery routes and steered by Maury's maps, he can trace his path on the sea in safety."

This is simply sublime. Storms have not been eliminated. But what has been eliminated, is ignorance, as well as the worry and dizzying fear that made this such a dark peril. In fact, it eliminated what was the most dangerous aspect of all—the fantastical element.

At least if you die, you know why. You have a great sense of security being able to preserve a clear mind, a fully enlightened soul and resigned to any of the effects of the great divine laws of the world, which even if it means there will be a few shipwrecks, maintain balance and safety.

CHAPTER 4

Polar Seas

Sometimes the most tempting thing for man is something useless and impossible. One of Man's most persistent maritime undertakings has been his attempt to discover a passageway in the regions to the North of America that would make it possible to go straight from Europe to Asia. The most basic common sense would have led anyone to realize right away that even if this passageway did exist in such a cold part of the world and in a region bristling with ice fields, it would be of no use and no one would want to pass through there.

It should be noted that this region is not as flat as the Siberian coast, where they can glide along in sleighs. It is on the contrary a thousand-league high mountain with horribly uneven terrain, deep gashes, seas that thaw only to freeze again in an instance and corridors of ice that change yearly, opening and closing back up. The passageway has just been found, in 1853, by a man, who, having penetrated so far that he could not turn back, pushed forward and passed through. Now we know. Imaginations calmed down and people lost interest in it.

When I call this endeavor *useless*, I was referring to the proposed goal of creating a commercial passageway. However, in pursuing this whim many things that are in no sense folly were encountered, things that are of great use to science, geography, meteorology and the study of the Earth's magnetism.

From the beginning what did they want? To open up a direct route to the land of gold, to the East Indies. Thus, England along with other states, envious of Spain and Portugal, hoped to catch them unaware at the very heart of their distant empire, in the sanctuary of wealth. During Elizabeth's reign, explorers, who had found or believed they had found a few particles of gold in Greenland, exploited the old Northern legend about treasure that was hidden under the pole and the piles of gold that are guarded by gnomes etc. And people were overcome. Based on such reasonable hopes, a great fleet of sixteen ships was sent, with sons from the noblest families volunteering to be on board. They fought over who would be allowed to go to this polar Eldorado. What they found was death, famine and walls of ice.

This setback mattered little. For more than three centuries, explorers worked unrelentingly and with astonishing perseverance. There were a series of martyrs. The first, John Cabot, was only saved by his crew's mutiny, which prevented him from going any further. Willem Barentsz died from the cold and Sir Hugh Willoughby died of starvation. Gaspar Corte-Real went down with all hands. Henry Hudson was thrown overboard by his crew, with no provisions and no sail in a rowboat and no one knows what became of him. Vitus Bering, having found the strait that separates America from Asia, died of fatigue, cold and misery on a deserted island. In our time, John Franklin was lost among the ice floes and he and his men were found dead only after having succumbed to that horrible necessity of last resort—cannibalism!

Entering these Northern waters humans encounter everything to discourage sea traffic. Well before the polar circle, a cold fog weighs on the sea, chills you to the bone, covers you in frost. The rigging grows taut; the sails come to a standstill. The deck becomes slick with ice and manoeuvring becomes difficult. Worrisome moving obstacles are hardly visible. From the top of the mast, in his small lodge covered in hoar-frost, the look-out—a veritable human stalactite—reports, at every moment the approach of a new enemy, a gigantic white ghost that is often two or three hundred feet above the water.

However, this gloomy procession that signals the arrival of the world of ice, this battle to avoid obstacles, makes them want to push further on. There is some sort of appealing sublime horror and heroic suffering in the polar unknown. Even those who have not attempted the crossing but have simply gone North and contemplated Spitsbergen are quite struck by it. All those peaks, ranges and chasms that carry its crystal brow up to 4,500 feet, are like apparitions in that dark sea. Against the dull snow, its glaciers stand out with vivid glimmers of green, blue and purple, with sparks and gemstones that create a dazzling diadem.

During that several-month long night, the aurora borealis constantly explodes in the bizarre splendor of this gloomy illumination. These are enormous and frightful conflagrations that fill the entire horizon, with their magnificent erupting jets—a fantastical Aetna flooding this scene of eternal winter with illusory lava.

Everything is a prism in this atmosphere of frozen particles where the air is thick with mirrors and tiny crystals. This gives rise to surprising mirages. Many objects are seen in reverse and for a moment appear to be upside down. The layers of air that produce these effects are in constant revolution. The ones that become lighter rise in turn and change everything. The slightest variation in temperature lowers, raises or reorients the mirror. Image and object merge, then separate and disperse, another unbroken image rises above it, a third one appears pale, grows dim and once more careens downward.

This is a world of illusion. If while daydreaming you enjoy following the ever-changing improvisation and interplay of clouds, go north. The same thing can be found, just as real and yet no less ephemeral, in this fleet of moving ice. Along the way, it provides this spectacle. The ice mimics all types of architectural styles. Here is the classical Greek style—porticos and colonnades. Egyptian obelisks appear, needles pointing up at the sky with fallen needles leaning up against them. And then here come the mountains, Ossa placed on top of Pelion, the City of Giants, which once they take on a more regular form offer you Cyclopean walls, as well as druidic tables and dolmens. Dark caves sink down deep below. But all this is decaying. Everything undulates and collapses in the shivering wind. You cannot enjoy it, because nothing is settled. At no time in this upside-down world does the law of gravity mean anything—the weak and the slight carry the strong. It is nonsensical art—child's play— on a huge scale, but one that can crush you.

Sometimes a dreadful incident occurs. Through this great fleet, which comes down from the North majestically and slowly, a giant with a base that lies far beneath the surface, plunging down six, seven hundred feet deep suddenly comes from the south, as it is violently pushed upwards by currents below. It pushes aside or knocks over everything. It reaches land, it arrives at the ice fields, but it is by no means hindered. In his book *Arctic Regions* from 1826, David Duncan wrote: "The ice field was shattered over an area of several nautical miles in a single minute. It split apart, it made a thundering roar like that of one hundred canons; it was like an earthquake. This mountain of ice rushed along towards us. Everything between it and us was crammed with shattered blocks of ice. We would have died, but it sailed along rapidly carried towards the North-East."

In 1818, after the European war, this war against nature—this search for the great passage— flared up again. It began with a solemn and unique event. The brave captain, John Ross, who was sent into Baffin Bay with two ships, was fooled by this dream world's phantasmagoria. He distinctly saw land that did not exist and maintained that it was impossible to pass through there. Upon returning from his trip, he was criticized; they said that he hadn't been bold enough. They even refused to let him take his revenge and reestablish his honor. A London liqueur merchant was so bold as to want to do more than the British Empire. He gave him five hundred thousand francs and Ross returned, determined to find a passage or to die trying. Neither eventuality came to pass! He stayed, however—and for how many winters— ignored and forgotten in those dreadful lonely expanses. He was brought home by whalers who, when they had come upon this savage, asked him whether he had by chance ever met the *late* captain John Ross.

His lieutenant William Parry, who was certain that he could find a passage on four different occasions made four obstinate attempts—by way of Baffin Bay and the West as well as by way of Spitsbergen and the North. He made several discoveries, pushed forward boldly with a combination sleigh and boat, which could both float or glide over ice floes. But these ice floes, which were invariably on their way from the South, would inevitably carry him back to his starting point. He was no more successful than Ross in finding a passage.

In 1832, a courageous young Frenchman, Jules de Blosseville wanted that distinction to belong to France. He risked his life and his money. He paid for it by dying. He was not even able to have the ship of his choice. He was given the Lilloise, which, according to his brother took on water on the very day of his departure. He repaired it with his own money, for forty thousand francs. In this hazardous vehicle, he wanted to attack the iron coast—Eastern Greenland. Apparently, he never even reached it. He was never heard from again. The English expeditions were prepared in a completely different way, with great caution and at great expense. But they were no more successful. In 1845, the unfortunate John Franklin, was lost among the ice floes. For twelve years they searched for him. England displayed an honorable stubbornness in this search. Other countries helped them out. Some Americans and Frenchmen lost their lives while looking for him. The peaks and capes of that desolate region bear not only Franklin's name but also those of Joseph-René Bellot and others who sacrificed their lives in order to save an Englishman. For his part, John Ross had offered to conduct the search for Blosseville. Dark Greenland is bedecked with such memories and its deserted spaces are no longer so deserted when we come upon these names that are testaments to the fraternity of man.

Lady Franklin showed admirable faith. She would never accept that she was a widow. She continually requested new expeditions. She swore that he was still alive and she was so persuasive that seven years after he disappeared, he was promoted to rear-admiral. She was right; he was alive. In 1850, the Eskimos say that they saw him with about sixty men. Soon, there were no more than thirty of them and they were no longer able to walk or hunt. They had to eat those who were dying. If Lady Franklin had been listened to, he would have been found. For she said, and common sense dictated, that they had to look for him in the South, because a man in such a desperate circumstance would not aggravate his situation by going North. The Admiralty, which was probably much less concerned with Franklin, than it was in finding this Northwest

Passage, always directed its search parties towards the North. His poor disconsolate wife ended up doing herself what others did not want to do. At great expense she commissioned a ship to go south. But it was too late. Only Franklin's bones were found.

In the meantime, longer and but more fortunate voyages were undertaken towards the Antarctic pole, where the combination of land, sea, ice floes and turbulent thaws that makes Greenland so horrific do not exist. This is a large limitless sea with strong and violent waves, an immense mass of ice that is much bigger than ours, with very little land. It is still unclear whether most of what was thought to be land with its ever-changing shores was in fact nothing more than a mere line of unbroken ice that had piled up. Depending on the winter, everything changes. Morel in 1820, James Weddell in 1824 and John Balleny in 1839 found an indentation and penetrated into an unobstructed sea that many others have not been able to find since.

The Frenchman Yves-Joseph Kerguelen and the Englishman James Ross had positive results when they found what was indisputably land.

In 1771, the former discovered the large Kerguelen Island that the English call *Desolation*. This two-hundred-league long island has excellent harbors and in spite of the climate, there is a rather rich animal life with seals and birds that can keep a ship supplied. At the time of his accession to the throne,

Louis XVI rewarded this glorious discovery by making Kerguelen an officer. This was the explorer's ruin. He was falsely accused of crimes that he did not commit and the ferocious rivalry of the noble officers of that time crushed him. Those who were jealous of him testified as witnesses against him. In 1782 he wrote the account of his discovery from within a prison cell that was six square feet.

In 1838, France, England and America sent three expeditions to the Antarctic in the interest of science. The illustrious Louis Duperrey had opened up the way for magnetic observations. They wanted to continue these observations at the pole itself. The English entrusted this assignment to an expedition headed by James Ross, the aforementioned John Ross's nephew, as well as his student and lieutenant. It was a model commissioning for which everything was carefully planned, chosen and anticipated. James returned without having lost a single man and without anyone getting ill.

The American Charles Wilkes and the Frenchman Jules Dumont d'Urville were not commissioned in the same way. The dangers and diseases were dreadful for them. James Ross, who was more fortunate when going around the Arctic Circle, entered into ice floes and found true land. He admits, with remarkable modesty, that his success was solely due to the admirable care with which his ships had been prepared. The Erebus and the Terror with their strong equipment, their saws, their prow and their iron breast beam opened up the ring of ice floes, sailed through the creaking crust and beyond it found an unobstructed sea with seals, birds and whales. A twelve-thousand-foot volcano, which is as tall as Mount Aetna, spewed flames. There was no vegetation and no way to access it—there was only a steep wall of granite upon which even snow did not stick. This is land; there is no doubt. The Aetna of the pole that was named Mount Erebus with its column of fire remains there as a testament.

Thus, in 1841 a core of land centralized the Antarctic ice.

Returning to our arctic pole, the months of April and May 1853 are important dates.

In April, the passage that explorers had been searching for, for three hundred years, was found. Its discovery was due to a lucky act of desperation.

Captain Robert Maclure, who had entered by way of the Bering Strait, and was trapped by the ice floes, starving after years, unable to turn back, ventured forward. He only went forty nautical miles and found himself in the Eastern Atlantic along side English ships. His daring saved him and the great discovery had finally been accomplished.

At the same time, in May 1853 an expedition left New York for the far North. A young sailor Elisha Kent Kane, who was only thirty years old, and who had already traveled all over the world, had just put forth a dubious and yet beautiful idea that greatly aroused American ambition. Just as Wilkes had promised to discover a new world, Kane pledged to find a sea, an unobstructed sea in the polar region. Whereas the English, in their traditionalism, were searching for a passage from East to West, Kane was going to go due North and take possession of that unexplored bassin. This idea captured people's imaginations. A New York fleet owner, named Grinnell, generously gave him two ships. Scholarly societies and the general public helped as well. Ladies worked with their own hands on the preparations with religious zeal. The crews, who were selected, were comprised of volunteers, who were asked to pledge three things: to obey orders, and to abstain from liquor and from using profane language. A first failed expedition did not discourage either Mr. Grinnell or the American public. A second one was organized with the help of certain London societies whose goals ranged from propagating the Bible to searching for Franklin.

Few voyages are more interesting. The influence that young Kane exerted is quite clear. Every line of his account is marked by his strength, his dazzling vivacity and a marvelous spirit of *full-steam-ahead*! He is certain of everything; he is fiery and yet positive. You sense that he will not wane when confronted with obstacles. He will go far, in fact as far as it is possible to go. The battle between such a temperament and nature's mercilessly slow pace in the North and its rampart-like terrifying obstacles is an intriguing one. He had hardly started out, when he was overtaken by the weather and forced to winter for six months in the ice. Even in springtime the temperature is only a cold 70 degrees! As the second winter was approaching on August 28th, he was abandoned—he was left with only eight of his original seventeen men. The fewer men and resources that he had the more fierce and harsh he became—all this because, he says, he wanted to better command respect. His good friends the Eskimos that helped feed him and from whom he is even compelled to take a few small objects contented themselves with three of his copper vases. In return, he took two women from them. An extreme and savage punishment. With eight sailors who had stayed with him under very difficult circumstances and with an inevitable decline in discipline, it was hardly prudent to have brought those poor creatures there. They were married. "Sivu, wife of Metek and Aningna, wife of Marsinga" cried for five days straight. Kane tries hard to make light of the situation and to make us laugh: "They were crying," he says "and were chanting their lamentations, and yet did not lose their appetite." The husbands and parents arrived with the stolen objects and reacted calmly to the situation, like intelligent men, whose only weapons against revolvers were their fish bones. They agreed to everything and promised friendship and an alliance. But, a few days later, they fled—disappeared! And harboring what feelings of friendship? We can be fairly certain. They will tell other wandering tribes how imperative it is for them to flee the white man. This is how one shuts out an entire world.

The rest of the story is quite dismal. The torments were so cruel that some died and others wanted to turn back. Kane would not give up—he had promised a sea, he had to find one. Plots, desertions, treason— all of this added to the horror of the situation. During the third wintering, with no provisions, no heat, they would have died if other Eskimos had not supplied them with their own fish. He hunted for them. In the meantime, a few of his men, who had been sent out on an exploratory mission, were lucky enough to see the sea that they so needed to find. At least they reported having caught sight of a large stretch of open water that was not frozen, with birds that seemed to be taking shelter in what looked like welcoming surroundings.

That was all they needed in order to return home. Kane left his ice-bound boat to the Eskimos who did not take advantage his small group or their extreme misery.

Weak and exhausted, he survived an eighty-two day voyage south only to die upon his return. Upon his death, this bold young man, who came closer than any other human being to the pole took with him the wreath that the scholarly societies of France had placed on his grave—the grand prize of geography.

In this account, where there are so many dreadful events, there is a single touching moment. It gives us an idea of the extent of the extreme suffering involved in such a voyage. If am referring to the death of his dogs. He had admirable dogs from Newfoundland as well as Eskimo dogs. More so than any man with him, these were his companions. During his long winters and endless nights, they kept watch around the ship. When he would venture out in the pitch-dark he would encounter the warm breath of these good-hearted beasts as they came towards him so that they could warm his hands. First the Newfoundlands fell ill—he attributes this to the lack of light, since when they were shown lanterns they felt better. But little by little a strange melancholy overcame them, and they went mad. The Eskimo dogs soon followed; even his dog Flora, the most well behaved and most thoughtful, became delirious like the others and succumbed. I believe that this is the only point in the harsh account that this firm heart seems to have been moved.

CHAPTER 5

The War Against the Races of the Sea

Looking back on everything that came before and on the entire history of exploration, one has two conflicting emotions:

First, there is admiration for the daring and genius with which man conquered the seas and brought his planet under his control.

Second, there is amazement in seeing that Man is so inept in everything concerning Man himself and in seeing that in his conquest of things, he was incapable of making use of people. These seafarers arrived everywhere as enemies, crushing young nations, which, had they been treated with care, would have been the means to accessing the best of each of these small worlds.

Here is man in the presence of the Earth that he has just discovered. He is there like an inexperienced musician standing before an enormous organ from which he can barely draw a few notes. As he emerged from the Middle Ages, after so much theology and philosophy, he became a barbarian, who could only smash the keys on this sacred instrument.

As we have seen, the seekers of gold started out by wanting gold and nothing else and by crushing man. Columbus, who was the most good-hearted of all of them shows this, in his own journal with a horrifying naiveté which makes one shudder in anticipation of what those who came after him did. As soon as he landed in Haiti, his first words are: "Where is the gold? And who has the gold?" The natives smiled at this and were astonished by this craving. They promised to search for some.

They even removed their own rings in order to satisfy this pressing hunger as quickly as possible.

He paints a moving portrait of this unfortunate race, its beauty, goodness and touching sense of trust. With all this, the Genovese had his miserly mission and his harsh way of thinking. The Turkish wars, the atrocious galleys with their slaves, the sale of men, this was everyday life. The sight of this unarmed young world, those poor children who were completely naked, those innocent and charming women, all this only inspired a single regrettably venal thought in him—they could be made into slaves.

However, he does not want them to be taken away: "After all they belong to the King and the Queen." But he says these ominous and very significant words:

"They are timid and born to obey. They will perform all the work that they are ordered to do. A thousand of them flee when faced with three. If your Highnesses order me to bring them back or to enslave them here there will be no opposition. I would only need fifty men.

Soon word came from Europe, the general decree regarding this people. They were to be gold serfs, all employed in searching for it, all subject to forced labor. He himself tells us that twelve years later, six-sevenths of the population had disappeared. And the Spanish historian Antonio de Herrera y Tordesillas adds that in twenty-five years the native population plunged from one million souls to fourteen thousand.

We all know what happened next. The miner and the planter exterminated an entire world, continually repopulating it at the expense of black blood. And what happened then? The black man alone thrived and continues to thrive in these hot and low-lying lands that are enormously fertile. America would be left to him. Europe did exactly the opposite of what it wanted to do.

Europe's colonial weakness became apparent throughout the world. The French adventurer did not thrive. He came with no family, bringing his vices and merging into the barbarian mass, instead of civilizing it. With the exception of two temperate countries where the English went in large numbers and with their families, they did not live overseas either. A century from now, India won't be aware that English had ever lived there. Did the Protestant or the Catholic missionaries have any influence? Did they make a single Christian? "Not a single one," the well-informed Eugène Burnouf told me. Between them and us are thirty centuries and thirty religions. If we try to tax their brain they will become what von Humboldt observed in American villages that today are still called missions: Having lost their native vigor without having taken anything from us, their bodies live but their minds are dead; they are sterile and will never again be of any use. They remain big, dazed and idiotic children.

Have our scholarly journeys and contact with civilized Europe benefited savages? I don't think so. Whereas the heroic races of North America die of starvation and poverty, the soft and gentle races of Oceania are disappearing due to the disgraceful acts of our sailors, who when they are at the other end of the world, throw off the mask of decency and no longer restrain themselves. This loving and weak population, where Bougainville found extreme abandon and where English merchant-evangelists made money but did not gain any souls, is disappearing, debilitated by our vices and disease.

In the past, the long stretch of Siberian coast was inhabited. In this very harsh climate, nomads lived who hunted animals with precious fur that both fed and covered them. Russian authorities foolishly forced them to settle down and become farmers, in an area where farming was impossible. Thus, they died away and there are no more people. Moreover, insatiable and improvident commerce that did not spare the lives of animals during their mating season also led to their annihilation. Today there is perfect solitude along a coastline that is a thousand leagues long. The wind may whistle and the sea may freeze over. The aurora borealis may transfigure the long night. Today only nature herself is witness to it.

The primary concern in the Arctic journeys to Greenland should have been to form at any cost a close friendship with the Eskimos, so as to ease their misery, adopt their children and bring them back to Europe, to create colonies in their midst, and establish schools for discoverers. In John Ross's account and elsewhere, it is obvious that they are intelligent and that they accept European arts very quickly. Their daughters would have married our sailors. A mixed population would have been born and this northern continent would have belonged to them. This was the means by which the passage that was so desired could have easily been found and by which it could have been regularized. It could have taken only thirty years to find it. Instead it took three hundred. And in the end they accomplished nothing, because in frightening off those poor savages who are moving towards the North and dying off, they have definitely crushed the men that belong to this place as well as the genius of this place! What does it matter to have seen this solitary place, if it becomes uninhabitable and unbearable for the rest of time?

It is obvious that if Man has treated Man in this way, he was no more merciful, no kinder to the animals. He carried out a horrific slaughter of the gentlest species. He made them savage and barbaric forever more.

All early accounts are in agreement in saying that at the time of our initial contact, many such species displayed nothing but trust and friendly curiosity. We could move through peaceful families of manatees and seals that allowed us to approach them. Auks and penguins followed voyagers around, enjoyed the warmth of the hearth, and at night, slid underneath sailors' uniforms.

Our forefathers readily, assumed and not without merit, that animals had feelings just as we do. The Flemish would attract shad by ringing small bells. When they would play music on boats it never failed to attract whales. The humpback whale especially enjoyed man's company, playing and frolicking all around him.

What man has practically destroyed through his persecution of animals is what was their greatest feature—marriage. Isolated and transient, they now only experience fleeting love, they have been reduced to a state of miserable celibacy which is increasingly sterile.

Fixed and true marriage was practically a universal aspect of the natural world. Marriage with a single mate who is faithful until death, exists among roe deer, magpies, pigeons, love-birds (a lovely type of parrot), brave kamichis and others. For other birds, it lasts at least until the young have been raised. Families are forced to separate at that point out of their need to extend the area in which they search for food.

Hares with their active lives and bats in their shadows are very loving towards their families. Even crustaceans and octopi love and defend their loved ones—if the female is caught, the male hastens to be caught as well.

Love, family and marriage quite literally exist among the gentle amphibians, to an even greater extent! Their slow pace and sedentary life both favor a fixed union. For the walrus (also known as the sea elephant) that enormous animal with a strange face, love is intrepid. The husband will allow himself to be killed in order to save his wife. She will do the same for their child. But what is unique and cannot be seen elsewhere, even in superior animals, is that the young walrus, who has already been saved and hidden away by his mother, will run to defend her when he sees her fighting to protect him and with admirable courage will do battle and die for her.

The German zoologist Georg Steller observed a strange scene, a domestic squabble that was completely human among another amphibian, the eared seal: A female had allowed her young to be stolen away from her. Her furious husband was beating her. She was groveling before him, kissing him as she burst into tears. "Her chest was bathed in tears."

Whales, that don't have the settled life of these amphibians, nonetheless willingly travel in pairs even in their meandering journeys through the ocean. Henri Duhamel du Monceau and Bernard de Lacépède say that in 1723, two whales that were encountered travelling together and who had been injured refused to be separated. When one was killed, the other threw himself on her body letting out an awful howl.

If there were just one animal in the world that should have been treated with care, it was the right whale, that admirable treasure upon whom nature heaped such riches. Moreover, this is a harmless creature, who wages war on no one and does not feed on the same species as we do. With the exception of their formidable tail, they are unarmed and have no defenses. And yet, they have so many enemies! Everyone becomes bold against them. Several species settle on and live off them and some go as far as to eat away at their tongues. Narwhals, armed with piercing tusks, plunge them into their flesh. Dolphins jump and bite at them. And sharks, with saw-like blows tear off bloody strips of flesh in passing.

Only two creatures, both blind and bloodthirsty attack the future by waging war in the most cowardly of fashions against pregnant females. They are the sperm whale and Man. The dreadful sperm whale whose head makes up a third of his body and is nothing but teeth and jaws, bites into her womb and eats her young from inside her body. As she howls in pain, he then eats her. Man makes her suffer even longer. He bleeds her and inflicts cruel wounds in quick succession. Slow to die, in her drawn out death throes, she flinches, she has a recurrence of strength and pain. She dies and her tail, as if it were galvanized quivers in a fearsome way. Her poor arms tremble. Once warm with maternal love, they seem to live again as if they were reaching for her young.

It is hard to imagine what that war was like, one hundred or two hundred years ago, when whales were plentiful, travelling the seas with their families, while crowds of amphibians populated all the shores. Great massacres were carried out, bloodshed on a scale that had never been seen even in the greatest battles. In one day fifteen or twenty whales were killed as well as fifteen hundred sea elephants! In other words it was killing for killing's sake. For, what benefit was there in this slaughter of colossuses when a single one has so much oil and so much blood? What did we want from this bloody deluge? To make the land become red with shame? To taint the sea?

We wanted to experience the pleasure of tyrants and of executioners; we wanted to strike, to reign supreme, to delight in our strength and fury, to savor pain and death. We often considered it a form of entertainment to torture and drive them to despair, often allowing these animals—who were too heavy or too gentle to take their revenge—to die slowly. Péron saw one sailor persecuting a female seal in just this way. She was crying like a woman, moaning and every time that she opened her bloodied mouth, he would strike her with a large oar, breaking her teeth.

In the New South Shetland Islands, Dumont d'Urville says, the English and the Americans exterminated all the seals in four years. In a blind rage, they would slit the throats of the newborns, and would kill the pregnant females. Often, they killed for the skins alone and wasted enormous amounts of oil that could have been used.

This carnage is a despicable lesson in cruelty, which disgracefully corrupts man. The most hideous instincts are brought out in this drunken butchery. What a disgrace towards nature! Thus, we can see— even under certain circumstances, in the most squeamish person—something unexpected and horrific emerge in everyone. In a friendly people, on the most charming European shore, a strange celebration occurs. They gather up as many as five or six hundred tuna, in order to slit their throats in a single day. Within an enclosure of boats, the long net called a madrague that is separated into several compartments and lifted up by a capstan eventually leads them into the death chamber. Around this compartment, two hundred swarthy men, with harpoons and hooks await them. The cream of society from within twenty leagues attends—the pretty women and their lovers. These women sit at the water's edge as close as possible, in order to have a good view of the bloodbath, thereby adorning the enclosure with a delightful circle. The signal is given and they strike. Those fish that look like men, leap up in the air, stabbed, speared, slashed into pieces, increasingly bloodying the water. Their distressing agitation and the fury of the executioners, the sea, which is no longer a sea but some sort of living, smoking foam—all this goes to people's heads. Those who came merely as spectators act—they stamp their feet and scream; they find that the killing is going too slowly. Finally, they limit the space. The teeming mass of wounded, dead, and dying is concentrated into a single spot: convulsive leaps, furious blows. The water gushes forth and the red droplets....

And this heightens the sense of intoxication. Even the women become delirious and forget themselves; they are carried away by the dizzying feeling. It is all over, she sighs, exhausted and yet unsatisfied, she says as she leaves: "What? That's all?"

CHAPTER 5

The Rights of the Sea

The great popular writer, Eugène Noël, who is able to impart everything he touches with clear and striking simplicity, has said: "We can make the Ocean into an immense food factory, a sustenance laboratory that is more productive than land itself. We could fertilize everything—sea, stream, river and ponds. Until now, we have only farmed land, now the art of farming water has arrived...Nations of the world, start making plans!"

More productive than land? How is that possible? Baude explains it very well in an important work on fishing that he has published. He says that fish are capable of the greatest growth with a minimum amount of food. To maintain them you need nothing or practically nothing.

Guillaume Rondelet tells us that a carp that he kept for three years in a bottle of water without feeding it was still able to grow to the extent that the fish could not have been extracted from the bottle. Salmon, during their two-month stay in fresh water refrain almost completely from eating and yet do not waste away. Their stay in salt water provides them with an average six pounds of flesh—a tremendous growth! This bears no similarity to the slow and costly development of our land animals. If you were to make a pile of what an ox eats in order to put on weight or even a pig, you would be alarmed to see the mountain of food that they need to consume.

Thus, the Chinese, for whom the subject of subsistence has proven to be dire, and who are so prolific, so great in number, with their population of three hundred million, appealed directly to that great reproductive force and rich workshop of nourishing life. All along its major rivers, great multitudes sought in the water a more dependable source of food than cultivated plants. The farmer always trembles—a gust of wind, frost, the slightest unexpected occurrence takes everything away and he is struck by famine. In contrast, the living harvest that grows at the bottom of these rivers invariably feeds countless families whose boats blanket the rivers and who, assured of catching enough food, abound and multiply just as the fish do.

In May, on the Empire's main river, an enormous trade in fish spawn develops, in which merchants come to buy this product in order to sell it all over to those who want to place the fertilizing element in their fish ponds at home. Thus everyone has his stock of fish, which can be easily fed with table scraps.

The Romans did the same. In the art of acclimation they went so far as to hatch the eggs of saltwater fish in fresh water.

Artificial fertilization, which was discovered by Jacobi in Germany in the last century, and is practiced in our century in England with great success, was reinvented here in France around 1840 by a fisherman named Remy from the region of Bresse and since then has become popular both in France and throughout Europe.

In the hands of our scientists such as Coste and Pouchet this practice has become a science. Among other things we have learned the regular relationship that exists between the sea and fresh water, by which I mean, the habits of certain saltwater fish that enter our rivers during certain seasons. No matter where they were born, as soon as eels reach the size of a pin, they hasten to swim up the Seine, in such numbers that they cause the river to turn white. This treasure, which if it were handled with care, would produce billions of fish each weighing several pounds, is shamefully destroyed. Bucketfuls of these extremely precious offspring are sold at cheap prices. Salmon are no less faithful. They invariably return from the sea to the rivers where they were born. Those that have been tagged reappear almost always without fail. Their love of their native river is such that if dams, or even water-falls block it, they throw themselves forward and make death-defying efforts to swim upstream to reach it.

The sea, in which life on this Earth began, would still be a kindly wet-nurse if man could only respect the order that reigns there and could refrain from disturbing it.

Man must not forget that the sea has her own sacred life, a totally independent role in the salvation of the planet. She greatly contributes to creating harmony and ensuring its preservation and salubrity here. For perhaps millions of centuries, before the birth of man, all this went on. The planet got along marvelously without him and his wisdom. His ancestors, those children of the sea flawlessly carried out amongst themselves the circulation of matter, exchanges and the succession of different phases of life, that all make up the rapid movement of constant purification. What can man contribute to this continual movement that occurs so far from him in that deep and obscure world? Very little good, but too much evil.

The destruction of a single species can detrimentally undermine the order and harmony of the whole. Let man reap a reasonable harvest from those who multiply abundantly—that is marvelous! Let him live off of individuals, but preserve the species. He must respect the role that each species plays as nature's functionaries.

We have already lived through two barbaric ages.

During the first, they said, as Homer did: "The sea is sterile." They only traveled on it in order to hunt for treasures that were the stuff of legends or often wildly exaggerated.

During the second age, man realized that the sea's wealth is above all the sea itself. And he laid his hands on it, but in a blind, cruel and violent way.

The Medieval loathing for nature was compounded by a mercantile and industrial brutality that was armed with terrifying machines that could kill from a distance, without danger and in massive numbers. With each advance in the arts, there were also advances in bloodthirsty barbarity and extermination.

An example: harpoons, launched by a machine, which strike like lightning. Another example: dragnets—those destructive nets—that have been in use since 1700. These enormous, heavy nets, which drag through the water harvesting everything including hope, have swept the Ocean floor clean. French fishermen were not allowed to use it but foreigners came to dredge right under our noses. Some species fled the Channel and went towards the Gironde. Others declined forever. The same will occur with an excellent and magnificent fish, the mackerel that is pursued barbarically all year round. Even the enormous reproductive capacity of cod cannot protect that species. Their numbers are decreasing even in Newfoundland.

Perhaps they have gone into exile somewhere in unknown lonely expanses.

The great nations of the world must come together to replace this savage state of things with a state of civilization in which man is more thoughtful and does not squander his wealth, while at the same time hurting himself. France, England and the United States must propose a Declaration of the Rights of the Sea and convince the other nations of the world to promulgate it together.

The old regulations, specifically for coastal fishing, are no longer of any use given modern navigation. There must be a code shared by all nations that is applicable to all seas, one that codifies not only the relationships between men, but also those between man and animals.

What man owes to himself, what he owes to animals, is to no longer engage in the type of fishing activity that is like a blind and barbaric hunt where more are killed than can possibly be taken away or where the fisherman kills the little fish for no profit which in a year's time could have amply fed him. Moreover, the death of the single fish would have made the death of a host of others completely unnecessary.

What man owes to himself and to them is to no longer dispense death and pain for no reason.

The Dutch and the English take care to kill herring immediately. The French, who are more negligent, throw them into heaps in their boats and let them die of asphyxia. This long agonizing death adulterates the fish; it diminishes its taste and firmness. The herring is steeped in pain, and he had the same fate as livestock that dies from disease. As for cod, our fishermen cut it up as soon as they catch it. As Jean-Jacques Baude has so astutely observed, those that are netted at night and have therefore known many hours of exertion and of desperate agony are inferior to those that are killed immediately.

On land, hunting seasons are regulated. Fishing should be as well, with respect to the season during which each species reproduces.

It must be planned just like the felling of wooded areas, where the yield must be allowed enough time to be restored.

The young and pregnant females have to be respected especially in species that are not overabundant as well as in superior beings that are less prolific such as cetaceans and amphibians.

We are compelled to kill—our teeth or stomachs prove that it is our destiny to have to bring about death. We must compensate for this by multiplying life.

On land, we create, we protect herds, we facilitate the reproduction of many beings who might never be born, would be less fertile or would die at a young age devoured by ferocious beasts. It is as if we were practically entitled to them.

In the waters, there are even more young lives that are eliminated. By defending, propagating and allowing them to grow in number we are establishing our right to live off the surplus. Reproduction in the sea is capable of being managed like an element and can be increased indefinitely. In that underwater world, man seems like the great magician, the powerful instigator of love and fertility. He is death's adversary, for even if he himself benefits from it, his awarded share is nothing in comparison to the streams of life that he can create at will.

As for the precious species that are on the verge of disappearing, especially for the whale, the world's largest animal and creation's richest life form, we need absolute peace for a half-century. The whales will then be able to undo the damage that was done to them. Once they are no longer pursued, they will return to their native climate, the temperate zone. They will resume their innocent life, grazing the living prairie of tiny elementary beings. Once they return to their rightful place, to their former habits and food supply, they will flourish once more, they will recover their gigantic proportions. We will once again see whales of two hundred and three hundred feet. Let their former mating rituals be sacred. This will go a long way to making them fertile once more. In the past they would rather be in a Californian bay. Why not let them have it? They will no longer seek out the awful ice floes of the poles, those miserable retreats where we still go after them in our madness, disturbing them and making their love from which we too could benefit, impossible.

Peace for the right whale, peace for the dugong, the walrus, the manatee, these precious species, who could soon disappear! They need a long peace, like the kind that was very wisely declared in Switzerland for the ibex, that beautiful animal that had been hunted down and almost destroyed. They were even thought to be lost forever, but soon they reappeared.

For amphibians and fish, for every creature, there needs to be a season of rest—we need the *Truce of God*.

The best way to make sure that they multiply is to spare them when they are reproducing, when nature is fulfilling her maternal work through them.

It seems that they themselves know that at that moment they are sacred. They lose their timidity, rise up towards the light, approach the shores and seem to think that they are sure to be protected.

This is the pinnacle of their beauty and strength. Their dazzling livery, their phosphorescence, point to the supreme radiance of life. This moment must be religiously respected in all species with the exception of those whose excessive fertility is a threat. Let them die later, that is fine! If they must be killed, kill them! But let them first have a chance to live.

Every innocent form of life has the right to its moment of happiness, when the individual, no matter how lowly, goes beyond the narrow limits of his individual Self, wants something beyond himself, and through this obscure desire is able to venture forth to live on into infinity.

May man cooperate in the effort! May he help nature! He will be blessed from the depths to the stars. His gaze will be like God's, if along with him man becomes the promoter of life and allows even the littlest ones to have a right to the pursuit of happiness here on Earth.

BOOK IV

Rebirth through the Sea

CHAPTER I

The Origins of Bathing in the Sea

The sea, which man has treated so poorly in this relentless war, has been, in spite of everything, both generous and beneficial to him. When the harsh land that man loves so has worn him down and exhausted him, the dreaded and accursed sea takes him in, bearing no resentment. She takes him to her bosom and restores his vigor and his life.

Didn't primitive life emerge from her after all? She has all its elements within her and all are at their marvelous peak. Why when we grow weak and want to recuperate wouldn't we go back to the boundless source that encourages us to draw from it?

She is good and generous towards everyone, but it seems that she is more beneficial and kind toward those creatures that are the closest to natural life—innocent children who suffer as a result of their fathers' sins and women, those victims of society, whose faults are the result of love and who although far less guilty than men are, carry much more of life's burden. The sea, which is a woman, takes pleasure in rebuilding them. She lends her strength to their weakness. She dispels their languor. She adores them and makes them beautiful once more, makes them young with the help of her eternal freshness. Everyday, Venus, who long ago emerged from the sea, is reborn through her—not the irritated, whining and melancholic Venus—but the true Venus, who was victorious in her triumphant powers of fertility and desire.

How can there be a link between our great frailty and this immense force, which is both beneficial and harsh? What type of union can there be between two parties that are so disproportionate? This is a good question. An art and initiation process are necessary. And to understand these, we must know about the time and the circumstance in which this art was first discovered.

Between two forceful eras—the power of the Renaissance and the power of the Revolution—there was a time of collapse, during which serious signs pointed to moral and physical enervation. The old world that was departing and the young world that had not yet arrived, left between them, a one or two-century-long intermission. Conceived in a void, weak and sickly generations were born. Excessive pleasures and excessive poverty decimated them as well. France, which fell into complete ruin three times in a single century, was finished off by an orgy of lunatics—the Regency. England, which still managed to thrive off of our ruins, seemed to be suffering just as much. The Puritan idea was growing weak and nothing else was emerging to replace it. Crushed during the reign of Charles II, it later went through the Walpoles' muddy quagmire. With the public collapse, the basest instincts emerged. That wonderful book, *Robinson Crusoe* made it possible to anticipate the imminent appearance of alcoholism. Another terrifying book in which medicine made use of all sorts of biblical threats and denounced the trend of avoiding marriage as a form of dark suicide brought about by a rise of egocentric depravity.

Muddled thoughts, bad habits, lethargic and unhealthy lives all translated physically into the relaxation of tissue, an unhealthy sagging of flesh, scrofula, etc. Charming complexions masked the most pathetic ills. Ann of Austria, who was renowned for her extreme freshness, died of an ulcer. The Princess of Soubise, that dazzling blonde, melted away, so to speak; she simply fell into shreds.

In England, a great nobleman, the Duke of Newcastle, who was full of curiosity, asked Dr. Richard Russell why England's noble stock was deteriorating and starting to degenerate, in other words why these lilies and roses were concealing scrofula. It is very rare that a damaged race can get stronger. And yet, the

English race did it nonetheless. For seventy or eighty years it gained strength and became extremely active. First of all, it owed its renewal to its flourishing business; after all there is nothing healthier than activity. Also, we must say that it was due to changes in eating habits, the way they brought up their children and their medical practices. Everyone wanted to be strong in order to be active, engage in business and win.

Genius was unnecessary. The great ideas of this renewal had been discovered, but they had to be applied. The Moravian Jan Komenský prefigured Jean-Jacques Rousseau by a century, when he said: "Go back to nature. Use it as a guide for education." The Saxon Hoffmann said: "Go back to nature. Use it as a guide in medicine."

Fortunately, Friedrich Hoffmann came along at around the time of the Regency and after the orgies of pleasures, which were only made worse by the orgies of medication. He said: "Avoid doctors. Be sober and drink water." This was a moral reform. Thus we saw in 1830, after the bacchanalia of the Restoration era, that Vincenz Priessnitz imposed the most severe penance upon the upper aristocracy of Europe—feeding them peasant bread and placing the most delicate ladies under waterfalls of melted snow in the middle of winter surrounded by Northern fir trees—in a hellish cold that in response brings about a hellish warmth. Man's love of life is particularly fierce;

his fear of death and devotion to Nature is particularly strong when he hopes to find respite in them.

In fact, why wouldn't water be man's salvation? According to Berzelius, man is at least four-fifths water and in the future man will resolve into water. Water is found in most plants in exactly the same proportions. And it covers four-fifths of the globe in the form of salt water. For land—the arid element—it is a constant source of hydrotherapy that cures its dryness. Water quenches its thirst, nourishes it, and makes its fruit swell as well as its harvests. Strange and miraculous fairy! With little, it does everything. With little, it destroys everything—basalt, granite, porphyry. It is the great force, but also the most flexible, lending itself to the transitions of universal metamorphosis. It envelops, penetrates, reflects and transforms nature.

In what awful desert or dark forest won't we go in search of the water that comes from within the earth? What a superstitious religion there is around these awe-inspiring springs that bring us the hidden virtues and spirits of the globe! I have seen fanatics whose only God was Karlsbad, that miraculous meeting place for the most contradictory of waters. And I, myself, was awestruck before the bubbling mud in which Acqui's sulphurous water abounds and stirs itself up with a strange throbbing that is only ever seen in living beings.

Thermal baths are life or death. Their action is decisive. How many sick people would have languished but instead, because of baths came to a quick end! Often these powerful waters bring about a sudden rebirth, restore one's health, even if just momentarily, and call forward in an awe-inspiring way the passions from which the ill was born. These passions return violently bubbling up fiercely, like the scalding springs that awakened them. Smoke, sulphurous vapors and the region's intoxicating atmosphere, all seem like the *aura* which would inflate and disturb the sibyl and forced her to speak. It is like an eruption within us, which causes those things we most want to hide to burst forth. In fact nothing is hidden in these babels where ostensibly for reasons of health, people ignore the laws of this world and enjoy the freedoms of the other world. Pale dead men and women, at gaming tables, begin their sinister night of unbridled pleasure from which they often do not wake up.

The sea breeze is a completely different matter. It can purify all by itself.

That purity also comes from the air. Mostly it comes from the rapid exchange that occurs between the sea and the air—the mutual transformation of those two oceans. There is no rest. Nowhere here does life languish and go dormant. Life is made, unmade and made over again by the sea. At every moment, the wild and intense sea passes through the crucible of death. The air, which is even more violent—battered over and over again by the wind, swept up by eddies of air concentrated to the point that it bursts into electrical whirlwinds—is in constant turmoil.

It is restful to live on land, but to live by the sea is a battle, an invigorating battle for those who can withstand it.

The Middle Ages was terrified and disgusted by the sea. "The Kingdom of the Prince of the Wind" is what they called the Devil. The noble seventeenth century took care not to live among unrefined seamen. Their castles with their dreary appearance and gloomy gardens were almost always located far—as far as possible—from the sea, in a place with no breeze, no view and surrounded by damp woods. English manors, which were also lost in the shadows of big trees and heavy fog, were often mirrored in the mud of unhealthy swamps. What is striking today in England is its many sea-side homes, its love of long stays by the sea and of swimming even in the middle of winter. All this is modern, deliberate and desirable.

The coastal populations that the sea fed were always more sympathetic towards her. Their instincts sensed her powerful capacity for life. They were struck first by her purgative virtues and had quite rightly observed that she helped neutralized the great ill of the time—scrofula and the sores that result from the disease. They believed that seawater's bitterness was excellent for getting rid of the worms that plague children. They gladly ate seaweed and certain polyps, such as alcyonarians, as if they had guessed that they were rich in iodine, which greatly aids the constrictive ability that purifies and firms up tissues. These traditional treatments were known and collected by Russell. They put him on the right path and helped him a great deal in answering the important question that the Duke of Newcastle had put to him. His answer came in the form of a critical and intriguing book. *De tabe glandulari, seu de usu aqae marinae* published in 1750.

In it he wrote an inspired thought: "It is not a question of curing, but of restoring and creating."

His intention was to perform a miracle, but a feasible miracle—to produce flesh and to create tissue. It's interesting that he preferred to work with children, who despite being compromised by race, could still be restored.

It was at this same time that the farmer Robert Bakewell had just discovered meat. Livestock, from whom up until then we had only taken milk, would henceforth provide more generous quantities of food. Those who increasingly threw themselves into action deserted their bland milky diets.

As for Russell, he discovered the sea, by which I mean he made it fashionable at exactly the right moment.

All this can be summed up by advice that pertains both to medical and educative practices. First of all, one must drink seawater, bathe in it and eat anything that comes from the sea in which her properties are concentrated. Secondly, children must wear the least amount of clothes possible. They must always maintain contact with the air. Air and water, and nothing else!

That last piece of advice was quite bold. To keep a child almost naked in a damp and changing climate, was to resign oneself in advance to sacrificing the weakest ones. The strong survived and the race that was perpetuated by them was all the more enhanced. Moreover, business, movement and navigation took children out of school and liberated them sooner, ridding them of an education, which forced them to always be seated and live like a legless person— England reserved this exclusively for the children of its lords, for those noble students of Oxford and Cambridge.

In his ingenious book that was solely guided by popular instincts, Russell had no way of knowing that in a single century all the sciences would prove him right and that each science would bring to light some new dimension that led to the discovery of a whole range of marine therapies.

The most precious elements of terrestrial animal life are found in abundance in the sea. They are whole and invariable, healthy, alive and are held in safe custody in order to restore life.

Thus, science was able to tell everyone: "Come nations of the world, come tired workers, come exhausted young women and children who are being punished because of your fathers' vices! Approach pale humanity and in the presence of the sea tell me in all honesty what you need in order to be restored. This restorative principle, whatever it may be, is found in the sea."

The universal foundation of life, the embryonic mucus, that living animal jelly in which man is born and reborn, in which he took and can continually recapture the soft consistency of his being, that treasure is found in such abundance in the sea that it has become the sea itself. She produces it, covers her plants and animals in it, heaps it upon them lavishly. Her generosity puts to shame the land's frugality. She gives, so learn how to receive. Her nurturing wealth will provide you with streams of her mother's milk.

They answer: "But our supporting structure, which is like our framework has been affected. Our bones are crooked, curved and twisted because of the poor quality of food that does no more than stave off hunger. Our bones are weak and fragile." Well, the limestone that they lack is so abundant in the sea that it fills her shellfish, her builder-madrepores and even creates continents. Through her fish it travels in schools and in great fleets—so great in fact that when they wash up on the shore this rich element is used for fertilizer.

And you, young lady, who are sickly and do not dare complain and yet are unsuspectingly inching closer to your grave? You are wasting away, draining yourself. But the fortifying power, the hygienic bracing effect, which reassures any living tissue, is found in the sea threefold. She has it spread over her surface in the iodized water. She has it in her kelp, which is constantly impregnated with it. She has it completely animalized in her most fertile tribe—gades, such as cod. Cod, with their millions of eggs alone, could iodize the entire earth.

Do you lack warmth? The sea has it in the most perfect form—that imperceptible warmth that all oily bodies contain, that is latent and yet so powerful that if it weren't evenly distributed, well-balanced and stable, it could melt all the ice floes, and would turn the pole into an Equator.

Beautiful red blood, warm blood, is the sea's triumph. Through this blood she has animated and armed her giants— which are so superior to any land creatures—with incomparable strength. She created this element, so she can easily recreate it for you. She can bring the color back to your cheeks, restore you—you pale drooping flower. She abounds with it, is bursting with pride from it. In the children of the sea, blood itself is a sea, which from the first beat rolls and gives off steam, while in the distance making the Ocean crimson.

The mystery has finally been revealed. All the constituent parts that are brought together in you are divided up within this great impersonal person. She has your bones, your blood, your vigor and your warmth; each element is represented by one or other of her children.

And she has what you do not have—a surplus, an overflow of strength. Her breath provides something gay, active and creative, something that might be called physically heroic. Despite her brutality, the great generator still pours out fierce joy, lively, fertile eagerness, as well as passionate savage love that beat within her.

CHAPTER 2

Choosing a Beach

The Earth acts as a doctor. Every climate acts as a cure. Increasingly medicine will be a form of migration, but a prescient form of migration. In the future we will act. We won't remain inert when we become ill with incurable diseases; rather we will anticipate them through education, good hygiene and above all through travel. Not the type of travel that one sees nowadays. But journeys that are skillfully planned in order to take advantage of the helpful and powerful invigorants that nature has in reserve all over the world.

The future's Fountain of Youth will lie in the following two things: *A science of migration* and *an art of acclimation*. Up until now man has been a captive, like the oyster on his rock. If he migrates even slightly outside of his temperate zone, it will only bring about death. He will not be free and truly a man until this distinctive art makes him the inhabitant of his entire planet.

Few illnesses can be cured under the circumstances and in the context in which they were born and produced. They stem from certain habits that these places preserve and that make them invincible. No physical or moral reform is possible for anyone who stubbornly persists in his state of original sin.

Once medical science has been enlightened by all the auxiliary sciences, it will eventually provide us with the methods and instructions that will lead us cautiously along this new path. Above all, transitional stages need to be handled carefully. Is it possible without preparation, without some sort of modification in lifestyle or diet to be abruptly transferred from a completely inland climate (such as Paris, Lyon, Dijon or Strasbourg) to a seaside climate? Is it possible to start bathing in the sea without first having breathed the coastal air for a long period of time? Is it possible without first having started some sort of cautious regime of hydrotherapy in the inland areas, to go out into the fresh air, risking nerve constriction and the gooseflesh that is caused by cold water and persists as one returns home (sometimes in heavy winds)? These preliminary questions will increasingly attract the attention of doctors.

The excessive speed of train travel is contrary to good health. To go, as we do, in only twenty hours from Paris to the Mediterranean and to go through such varied climates on an hourly basis is the most careless thing a nervous person can do. Such a person will arrive at Marseille delirious, extremely agitated and dizzy. When Madame de Sévigné used to take a whole month to go from Brittany to Provence, she would make the transition between these two brutally contrasting climates with the utmost of care, little by little and very gradually. She would pass imperceptibly from the western coastal region into the eastern coastal region by way of the entirely terrestrial climate of Burgundy. Then, slowly making her way down the upper Rhone through the Dauphiné, by way of Valence and Avignon, she confronted the great winds with fewer problems. Finally resting in Aix, in the interior of Provence, away from the Rhone and the coast she became Provencal by way of her lungs and her breathing. Only then, would she approach the sea.

France has the enviable advantage of having two seas. Based on seasons, temperament and the seriousness of the illness, this makes it easy to alternate between the salty tonic of the Mediterranean and the more clammy and gentle tonic—notwithstanding the storms—that the Atlantic Ocean offers us.

On either one of these seas, there is a graduated scale of resorts that are either more or less gentle, more or less invigorating. It is very interesting to observe these two scales and follow them by going from the mildest to the most intense.

The scale along the Atlantic coast starts at the raging, bracing, windswept and stormy waters of the Channel, becomes extremely mild in Southern Britanny, even more adapted to human needs in the Gironde, and turns immensely mild in the enclosed Arcachon Basin.

The scale along the Mediterranean, which is virtually circular, has its most extreme point in the dry and intense climate of Provence and Genoa. It becomes weaker towards Pisa, finds its balance in Sicily, and in Algiers reaches a remarkable degree of stability. When returning in the other direction, we find the extreme mildness of Valencia and Mallorca as well as the small ports of the Rousillon that are so well protected from the North.

Two of the Mediterranean's characteristics make this sea especially beautiful: its extremely harmonious surroundings as well as the intense transparency of the air and the light. This is an extremely bitter and salty blue sea, which loses three times more water through evaporation than is received from rivers and streams. She would have been completely reduced to salt and would become as acrid as the Dead Sea, if smaller currents like the one from Gibraltar did not constantly temper her with Ocean waters.

All of her shores that I have seen were beautiful, although a little acrid. There is nothing ordinary there. The traces of subterranean fires that are every-where, the dark plutonic rocks, are never dull, like the long sand dunes or the watery sediments of cliffs. If the famous orange groves seem monotonous, in the sheltered spots the African vegetation, like aloe and cacti, the fields with exquisite hedges where myrtle and jasmine predominate or finally the fragrant moors that are wildly aromatic are all on the contrary quite charming. Although it is true that above your head, more often than not bare and barren mountains are ever present on the horizon. The foot of these mountains, their extreme roots as it were, that extend into the sea, can be distinguished along the bottom of the sea. One traveler wrote: "It seemed that my boat was rowing between two types of atmospheres, as if there were air above and below it." He described the varied plant and animal life that he was contemplating through the crystalline sea in the water of Sicily. Less fortunate, by the sea near Genoa, with water that was equally transparent, I could only see a desert. The arid volcanic rock along the shore, with its black marble or those that were an even more lugubrious white, in my mind represented natural monuments like ancient sarcophagi and toppled churches at the bottom of this brilliant mirror. At times, I thought I saw views of the cathedrals of Florence and Pisa. At other times, it seemed to me that I saw silent sphinxes and as yet unnamed monsters. Whales? Elephants? I don't know— chimera and strange dreams but no sign of real life.

As it is, this beautiful sea with her powerful climates toughens man up quite admirably. She provides him the most resistant kind of dry strength, the kind that creates the sturdiest races. Our Northern Herculeses are perhaps stronger, but they are certainly not as robust and have more difficulty acclimating to different regions, than the Provencal Catalan, Genovese, Calabrian or Greek sailor has. The latter with their coppery and bronzed skins have passed into the metallic state. This rich skin color is not accidental, but rather is caused by a profound absorption of sun and of life. A wise doctor, who is a friend of mine, would send his pallid patients from Paris and Lyon to go sunbathing there. He himself would expose himself on a rock for several hours. He only covered his head and the rest of his body acquired the most beautiful African complexion.

Invalids, who are very sick, will go to Sicily, Algiers, Madeira or to the Canary Islands. But the regeneration of the weak, worn out, pale urban populations, will perhaps be better achieved in less monotonous climates. They can be expected to recuperate in regions that have given off the greatest amount of energy on Earth—the steel of the human race, Greece and the race of sharp, cutting and indestructible flint stone that produced Columbus, Doria, Massena and Garibaldi.

In the far north, our harbors, such as Dunkerque, Boulogne and Dieppe, where the Channel's winds and the currents meet, are still factories that generate and regenerate men. That great wind and that great sea, in their external battle, could revive the dead. There are truly astonishing rebirths. With the exception of those whose condition has seriously degenerated, recovery is instantaneous. The entire human mechanism, whether willingly or not begins to work hard—it digests and breathes. Nature is demanding on it and is capable of making it function well. The extremely robust and verdant plant-life, which thrives even on the shore in the strongest of ocean winds, put our languor to shame. Every little Norman port-town is merely an opening in the cliffs where the unrelenting Northwest wind (the *Norouais* as the true Normans say) whistles and blows and revives us. Of course, all of this is less brutal at the entrance to the Seine, under the apple trees of Honfleur and Trouville. As it flows by, this good river gently bows to the left and carries with it the influence of its friendly and kind character.

Earlier, we saw the passionate and often frightful sea of Granville, Saint Malo and Cancale. This is the most instructive place for young people. This is where man takes up the sea's challenge and where the struggle occurs which will make the strong even stronger. The greatest of naval manoeuvres must occur in these waters between the Normans and the Bretons.

If on the contrary, the person in question is damaged and fragile, if we are speaking of a weak and sickly child or a woman who has been loved too much, who is worn out by love's work, we would look for a more gentle spot, so as to better protect this treasure. Among the small sleepy islands and peninsulas of the Morbihan, you will find a beach that is completely calm and water that is not quite so cold, without going too far south. All these islets form a labyrinth that is more confusing than the one in which, long ago, a king hid his Rosamond. Entrust yours to this secluded sea. No one will be any the wiser with the exception of the old druidic stones, which along with a few fishermen, dwell alone in these wild and gentle places.

"But," she says, "how do people there live?"

"Mostly, from fishing, Madame."

"And what else?"

"From fishing."

It is not very far from Saint Gildas, the abbey where the Bretons say that Heloise came to join Abelard. They make do with very little, with the sober and solitary diet of Robinson Crusoe and Friday.

More civilized, friendly and charming places can be found by going south to Pornic, Royan and Saint Georges and Arcachon.

Earlier I spoke of Saint Georges, the gentle beach with its bitter scents. Arcachon is also very gentle in its resinous pine groves that give off the wonderful scent of life. If it weren't for the invasion of Bordeaux's high society, those crowds, which on certain days surge and rush, this is the place where one would like to hide away one's dearest invalids, those tender and delicate objects that we fear exposing to the tumult of this world. This spot, with its inland basin offered the contrast of profound and absolute calm, only a few steps away from a terrifying sea. On the outside there is the lighthouse and the raging Bay of Biscay. On the inside, there are sleepy waters and the languor of a silent tide that makes no more noise than that dear foot on the springy cushion of soft seaweed, which reinforces overly soft sand.

In an intermediary climate, which is neither North, nor South, nor Brittany, nor Vendée, I visited and revisited with great pleasure the friendly and serious refuge of Pornic with its good-hearted seamen and pretty girls who are so charming under their pointed bonnets. It is a restful little place to which the sea comes subdued, obliquely and indirectly because of the long island or rather peninsula of Noirmoutiers that faces the town. Almost immediately this sea comes upon this spot humanized. She seems to be spinning flax or moire with her rippled waves. In this basin that is several leagues wide, the sea has dug out little basins, narrow coves with gentle slopes for women as well as tubs for children. These lovely sandy beaches are separated by respectful rocks that conceal them from indiscrete eyes. They are delightful with all their little mysteries. You can see some marine life there, although it is much less rich than in the past. The refuge is useful, but it also does harm. Aquatic life cannot receive a rich enough supply of food in this terribly calm basin and therefore it has deserted this place. This sea draws less and less of its waters from the Ocean's great tides. It tones down its sounds. They are muffled. It is a very charming partial silence. Nowhere, have I found the freedom to dream and the delight of a dying sea any sweeter.

CHAPTER 3

The Residence

Allow someone who is far from an expert, and yet who has still managed to acquire some experience at great cost, to give you some advice on issues, which books don't discuss and with which doctors have rarely concerned themselves until now. So that this advice is not too abstract, I will address it to an invalid who would like some guidance. Is this an imaginary person? Not at all. I am speaking of a person whom I have really met on several occasions throughout my life.

This is a sick young woman or one who is on the verge of being sick. She is weak, and has a child who is even weaker. They made it through the winter and spring with great difficulty. However, there is no serious degeneration, only frailty and anemia. Only a certain difficulty in living. They are being sent to the sea to spend the entire summer.

This is a great expense for those of little means who are not well-to-do. It is a tiring inconvenience for the lady of the house. It is a painful separation especially for spouses that are very close. They negotiate! They would like to reduce the sentence. Wouldn't a single month be enough? But the very wise doctor insists. He believes that more often than not a short stay does more harm than good. The sudden and harsh impression made by the swims, without preparation is likely to shake even the most robust health. Any reasonable person should first acclimate herself and should breathe the air in. The month of June is perfect for this. July and August are for bathing. September and sometimes October, which are refreshing after the hot summer weather, reduce the excitement caused by the saline acridity, reinforce the results of the treatment and with their strong cool winds, even harden one against the cold winter weather.

Few men are free for the whole summer. At best, the husband will be able to join his wife for one or two months, in August or September. No matter how inclined he may be to sacrifice any secondary interest for her, he must stay behind for her sake. In the hectic life of the working man, there are certain chains that can only be broken to the detriment of the family. Therefore, she must leave alone. And so they are divorced!

Alone? She has never been alone before. It would be more reassuring for her if she were going along with a family of rich friends that were traveling as a whole group—husband, wife, children, and servants. If I may be so bold as to give my opinion on the subject, I would say: "Have her go by herself."

This trip in the company of others is cheerful and pleasant at first, but often has completely unanticipated consequences. They disturb each other, they quarrel, they come home as enemies—or even worse when they return their friendship is too close. The idleness that goes along with bathing too often has unforeseen results that one regrets for the rest of one's life. Of all the consequences, the least unpleasant – and yet in my opinion not the least significant—is that people who if apart would have had a better experience of the sea and would therefore have returned with a more favorable and intense impression of it, will in fact, if they live together continue their big city lives (frivolity, vulgarity, false gaiety, etc). When one is alone, one keeps busy and one thinks. In a group, one chatters away, one speaks ill of others. These rich, fashionable friends will take the young woman along as they engage in their pastimes. She will experience the agitation caused by these activities; her life will be more restless and unhealthier than the one she had in Paris. She will be far from achieving her intended goal. Madame, take all this into consideration.

Be brave and be careful. It is only in serious solitude, in the innocent little life that you will have with your child, there by the sea, a life that is perhaps child-like, but is also pure, noble and poetic, it is only, I repeat in such a life that you will truly find the desired renewal. The refined and loving sense of fairness that leads you to avoid pleasure while another person who stayed home, is working hard for your family, will make a great difference, believe me. The sea will love you all the more, if she is the only friend that you want to have. During this period of rest, she will lavish you with her wealth of life and youth. Your child will grow like a fine tree, and your charm will blossom. You will once again be young and adored.

She resigns herself to leaving. She leaves. The seaside resort has been recommended. It is well known. One can evaluate the true quality of the waters through chemical analysis. But there are a myriad of particular local characteristics that cannot be discerned from a distance. The doctor is rarely aware of them. The busy city-dwelling man has neither the opportunity nor the free time to make a detailed study of these towns.

Some worthy guides have been published for some of the bigger towns. They indicate the innumerable illnesses that can be cured in the recommended resort. But few, too few of them specify the essential thing that we seek in these places—the uniqueness of the location. They don't dare clearly state positive and negative points, nor do they rank resorts. They offer generalized praise, but it is so generalized that it is of very little use.

What sort of exposure does that particular resort have? If you look at the map, the coast is oriented towards the South. But this does not tell us anything at all. It is possible that a particular curve in the terrain places your residence under an extremely cold influence such as a stream that throws itself into the sea, or a small hidden and treacherous valley, which blows the North wind on you. On the other hand, it is also possible that because of a fold in the terrain, the West wind sweeps through drowning you in a stream of air.

Are there marshes in the area? The answer is almost always: Yes. But it makes a great deal of difference if they are salt marshes that are renewed and purified by the sea, as opposed to stagnant fresh water marshes that give off feverish emanations, after periods of drought.

Is the sea completely pure or mixed there? If it is mixed, in what proportions? This is a great mystery that they are afraid to shed light on. However, for the nervous or inexperienced person who is starting a regimen of bathing in the sea, the gentlest waters are best. One wants the purest water, the least salty and least acrid air, as well as a beach that is not too bleak and offers the pleasures of the countryside—these are the best conditions.

A major and vital issue is the choice of residence. Who can direct you in this choice? No one. You yourself must see and observe. You will derive very little insight from those who have visited the area or who even stayed there for some time. They praise or criticize based less on the true merit of the place but rather based on how much they enjoyed it and the friends they left behind. They will refer you to these friends, who welcome you into their home wonderfully. And, after a few days you will see the drawbacks. You will find yourself living in the least suitable house. One that is sometimes even unhealthy and dangerous. No matter, you are bound to them, now. You would hurt the feelings of the person who sent you there, as well as that friendly, good-hearted and hospitable family, who took you in.

"So then, I will maintain my freedom. And, as soon as I arrive, if there is an honest and well-respected doctor there, I will ask him to enlighten me."

"Honest! That is not enough. He would need to be bold and heroic if he were going to speak unequivocally on this topic. He would become the mortal enemy of the entire local population. It would be his downfall. He would be an outcast in the area. He would live like a pariah who would consider himself fortunate if every once in a while he were ill-treated.

I cannot stand those absurdly flimsy buildings that speculators have constructed in such variable climates.

These small cardboard houses are the most dangerous traps. Since we arrive during the hot summer months, we accept this bivouac. But often we stay on through September and sometimes even on through October in the strong winds and rain.

The landowners of the area, who are moreover in very good health, build good, solid and secure homes for themselves. And for us, poor invalids, they build wood shacks, absurd chalets (not like in Switzerland where they are covered with moss) which are exposed to the elements and in which nothing is joined. They are really trying to take advantage of us.

In these villas that appear luxurious but are in truth wretched, nothing is provided for. There are sitting rooms, ceremonial rooms with views of the sea, but no pleasant interior. There is none of that gentle comfort that a woman needs. There is nowhere for her to retire to. She lives as if in the midst of a partial storm and at every moment suffers sudden changes in temperature.

Moreover, the solid home of the fisherman and even of the bourgeois is often low, humid, uncomfortable and at times its lay-out is even indecent. Often these houses don't have thick double ceilings, but rather they have a single layer of wood flooring, through which the cold air from the ground floor rises. This leads to colds and rheumatism, gastritis and hundreds of other illnesses.

No matter your choice, Madame, between these two dwellings, do you know what I really want for you above everything else? Go ahead and laugh, it makes no difference to me. Even though it is June, you should have an excellent fireplace that is windproof. In our beautiful France with its cold Northwest, its rainy Southwest, which predominated this year for merely nine out of twelve months, you need to be able to make a fire all year round. On a damp night when your child comes home shivering and can't seem to get warm before bed time you need a moment of bright fire.

Two things must first be provided for in any abode—fire and water. The water must be acceptable although this is rather rare by the sea. If it is very bad, try to replace it with beer or some other local beverage that allows you to do without water.

If only I could build you the villa of the future that I have in mind! I am not talking about the splendid mansions, the palaces that the rich will want to have built by the sea. I am speaking of the humble homes of those with meager resources. This is a new art that is begging to be created and one which most seem to think is not possible. What has been attempted are reproductions of types of homes that are inconsistent with our climate and life by the sea. Those belvederes damaged by flimsy ornamentation are fine for sheltered spots, but here they make you tremble, because you think the wind is going to carry them away. Chalets, which in Switzerland stretch out immense roofs that protect against the snow and store hay, have the serious disadvantage of blocking out too much light. In our Northern Seas the sun must not be kept out but carefully collected. As for those replicas of chapels and of gothic churches that are so uncomfortable for living in, let's not even waste our time with those ridiculous playthings.

At the sea, the first thing to look for is great solid, sturdy and thick walls that precludes the rattling and rolling that can be felt everywhere in those fragile constructions. You need a sound foundation so that during even the worst storms, a timid woman has the peace-of-mind, the smile and the joy of a contrast that causes her to say: "This house is so cozy!"

The second point of concern is that the side of the house that faces land should be so completely protected that you can forget the sea and that despite the great motion of the waves you can find peace and quiet. To meet these two needs, I would prefer the shape that best prevents the wind from taking hold—a half-circle, like a crescent, whose convex side would give me a varying panorama of the sea and would get sun all day long allowing me to see the sun go round from window to window.

The points of the crescent would protect the interior of the concave side of the half-circle so that they wrap around the lady of the house's lovely little flowerbed. This flowerbed's gradual slope would allow you to create a garden of a certain size that is protected from the sea's wind. Often a fold in the terrain neutralizes its influence.

They say that "flora flees the sea," but what it is fleeing is man's neglect. I can still see a farm in Étretat—facing the rough sea at the very top of the cliffs, right in the heaviest winds—with an orchard and admirable trees. What sort of protection did they have in place? Merely an embankment five feet tall, a hedge, on which grew any plant that happened to grow there. Behind the embankment an entire row of solid elm trees that sheltered all the rest. I could have cited examples of such places in Brittany as well. We all know the amount of fruits and vegetables produced in Roscoff to the point that it even supplies Normandy at good prices.

Getting back to the building, I think it should not be too tall—only a ground floor and a second storey with bedrooms. The attic should not be too big, but rather a few low rooms that insulate the building's roof.

Thus, the house will be small. On the other hand, it must have thick walls, it must have two rows of rooms, with quarters looking out onto the sea and others facing land.

The ground floor, facing land, would be a bit sheltered by the second storey that would jut out by only four or five feet. Thus in the interior of the crescent there would be a sort of porch for when the weather is bad. Downstairs, on the ground floor, there would be a dining room, perhaps a small room for travel and natural history books and another room for the tub. I don't mean there should be a real library or a luxurious bathroom. The bare essentials, simplicity and practicality and nothing more.

On harsh days when the beach is not bearable for someone with a weak chest, I would like to see this lady sitting, reading or working in her flowerbed, in complete safety. There she would have living things such as flowers, an aviary and a small pool filled with sea water where each day she could bring her discoveries—those little objects of curiosity that fishermen would give her.

As for the aviary, I would prefer that it be the opened type that I suggested in another book, *The Bird*, where birds seek shelter at night as well as a bit of food. It is closed at night to protect them from owls and then re-opened in the morning. They return regularly to it. I even think that if the aviary was big enough and we could put the tree they are used to nesting in within it, they would gladly do so, under your protection and would even entrust you with their young

This is a solemn life, a charming life. What exquisite solitude this little intermission in life, this short period of widowhood offers! The situation is new.

No more household duties, none of the daily routine. With the child, she feels even more isolated than she would have been without him. If she did not have this little companion, another companion would join her, namely daydreams that only lead to pointless musing. But her child, her innocent guardian, won't allow this. He keeps her busy; he makes her talk. He reminds her of her home. With him, she always maintains that feeling that someone is working back there for them, someone who is counting the days as well.

Bloom, you pure and lovable flower. You are younger today than you have ever been and under your child's protection, you will go back to being a free young girl, whose freedom is particularly sweet.

CHAPTER 4

The Initial Yearning for the Sea

It is a great and sudden transition to leave Paris in June for a deserted beach. Paris is stunning at this time of year with its magnificent gardens and its chestnut trees in bloom. June would be extremely beautiful on the coast if you could both be there, before the arrival of the invading crowds. But when you are alone, in a tête-à-tête with the sea, the distinguished company of this great solitary figure can sometimes be quite sad.

The first trips to the beach do not make a favorable impression. It is monotonous, wild and arid. The uncommon grandeur of the spectacle makes you feel weak and small in comparison. It is a bit heart-rending. The frail chest that was only breathing indoor air and that suddenly is in the universe's chamber, exposed to the sun and strong winds, feels like it is suffocating. The child plays, comes and goes. She sits still and she shivers from the cold wind. The warmth of the nest that she left behind comes to mind. And yet the child is having fun. This consoles her a little.

All this will change Madame. Gain some strength. Your impression will be completely different when as you get to know the sea better, you become aware that she is very populated. That painful constriction that you feel in your chest will automatically disappear. You have to grow accustom to that fresh air that is salty and bitter and far from refreshing. You have to get used to it slowly and not attempt to breathe it in deliberately. Little by little, without being conscious of it anymore, in some sheltered corner, while playing with your child, you will breathe easily and you will fill your lungs. But, in the beginning, don't stay at the beach for very long. Head for the interior of the region during your walks.

The land, your customary friend, is calling you back. The pine forests compete with the sea in their salubrious emanations. Theirs, which are so resinous and bracing, like the sea's, have the advantage of not being acrid. They penetrate our entire being, entering into us through every pore, modifying our blood, purifying it and imparting us with our own subtle odor. In the moors behind the pine trees, medicinal plants and the slightly tough herbs that you tread upon lavish you with scents, which are neither insipid nor intoxicating (like those of the dangerous rose), but instead are pleasantly bitter. Sit among these scents and like them, you will be well-protected by that fold in the landscape. Don't you get the feeling of being a thousand leagues from the sea? Breathe these pure spirits in, breathe in the souls of these wild flowers, your sisters in purity. Pick some of them, if necessary Madame. It is a pleasure for them. A bit harsh, but yet so sweet! Their virginal fragrance has the uniquely mysterious power of being able to calm and strengthen. Don't be afraid to conceal them against your bosom and over your heart.

Let's not forget to mention that these sheltered moors are scorching hot at certain hours of the day. They absorb, they concentrate the sun's rays. A weak woman would dry up, there. A young girl, full of life would become flush, would boil over with agitation and would come down with dreadful fevers. Her head would become muddled with astonishing and dangerous delusions. You must choose cloudy days that are damp and mild, when going there. Or else, you must get up early when everything is cool, when the thyme still has dew on it, when the nimble rabbit is still roaming about exploring his territory.

But let's get back to the Ocean. When the tide is going out, she is exposing herself and in a way is offering you the rich life that she nourishes within her. You must follow the water step by step, moving forward on the damp sand. Don't be afraid. At most, the diminished incoming tide wants to kiss your feet.

If you look you will see that this sand is not dead and that, here and there, several stragglers, which the ebb caught off-guard, are moving about. On certain beaches, small fish are concealed there. At the river's mouth, eels wriggle beneath the sand and create tiny earthquakes. A crab that was struggling to find a meal or was busy fighting wants, with a bit of tardiness, to go back to the sea. His escape leaves a strange mosaic on the sand from the zigzags of his sidelong movement. At the point where the trace ends, you will find the crab nestling as he waits for the incoming tide. Solens (also known as razor shells) have dived into the sand, but their retreat is revealed by the air holes that they use to breathe through. The Venus shells' dwellings are betrayed by the fuci that are attached to their shells sticking out of the sand. The undulations in the ground tell you where the passageways of the warrior annelids are; their arsenal would charm you, as would the rainbow of their changing colors when seen through a microscope.

The greatest spectacle comes during spring tides. The Ocean, which rises a great deal, at ebb tide withdraws particularly far. She unveils herself, exposing immense and unknown stretches. The mysterious sea floor, which we have dreamed so much about, appears. You will catch a glimpse of the movements, life and secret hideaways of the astonished populations, who thought they were safe and sound and who never, or almost never have been exposed to the sun and have certainly never been exposed to the eyes of man.

Be reassured frightened masses. This is the curious but compassionate eye of a woman. It is not the hand of the fisherman. What does she want? Only to see you, to give her regards, to show you to her child and to leave you in your natural element while wishing you good health and prosperity.

Sometimes, you don't have to roam very far. Everything can be found in a single spot. In hollowed out rocks, the Ocean takes pleasure in recreating itself in miniature form, which is no less complete—a world that is only a few square feet wide. You sit and observe it. The longer you look, the more lives appear, which at first went undetected but then become apparent. You could stay there forever, if the master, the impervious sovereign of the beach, did not chase you away with the incoming tide.

Tomorrow, we'll return. It is like a school, a museum; it is unending amusement for both mother and child. It is there, for the first time, that the woman's penetrating shrewdness and her loving heart, grasp and understand. Her maternal instincts tell her everything, how life moves forward, creating itself, giving birth to itself. Do you want to know why her instincts reveal the act of creation so quickly to her? Why she enters into the mystery of nature, without hesitating, like someone returning to her own home? Because she herself is nature.

Below the unctuous water, seaweed, oily and nourishing, along with other tiny plants with refined and lovely designs, are like a patient prairie, there to feed the livestock, the mollusks that graze upon them. Limpets, whelks, turbots, purple mussels and pink or lilac-colored tellins, all these calm souls will wait. Acorn barnacles that are better protected in their fortified city just close their four shutters. They will still be there tomorrow. Does this mean that with their lethargy they don't dream of moving? That they don't have a muddled sense of and love for the unknown? That they don't have a sense that some good-hearted soul, won't come at certain times to refresh and nourish them? Oh! They imagine this, and they wait. Widowers of their grand spouse the Ocean, they know she will return towards land in order to caress them. They look towards her, in anticipation and those of them who have fixed houses are careful to place their door in that direction and stand ready to open it. Even if she is a little violent, so much the better, they are all the more delighted, very content with that living tide that will cradle them mightily.

"Look, my child, as we approach, those motion-less creatures are the only ones remaining. But others, which are livelier have fled. Now, they are reassured.

The shrimp skip along and make the water iridescent with their light and delicate palps. They take on the responsibility of making the waves and the storms that are in proportion to such an ocean. The slow and unsteady spider crabs are betrayed by their timid brand of daring. They climb towards the light to the warm surface. Cautious characters, crouching beneath the kelp, beneath the purple coralline, the crab moves forward, curious and after a furtive glance, dives back into this forest."

"But what do I see? What is that? A big motionless shellfish is coming to life and attempting to move forward... Oh! That is not natural. This is a gross fraud. The intruder gives himself away by his strange stumbling.... Who wouldn't recognize you, you beautiful mask, Sir Hermit Crab, clever crab who pretends to be an innocent mollusk. Your guilty conscience is bothering you and puts you in this state."

On the shore of our miniature ocean, the animate flowers open their corolla, impervious to any movement. Near the heavy anemone, those charming little fairies, the annelids appear and perform in the sun. A disc—a white, lilac-colored or sometimes flesh-colored umbrella—emerges from a twisted tube. This umbrella, which has been cast off and thrown off to the side, is an incomparable object in the plant world. Not one of them looks like her sister; each one is inimitable in its delicate silkiness.

There is one with no umbrella, but with a floating host of slender, fluffy fibers that are slightly tinged in silvery gray. Five longer fibers extend out that are a handsome cherry color. They undulate, intertwine, come undone, and entangle themselves in the silvery hairs, creating charming underwater illusions. This is nothing to the crude senses of a man, but it is quite something for a woman whose sensory life, that delicate and sickly genius within her, is stirred by everything. She senses something and recognizes herself in these colors that alternately redden and fade. She senses the flame of life, blazing, shining and dieing out. What a touching vision! She, once again, looks deeply into this charming little ocean and there she has a better perspective on Nature, that fertile but stern mother, who seems to find fierce joy as she consumes herself.

She remains contemplative, gripped by this thought. A woman would not be a woman, in other words, she wouldn't be the charm of the world, if she did not have a touching gift: Affection towards all forms of life, pity and her lovely tears.

She was not crying yet, but was on the verge of tears! Her child saw this. Being, as children tend to be, attentive and quick-witted, he became silent. They returned home without saying a word.

This pleasant day was the first day that she began to teach him, with her heart, to read the language of nature. And from the very first moment this language had spoken words whose mysteries were so moving, that her poor heart was affected.

It was getting dark. The dawdling sea bird pressed on as quickly as possible, returning to land and to his nest. While going back home by way of the cliffs and the garden, where it is already dark, the first screech of a night bird—sharp and sinister—can be heard. But the aviary, which offers refuge, was closed tight; the birds were sleeping with their heads under their wings. She made sure they were safe and saw to it herself that everything was secure. With a sigh, her heart is relieved and she kissed her son.

CHAPTER 5

The Rebirth of Beauty

Even if, as some French doctors say, bathing in the sea only has a mechanical effect but does not provide our blood with any new constituents and is merely one type of hydrotherapy, then one must admit that of all forms of hydrotherapy, it is the most strenuous and the most dangerous. If this water, which is so rich in life, provides no more life than fresh water, it is foolish to undertake such experiments out in the open air, exposed to the dangers of the winds, sun and thousands of unforeseen events.

Anyone who sees the poor creature who is coming out of the water after one of her first swims, and sees her looking pale, haggard, and frightful with a deadly shiver, can sense how harsh such an attempt is, and how dangerous it can be for certain constitutions. Rest assured that no one would confront such a trying experience if at home one could substitute it, with a gentle and cautious form of hydrotherapy that lacks these dangers.

Add to this, that the already powerful effect of such an experience is made even worse for a nervous woman by the presence of a crowd. It is a painful display in front of a critical group of people, in front of rivals who are thrilled to find her ugly for once, in front of thoughtless men who laugh stupidly and mercilessly and who observe, lorgnette in hand, the poor humiliated woman who has had the misfortune in her confusion of dressing haphazardly.

In order to endure all this, the invalid must have faith, a strong faith in the sea. She must believe that no other remedy will work. She must want to soak up the virtues of these waters at all costs.

"Why not?" say the Germans. "If the first moment of bathing causes contractions and closes up your pores, the second—that warm reaction that comes afterwards—opens them up again, dilates the skin and makes it quite susceptible to absorbing the life within the sea."

The two processes occur almost always in five or six minutes. Beyond that point, bathing can often have negative effects.

Moreover, one must not come to the violent emotions of bathing in cold water without being prepared for it by having made a habitual practice of taking warm baths that facilitate absorption. Our skin, which is covered with tiny mouths and which in its own ways absorbs and digests like a stomach, needs to get used to powerful food, drinking in the sea's mucus, that salty milk, which is her life and from which the sea creates and recreates beings. In the gradual sequence of hot baths, to warm baths, to practically cold baths, the skin will acquire this habit. It will acquire a thirst for it and will drink it in more and more.

On the harsh occasion when you bathe in the cold sea for the first time, at the very least you must avoid the unbearable gaze of the crowd. It should be done in a safe place with no more than the essential number of witnesses, a devoted person who can come to the rescue if need be, keep watch, give moral support and who can, at the critical moment when the swimmer returns, give a rub down with very warm woolens and provide a hot beverage in which there are a few drops of a powerful elixir as a light tonic.

"But," you will say "it is less dangerous if everyone can see the bather. We are far from being like Bernardin de Saint-Pierre's Virginie, who despite being in extreme danger, preferred to drown than to swim." You are wrong. We are more nervous now than we have ever been before. And the impression I am speaking about is so vivid and so revolting—of course I mean only for certain people—that it can result in lethal consequences such as aneurysms and apoplexy.

I love the people, I hate crowds, and I especially hate noisy crowds of pleasure-seekers, who depress the sea with their gaiety, their fashions and their ridiculous behavior. What! The Earth is not big enough? Do you have to come here to wage war against poor invalids and debase the sea's majesty, her savage and true grandeur!

I happened to have the misfortune of spending a day sailing from Le Havre to Honfleur on a boat crowded, in fact overcrowded, with these imbeciles. During this very short trip, they found the time to get bored and organized a dance. Someone, (perhaps a dancing master) had his kit on hand and played contradanse in the presence of the Ocean. In truth, you couldn't hear a thing. You could just barely make out a single shrill note grating through the solemn, tremendous bass that was rumbling around us.

I can easily imagine the lady's dismay when, in July, she sees her beloved solitude disturbed by this invasion—so many poseurs, so many dandies, idle chatterers and prying eyes. Freedom has come to an end. Even the most isolated home reverberates at night with the sounds coming from elegant guingettes, cafés and casinos. During the day, hordes of precious young women, in yellow gloves and polished boots flutter about on the beach. Anyone who is on her own stands out. Alone? Why? They wonder. They approach; through the child they try to strike up a conversation.

They pick up some shells for him. Consequently, the lady, who is embarrassed and overwhelmed stays home or decides to only go out in the morning. This sparks thousands of malicious comments. Rumors get back to her. She starts to worry. These nuisances, who she keeps at a distance, are sometimes influential people, who could damage her husband's reputation.

More than any other activity, bathing in the sea fires the imagination. All this perturbs her July and August nights; they are fiery and restless. If in the morning, she finally falls asleep, she still finds no peace of mind. Bathing, far from refreshing her, adds irritating salt to the blistering heat. She has not recovered the strength of youth, but rather its seething ferment. Still weak and quite nervous she is all the more troubled by this inner-storm that is far from concealed. The merciless sea brings about and reveals all this excitement, which one would like to keep secret, for all to see on her skin. Her skin betrays the secret with a slight rash of red patches. All these little problems, which afflict children even more, and which mothers cherish in their children as signs of restored health, are humiliating when they, themselves have them.. They are afraid of not being loved as much, because of them. How little they know men! They don't realize that the greatest form of attraction, the thing that stimulates love most intensely is not so much beauty as it is upheaval.

"But, what if he found me to be ugly!" This is what she says every morning when looking in the mirror. She both fears and desires the arrival of the man she loves. And yet, she feels quite alone, she is afraid without knowing why, and this in the midst of this crowd. She no longer dares to wander, walking in remote areas. She becomes increasingly agitated. She comes down with a fever; she takes to her bed.... Scarcely twenty-four hours later, she finds him by her side.

Who informed him? Not her. But, in his big hand-writing, a tiny hand wrote: "My dear papa, come quickly. Mama is in bed. The other day she said: 'If only he were here!'

He appeared. She is cured. Here is a blissful man! Happy to see her recover, happy to be needed, happy to see her so beautiful. She has become tan, but how young she looks! What life there is in her charming gaze! What a gentle radiance of health in the silken texture of her beautiful hair that is loose and undulating.

Is what we have just read a tall-tale? This swift rebirth of life, beauty, affection, this charming adventure in which you find a young mistress in your wife, who is moved and so happy because of your arrival— is this miracle sheer fiction? Not at all. This is the pleasant sight that one often sees. It is perhaps rare for the rich, but that is not the case in families, who are hard working and captive in their duties. Their forced separations are painful. These escapes, that finally make a reunion possible, have a charm that cannot be denied. There is no shame in being happy.

When you realize the tremendous tension of modern life for workingmen (in other words for everyone except a few idlers) it brings great pleasure to observe these joyful scenes when a reunited family has its hearts filled with joy. Those who are heartless will say it is bourgeois and prosaic. The form matters little, when the substance is so touching. The anxious merchant, who from one payment date to another, saved the boat in which the fate of his family resides, the administrative victim, the clerk who has been worn down by the injustice and tyranny of the office, those captives left behind their chains and in this short-lived peace and quiet, a kind and affectionate family would like to make them forget it all. The mother and child are very skilled at this. With their gaiety, their caresses, and with the distractions that the sea offers, his sad spirits are done away with and other thoughts are awoken in him. It is their victory. They lead him about, have him visit *their* beach, contemplate *their* sea, take pleasure in his admiration, because all of this is *theirs*. They took possession of the ocean in which they bathe and enjoy sharing it with him.

The wife, once again, becomes quite friendly and kind towards the same crowds that until then had made her anxious. She feels so much better, in such harmony! She not only feels secure, she feels bold. She establishes close ties with the sea and with the waves. She maintains that she will swim—"she wants to tame the sea." This is slightly over-ambitious. First of all, she is out done by her competitor, her child, who is far more nimble and daring. Thinking that she is being held up, she swims. Otherwise, she is afraid and sinks down....

She will get better thanks to bathing. For she has fallen in love with the sea and she envies her. This sea, after all, does not evoke mediocre passions. Some sort of intoxicating electricity that we would love to absorb entirely is within her.

CHAPTER 6

The Rebirth of the Heart and of Fraternity

Three forms of nature expand and enlarge our soul, make it extend and sail through the infinite: the unsettled ocean of the air, with its festival of lights, its vapor, its half-light and its moving phantasmagoria of rapidly fading and capricious creations; the fixed ocean of land, with its undulating surface that can be observed from the top of tall mountains, upheavals that bear witness to its ancient mobility, the sublimity of its peaks and their eternal ice; and finally, the ocean of water. Less mobile than the first, less fixed than the second, it obeys celestial movements in its well-regulated swaying.

These three things constitute the scale through which the infinite speaks to our souls. However, let's make note of the differences between them.

The first of these oceans is so mobile that we can hardly observe it. It misleads, deceives and amuses us. It dissipates and interrupts our thoughts. At times it provides immense hope—a day in the midst of the infinite. We will see God's very core.... No...it is all so fleeting, and our heart is filled with sorrow, disquiet and doubt. Why did you allow me to glimpse this sublime illusion of light? I will never forget it and now the world seems obscure in comparison.

The fixed ocean of mountains is not as elusive. On the contrary, it blocks our every step and it requires difficult and healthy exertion from us. The price of contemplation is an enormously strenuous act. And yet, like the transparence of the air the opacity of land often tricks us and leads us astray. We have all heard the story of Louis-François Ramond de Carbonnières, who for ten years, looked in vain for the Mont Perdu in the Pyrenees, a peak that can be seen but that no one had reached.

There is one extremely big difference between these two elements—land is silent and the Ocean speaks. The Ocean is a voice that speaks to distant stars and responds to their movement in its deep and solemn language. It speaks to the land and the shore, conversing with their echoes in poignant tones. In turn plaintive and threatening it rumbles or sighs. Above all, it speaks to man. Since the Ocean is the fertile crucible in which creation began and within whose strength it continues, it possesses creation's animated eloquence. This is life speaking to life. The beings, which are born from the Ocean in the millions and billions, are its words. It speaks, even before the white and foaming sea of milk— from which they emerge— with its fertile marine jelly, is organized. All this, combined together is the great voice of the Ocean.

What does it say? It speaks of life, the eternal metamorphosis. It speaks of a fluctuating existence. It puts the petrified ambitions of terrestrial life to shame.

What does it say? Immortality. An indomitable force of life can be found in the lowest rungs of nature. And yet, their souls are so much more superior!

What does it say? Solidarity. Let's accept the rapid exchange, which occurs between the different parts of an individual. Let's accept the superior law that unites the living members of a single entity: humanity. And beyond that, let's accept the supreme law that means that we cooperate and create, with the great Soul, that we are associated (to the best of our ability) with this world's loving Harmony and that we show solidarity with the life God has created.

The sea articulates these serious words, quite distinctly in voices that we perceive as being unclear. And yet, man, who has been deafened by common everyday sounds, who has been overwrought and made prosaic, has trouble hearing them when he gets to the shore. Even in the best of men, the sense of superior life has been diminished. He is wary of it. Who will have a hold over him? Nature? No, not yet. Having been mellowed by his family, the innocence of his child, the tenderness of his wife, at first man's interest is rekindled in the concerns of humanity. This shows that souls have genders and feel things in very different ways. She is moved more deeply by the sea, by the poetry of the infinite. He, on the other had, is moved by the men of the sea, the dangers they face, their daily drama and their families' ever-changing fate. Even though his wife is tenderhearted towards the problems of individuals she does not take a serious interest in the problems of an entire class. Any hard-working man, who comes to the coast, fixes his attention mainly on the life of working men—the fishermen and sailors with their harsh and dangerous lives in which the risks are great and the benefits are few.

I see him, while his wife is getting up and the child is being dressed, walking along the shore. On a cold morning, after a night of heavy rain, one by one, the boats return. Everything is soaked and chilled, these people's clothes are dripping wet. Young children also spent the night at sea. What did they bring back? Not much. And yet they came back alive. In last night's brutal wind, the boats were taking in water. They saw death at close range. This is a good opportunity for the man, who was bemoaning his fate just yesterday, to reflect upon himself and say: "My fate is not as harsh as theirs."

At night, during a dubious looking sunset, with copper-colored clouds rising over a sinister-looking sea, he sees them set off once again. "But aren't we in store for some bad weather?" he asks them. "Sir, you have to make a living." They set off, and their children with them. Their wives, who are extremely solemn, followed them with their eyes and more than one was softly saying a few prayers. Who wouldn't do the same? The stranger himself makes a wish. He says: "This night will be a rough one. We would like to see them return."

In this way, the sea opens up the heart. And even the hardest of hearts are taken by it. No matter what, one finds one's humanity. Oh! There are more than enough reasons! Every type of human misery can be found in the brave, intelligent, honest, inhabitants who are without comparison the best of our country. I have lived quite a bit on the coast. Any form of heroic virtue that in the interior might be considered a rare thing, is commonplace here. And what is most intriguing is the lack of self-importance! In France, only those in military life are overly proud. On the coast, the greatest dangers count very little. It seems obvious to simply defy these dangers each day without ever boasting. I have never seen more humble (I almost said timid) men than those pilots on the Gironde, who intrepidly and continually leave from Royan and Saint-Georges to do battle with Cordouan. There, just like in Grainville (and everywhere else), the women alone spoke, yelled, settled everything as they took care of day-to-day affairs. These brave men, once on land, did not say a word and were as quiet as their valiant spouses were loud and superb, as they exercised their paternal authority on their children. The husband followed the advice of the Roman poet to the letter: "Happy to be nobody in my own home."

Their women, who show great concern for strangers and their community, also had regal hearts that were magnificent and generous in vital moments. In Saint-Georges they used to give all their sheets for shredded linen for the wounded of the battle of Solferino. In April 1859, in Étretat, when three Englishmen had had a wreck near the coast, in an inaccessible area, all the locals rushed to their rescue and were in despair as long as they were in danger. Men and women displayed all the signs of intense sensitivity. Once rescued, they were taken in with cries and tears. They were sheltered, dressed and came away with a wealth of new friends and gifts.

Oh, the good people of France! And yet, until now their life has been sad and difficult! Under the naval recruiting system (which, moreover is so useful and from which we derive such strength), at any given moment they leave the benefits of their merchant ships for the strict training of the Navy. Forty years ago, manoeuvres were still accompanied by songs. Today they are done in silence. The bonuses that are awarded for whales only benefit the fleet owner. Cod supplies have diminished, the number of mackerel has dropped and herring has taken its distance from man. A very precious little book, *The Story of Rose Duchemin in Her Own Words*, gives a gripping picture of this life of misery. The clever Alphonse Karr, who wrote the book under the dictation of this fisherman's wife, was tactful enough not to change a single word.

The town of Étretat is not strictly speaking a harbor. It lays low at sea-level and is protected by the sea merely by a mountain of pebbles, a barrier whose sole architects were the storms, which pushed forward and added on to it new jetties of pebbles. There is no shelter. Thus, according to the ancient and strict Celtic practice, each boat that arrives must be pulled up onto the quay by a rope that is wound around a capstan. The capstan, with its four bars, is turned by the fisherman's family. Since the boys are at sea this means his wife, his daughters and their friends. It is easy to understand the difficulties involved. The heavy boat, when it is being pulled up, hits rock after rock, obstacle after obstacle and only surmounts these with little leaps. Each jolt shakes these women's chests. One can literally say that this extremely difficult return is impressed upon their strained flesh, onto their bosoms and their very hearts.

At first, this made me sad. I was hurt. My first instinct was to join in myself and help them. Such an action would have seemed peculiar and some sort of self-consciousness stopped me. But, everyday, I assisted them at least in my heart. I would go there, I would watch. These young and charming girls (who were rarely pretty, but charming nonetheless) did not wear the short red slips that were part of the traditional dress on the coast. Instead they wore long dresses. For the most part, both their race and minds were refined and several were quite delicate. They were more like young ladies. Bent over as they performed this demanding task, which was filial and therefore elevated, they did not lack grace or pride. In this very trying endeavor, their young hearts did not allow for a single weak moment—not a single complaint or sigh.

This small, ever-so small quay of pebbles still managed to be too big. I saw many abandoned and unnecessary boats. Their catch was unproductive. The fish had fled. Étretat languished, perished, just as nearby Dieppe was languishing. Increasingly, it is reduced to having to rely on bathers. It is staking its life on bathers, as well as on a housing gamble, since depending on whether these dwellings are rented or empty, they can bring in money one day and the next are a drain on finances. No matter how much Parisians and especially Paris's high society pay out, this inter-action is a curse for this area.

Our Norman population, who discovered America, who from the 14th century on, conquered the African coast, loves the sea less and less. Henceforth, many have turned their back to the coast and are looking towards the interior. The descendant of the man who first threw the harpoon has resigned himself to woman's work, and has become a pale cotton-spinner in the textile mills of Montville or Bolbec.

It is up to science and the law stop this decadence.

If science, with its ability to lead, is firmly followed, it will create the means by which the sea can be managed and will rebuild the fishing trade, which as we have seen, is the training ground for our Navy. Law, which is not exclusively influenced by the land's interest, will maintain our sailors as the pride of the country, an elite group that are in no way comparable to the great masses from which we draw our soldiers and who will be the true soldiers that could in certain circumstances cut the world's Gordian knot.

This is what I dreamed about on the small quay in Étretat in the dark summer of 1860 when the rain was pouring down, while the unyielding capstan grated, the rope creaked and the boat slowly made its way forward.

That boat that is our century is also being dragged along and is having a great deal of trouble making its way. Just like in 1730, there is sluggishness and fatigue. It would be wise if we helped by placing ourselves at the bar. But so many are wasting time, are playing with seashells and pebbles.

They say that Scipio, the conqueror of Carthage, and Terence, an escaped prisoner from that ruined world, used to collect shells along the sea, two good friends who were completely oblivious to the past and left it behind them. They took pleasure in forgetting it, wiping their lives clean, and returning to childhood. Ungrateful Rome, destroyed Carthage, their two homelands, weighed very little upon them, hardly left a trace on their souls, no more than a ripple on the incoming tide.

This is not our desire. We do not want to be children. We do not want to forget, but rather, with tenacious passion, we went to help in the tiring manoeuvres of this great exhausted century. We want to pull the boat forward and with our strong hands push the capstan of the future.

CHAPTER 7

Vita Nuova *of Nations*

In December 1860, while I was finishing this book, I received from Italy—the resurrected one, the glorious mother of us all—a beautiful New Year's gift. News, in the form of a pamphlet arrived for me from Florence.

This is a country from which important news often emerges. In 1300, it was Dante. In 1500 it was Amerigo Vespucci. In 1600 it was Galileo. What will today's news from Florence bring?

Oh, at first glance, it seems insignificant! But who knows? Perhaps the consequences will be enormous! It's a speech that is only a few pages long, a medical brochure. Nothing in the title attracts your attention—rather it might dissuade you from reading it. And yet, there is in it the seeds of something whose consequences are incalculable and capable of changing the world. Opposite the title page, I see the portrait of two children in a Florentine hospital, one who is already dead and the other who is dying. The author is a doctor, who—and this is quite rare—was so taken with his young invalids, these poor unknown children, that he wanted to express his pain and regrets in writing.

The first boy, who was seven or eight years old, with a refined and austere nobility and who seemed bitter about his great incomplete destiny, has a flower on his pillow. His mother, who was too poor to give him anything else, would bring him flowers whenever she came to visit. He protected them with such care, was so obsessed with them that he was allowed to keep that one.

The other child, who is smaller, with the moving charm of a four or five-year-old, is obviously about to die. His eyes are wandering as if in his final dream. These two children had shown affection for one another. Without being able to speak, they liked looking at each other and the compassionate doctor had placed them across from one another. He brought them together in the engraving just as they had been when dying.

This is very Italian. Elsewhere, showing weakness or tenderness is not allowed. One would be afraid of ridicule. Not in Italy. The doctor writes for the general public as he would if he were all alone. He pours out his heart without reservation, with a feminine trust and confidence that makes you smile and cry. Admittedly, the language has much to do with it.

It is a charming language for women and children, so tender and yet dazzling, beautiful even when speaking of painful topics. It is as if it were raining tears and flowers.

Then, he stops and apologizes. If he spoke in this way, it is not without reason. "The reason is that these children would not have died, if they could have been sent to the sea." His conclusion: A children's hospital should be established on the coast.

This is quite a clever man. He touches his reader. The rest will follow. Now, men are paying attention and are moved, ladies are in tears. They pray, they want, they demand. They cannot be denied. Without waiting for the government, a private association immediately established the Children's Baths in Viareggio.

We all know that lovely road, after passing harsh Genoa and the magnificent harbor of La Spezia, when we enter Tuscany, with its Virgilian olive trees. Halfway to Livorno, a gentle coastline provides this solitary little port that henceforth this charming foundation hallows.

Florence, is where the idea of charity had its origin in Europe, since they had hospitals before the year 1000. In 1287, when the divine Beatrice inspired Dante, her father established the Santa Maria Nuova Hospital. During Luther's less than enthusiastic travels through Italy, he nonetheless admired its hospitals and the beautiful Italian ladies, who with their veils and without vainglory went there to serve the sick.

This new foundation will be a model for Europe. We owe it to the children. They bear the brunt of the hellish life that we lead, that life of dreadful work and more importantly of deadly excess.

We cannot deny the profound degradation that has affected our Western races. The reasons for this are many. The most striking is the enormity and rapid pace of our work. This is most unavoidable, imposed upon us by the trade. But even those people, whose trade does not demand it, are nonetheless in a rush. Some sort of passion for moving faster and faster is now in people's character, in their temperament and in the acridness of the blood. In comparison, every other century has been lazy and sterile. Our results have been great. From our brains, a marvelous stream of sciences, arts, inventions, ideas and products has flowed. And we are flooding the globe, the present and the future with them. But at what cost does all of this come? At the cost of a horrible effusion of strength and of a cerebral drain that in turn strains our ability to reproduce. Our accomplishments are prodigious and our children are wretched.

It is worth noting that this great effort, this excessive production is the work of a small number. America is doing little and Asia nothing. And even in Europe, itself, everything is done by a few million men, from the far-Western part of the continent. The others mock them for wearing themselves out and believe that they could easily take their place. Poor barbarians, do you really believe that some Russian, or some Western pioneer from the United States could become an artist, an English mechanical engineer or a Parisian optician, at any point in the future? We are the way that we are as a result of centuries of refinement and education. We have a long tradition. What would happen if we were to die out? No one is ready to be our successors.

Even if we are ready to accept this annihilating work and this self-destruction of our fertility in the interest of human kind, we cannot in good conscience want to cause the ruin of our children and take them down with us. And yet, this is exactly what is happening. They are born prepared. They have our arts in their blood, but they also have our fatigue. With their frightening precociousness, they know how, they are capable, they would act. But they do nothing. They die.

During his childhood, man, like a plant or anything else, needs rest, fresh air, and sweet freedom. In this case everything works against him, our strength as much as our weaknesses. Everything seems to have conspired to suffocate our children. Do we love them? Undoubtedly, yes. And yet, we are killing them. Whether we know it or not, this agitated and violent society is waging a veritable war against childhood.

There are times of crisis when childhood hangs

by a thread, especially during development. In these times, life seems to be hesitating. It seems to wonder: "Will I endure?" At these key moments, contact with too many people, living in cities and among crowds, is death for these fragile creatures. Or—and this is even worse—it is the beginning of a long string of diseases. A wretched life begins in which after falling, lifting himself up and then falling again, in the majority of cases the youth will crawl along and be in need of charity.

We have to put a quick end to this. We have to make plans for the future. We have to extract the child from this dangerous environment, take him away from man, give him over to Nature and have him breathe in life with those sea breezes. Sick children will get better there. The foundling will grow up there. Strengthened, fortified, many would become seamen and thus instead of being frail factory workers or continual patients in hospital wards, the State would get a robust and bold sailor.

Furthermore, why the State? Florence proved to us that a regal heart is as good as royalty. And women are royalty. It is up to them to make demands.

If I were a beautiful young lady, I know what I would do. In my splendor and magnificence, one day at one of those moments when a lover attests, protests, swears and feels the need to give, I would say: "I take you at your word. But I don't think that I can be amused with ordinary gifts. I detest your heavy cash-mere shawls that are made, nowadays in India based on London designs. I don't think much of diamonds. Soon, diamonds will be run-of-the-mill. Mr. Berthelot, who is remaking exact replicas of nature, and who is creating many living things, will with even greater ease lavish us with diamonds. I like things that last. I want a good house on the coast that is slightly sheltered, sun drenched and can accommodate fifty children. There is no need for much furniture. Once they are settled there, they will never want for food. There won't be a single lady who goes to the sea, who won't take great pleasure in helping this cause. If the Beatrices of Florence established such houses, why can't France's do the same? Are we any less beautiful, and are you men any less in love?"

"If, as you tell me from morning until night, the sea has made me more beautiful, then you owe its shores a keepsake. And if you love me, then I suppose that you must find happiness being my associate in creating something, in starting this little world for children near the great wet-nurse with me. May the sea keep this lasting token of affection and of pure love! May her lively work be a testament to the fact that we were united by a sacred idea in the presence of the infinite."

Thus, one woman would begin. And another would continue, our shared mother, France. There would be no more useful institution and no more important sacrifice. Moreover, only a few would be necessary. Transferring a few establishments from the interior would be sufficient. In fact, there would be a reduction in such institutions, because these inland establishments are a pure waste of money; they could be described as factories that turn out invalids who, throughout their lives, will always need to beg more help.

In Ancient Rome, they never questioned the importance of public health in the lives of the whole society. When we see their munificence and the work they did to bring healthy water even to minor cities, with their amazing aqueducts, like their Pont-du-Gard, the immense baths where the masses came to bathe for free (or at most for a small donation), you have an immense appreciation for their great wisdom. They also had seawater pools in which they swam. Would we hesitate to do what they did for their idle and unproductive plebs, in order to safeguard our unique creators that are at the basis of the world's future advances?

I am not just referring to children now, but to everyone. Today, within every city, there is another congested city—the hospital to which the weakening worker continuously returns, over and over again. This costs a great deal...and to whom? In the final analysis it costs the other workers, who carry the burden of all public expenditures. He dies young, leaves his family in the public's hands. Prevention is much easier than the cure. The person we can do the most for, is not the invalid but the man who will become one, the man who is completely drained. Ten days of rest by the sea would restore his strength and would preserve a sturdy worker. Transportation, simple lodgings for such a short summer stay, inexpensive meals at common tables, would all cost infinitely less than a long stay in a hospital. And the man would be saved, along with his family and children. He is irreplaceable. For, as I said earlier, each one of these men is the latest product of a long industrious tradition. In fact, he is a work of art, human art. An unknown form of art in which humanity continues to advance, to shape itself, as a creative force.

Who will give me the privilege of seeing the Earth's elite—this host of inventive, creative and productive men of the people, who sweat and strain for the world—continuously restore their strength in God's great swimming pool! All of humanity would benefit since it would flourish through the great amount of work these men do. And therefore, it owes these men every pleasure, every luxury, every light. Humanity thrives through their good offices, lives off their marrow and their blood. If we gave them renewal through nature, fresh air and the sea—a day of rest—it would be only fair. It's an act of kindness towards the human race, for whom they are so necessary and who if they were to die out tomorrow, would be orphaned.

Take pity on yourselves, poor men of the West. Help yourselves in a serious way; see to the salvation of us all. The Earth begs you to live. In order to restore you, it offers the best of itself— the sea. The Earth would be lost if you were lost. For, you are its genius, its inventive soul. It lives through your life and if you were to die, it too would die.

THE AMERICA AWARDS
for a lifetime contribution to international writing
Awarded by the Contemporary Arts Educational Project, Inc.
in loving memory of Anna Fahrni

The 2012 Award winner is:

IVO MICHIELS [Belgium] 1923

Previous winners:
1994 Aimé Cesaire [Martinique] 1913–2008
1995 Harold Pinter [England] 1930–2008
1996 José Donoso [Chile] 1924-1996 (*awarded prior to his death*)
1997 Friederike Mayröcker [Austria] 1924
1998 Rafael Alberti [Spain] 1902-1999
1999 Jacques Roubaud [France] 1932
2000 Eudora Welty [USA] 1909-2001
2001 Inger Christensen [Denmark] 1935–2009
2002 Peter Handke [Austria] 1942
2003 Adonis (Ali Ahmad Said) [Syria/Lebanon] 1930
2004 José Saramago [Portugal] 1922-2010
2005 Andrea Zanzotto [Italy] 1921
2006 Julien Gracq (Louis Poirier) [France] 1910-2007
2007 Paavo Haavikko [Finland] 1931
2008 John Ashbery [USA] 1927
2009 Günter Kunert [GDR/Germany] 1929
2010 Javier Marías [Spain] 1951
2011 Ko Un [South Korea] 1933